Andrew Banasiewicz

Probabilistic Benchmarking

Norm-Setting in the Age of Big Data

DE GRUYTER

Despite careful production of our books, sometimes mistakes happen. Unfortunately, the copyright information was incorrect in the original publication. This has now been corrected. We apologize for the mistake.

ISBN 978-3-11-099979-2
e-ISBN (PDF) 978-3-11-100129-6
e-ISBN (EPUB) 978-3-11-100149-4

Library of Congress Control Number: 2024939882

Bibliographic information published by the Deutsche Nationalbibliothek
The Deutsche Nationalbibliothek lists this publication in the Deutsche Nationalbibliografie; detailed bibliographic data are available on the internet at http://dnb.dnb.de.

© 2024 Andrew D. Banasiewicz
Cover image: matejmo/iStock/Getty Images Plus
Typesetting: Integra Software Services Pvt. Ltd.

www.degruyter.com

The ideas summarized in this book are dedicated to those always in my heart and in my mind: my wife Carol; my daughters Alana and Katrina; my son Adam; my mother-in-law Jenny; the memory of my parents Andrzej and Barbara, my sister Beatka, and my brother Damian; and my father-in-law Ernesto.

Preface

What is a good outcome? Assessment of organizational outcomes, such as sales growth or return on investment, or states, such as exposure to the risk business disruption or shareholder litigation, is inescapably relative, because comparison is hard coded into human nature, and it is a common part of social life. In fact, our natural inclination to compare gives rise to an interesting phenomenon, characterized here as assessment paradox: to be truly meaningful, exact magnitude-expressed values often need to be 'translated' into qualitative, assessment-laden categories, such as 'above average' or 'subpar.' That need is paradoxical because it runs counter to the intuitively obvious idea that exact magnitudes are more informative – after all, exact values generally imply continuous measurement scale which, in abstract information processing terms, is more informative because it allows a wider range of mathematical manipulations than is allowed for categorically expressed values. And yet in the fundamental human sensemaking context, it is the manifestly less informative categorical designation that ultimately is more immediately clear in terms of what, exactly, it communicates. In the end, it is not the magnitude of as such, but the interpretation of that magnitude that is truly informative.

The preceding reasoning is at the core of the appeal of benchmarking, a comparative assessment process built around contrasting magnitudes of interest with appropriate standards of points of reference. Benchmarking is ubiquitous – in fact, it could even be argued that it is fundamental not only to organizational decision-making, but to numerous other facets of life, such as healthcare, manufacturing, and service delivery. And yet, the idea of benchmarking lacks conceptual cohesiveness and operational specificity – in many regards, it is whatever one wants to be in a particular situation. In some contexts, benchmarking is framed in terms of quantitative contrasts, while in some others it is framed as an impossibly broad undertaking that lumps together under a single umbrella of meaning assessment-minded approaches that range from qualitative best practice seeking evaluations to rigorous quantitative contrasts. It is easy to see how such lack of definitional and operational clarity can hamper broader utilization of that important sensemaking tool, as the absence of a singular definitional framing and explicit concept operationalization creates a potpourri of incommensurate, one-off approaches and benchmarking outcomes.

The common practice of implicitly equating benchmarking with any and all forms of comparative assessment also blurs an important distinction between point-in-time, cross-entity, or 'us vs. others' contrasts, and cross-time 'now vs. then' comparisons. When considered from the perspective of comparative assessment, benchmarking can be seen as a mechanism of the former, i.e., 'us vs. others' types of comparisons; baselining, a complementary though comparatively lesser known and less frequently invoked idea, can be, on the other hand, seen as a mechanism of the 'now vs. then' minded comparative assessment. When thoughtfully structured and deployed, the combination of conceptually clear and operationally explicit benchmarking and baselining can create a

https://doi.org/10.1515/9783111001296-202

foundation of an unbiased and systematic mechanism of an ongoing comparative assessment of organizational outcomes and states of interest. It is the purpose of this book to offer the necessary conceptual framings and methodological details.

The ensuing overview is divided into three parts: Part I offers a general review of past and current benchmarking and baselining framings and practices, along with technical concepts that are at the core of cross-entity and cross-time comparisons. Part II lays out the general conceptual framework that outlines the structure of comparative assessment in general, and describes the roles played by benchmarking and baselining, as two distinct but complementary mechanisms of comparative assessment; also addressed are specific methodological considerations that are necessary to valid and reliable deployments of those ideas. Part III offers case studies that highlight the key ideas and benefits of carefully structured benchmarking and baselining applications.

I would like to close this brief introduction with what I see to be the nature of this book: in simplest of terms, it is meant to offer a complete guide to setting up robust comparative assessment organizational capabilities, geared toward providing decision-informing insights in an unbiased, consistent, and ongoing manner. To that end, while the intent was for this book to be as nontechnical as possible, some technical details are necessary in order to offer application and deployment-ready overview of the ideas of benchmarking and baselining; those details, however, were kept to the absolute minimum, and the associated explanations were structured to make them easily understandable. All in all, while this book outlines the general theoretical rationale and lays out operationalization-guiding methodological details, it is written from the perspective of a practitioner looking to put those ideas to work.

Andrew Banasiewicz
May 2024
Bristol, RI

Contents

Part I: **Laying the Foundation**

Chapter 1
Modern Tools of Organizational Assessment

What is a good outcome? It is tempting to say, 'I will know it when I see it,' but that is not quite the case. While many organizational outcomes may indeed lend themselves to objective measurement, conclusive assessment of some of those outcomes can be paradoxical, as numerically explicit values may turn out to be surprisingly informationally ambiguous. Is 8% ROI 'good'? Oftentimes, answering such a question calls for the use of some type of comparative assessment standard, a benchmark. But, while the idea of benchmark-based assessment is often taken to be intuitively obvious, it can in fact turn out to be all but that, especially when a benchmark of interest needs to be derived from applicable data. Moreover, the general idea of benchmark-based assessment is often confounded with the seemingly closely related idea of best practices, even though quantitative benchmarks are fundamentally different from qualitative best practices.

This introductory chapter takes a broad view of the idea of standard-based assessment of organizational outcomes and states of interest by, firstly, drawing a clear line of demarcation between quantitative and qualitative assessments, and, secondly, by framing the idea of quantitative assessment standards in the context of two distinct approaches: spatial benchmarking and temporal baselining. The goal here is to outline a general conceptual framework that captures the key distinctions between spatial and temporal aspects of assessment, static vs. dynamic modes of estimation, and existing vs. created origins of assessment standards.

What Is a Good Outcome?

Should 10% return on investment (ROI) be considered a 'good' outcome? How about 15% or 20%? What about 1-in-20 odds of critical infrastructure failure? Should it be deemed 'low' or 'high'?

Such basic questions highlight an interesting phenomenon of interpretational uncertainty of quantitative estimates, framed here as *assessment paradox*. It might sound counterintuitive, but numerically expressed assessments of measurable outcomes, such as ROI or the likelihood of incurring shareholder litigation, can be both precise and vague: Precise because numeric expressions are generally magnitudinally unambiguous, but vague because the meaning implied by those magnitudes may not necessarily be clear. For instance, it can be assumed that an average person understands the meaning of, let's say, 10% or 1-in-20 odds, but understanding the direct meaning of those and like magnitudes may immediately yield conclusive insights, such as strong vs. weak returns or high- vs. moderate-risk exposure – often, more in-

https://doi.org/10.1515/9783111001296-001

formation is needed to draw such conclusions. And hence the paradox: The pursuit of more numerically precise assessments can lead to greater interpretational ambiguity.

A little bit of reflection suggests a simple reason: While some numerically expressed magnitudes have universally clear interpretation, others need some type of a frame of reference to become informationally meaningful, even if the two are expressed on the same scale. For example, while estimates such as 5% chance of rain are generally understood as implying low probability, other estimates such as 5% chance of incurring shareholder litigation do not necessarily suggest low or high risk. Even though both assessments are bound by the same 0–100% range, the latter of the two estimates usually requires additional contextualization, because its interpretation is more nuanced than the self-evident numeric meaning conveyed by the probability of precipitation. The key difference maker here is the scope of assessment: Probability of rain is an aggregate, or system-wide estimate, while estimates such as likelihood of incurring shareholder litigation commonly capture disaggregate, or entity-specific assessments. And thus, while the former's meaning is self-evident, the latter begs a follow-on question of how that entity's estimate compares with some relevant benchmarks, such as an overall average probability of incurring shareholder litigation.

In a more general sense, the assessment paradox highlights an interesting aspect of human sensemaking: On the one hand, we tend to seek precision, but on the other hand, our natural, i.e., in-the-mind sensemaking processes are predominantly geared toward reducing highly granular – e.g., 5.75% ROI – inputs into coarser but conclusive categories such as 'above average' vs. 'below average.' It is ironic that efforts to produce high-resolution, in the manner of speaking, measures ultimately give rise to the need to collapse those high informational resolutions into coarser but more meaningful value-laden conclusions. Informational sensemaking-wise, to be actionable, precise estimates, commonly expressed as *absolute* numeric values, need to be re-framed as *relative*, typically positively or negatively valenced, conclusive categories.

That re-framing can be accomplished in one of two general ways: One is to use pre-determined categories, and the other is to utilize some type of an evaluative point of reference, commonly referred to as *benchmarks*.

A common example of predefined categories is a simple schema that divides the continuum of outcomes into discrete, meaning-suggesting groupings such as 'low,' 'medium,' and 'high.' The number of categories and numeric ranges defining each individual category can be based on a myriad of factors, such as organizational goals, preference, and experience; usage-wise, pre-defined categories' schemas tend to remain fixed over time, which enables easy cross-time comparisons.

Alternatively, numerically explicit estimates can be re-framed into conclusive categories by evaluating observed outcomes of interest in the context of a chosen point of reference, i.e., a benchmark, such as average ROI. As used in practice, benchmarks can be formal or informal – the former are typically computed using appropriate data, when available, while the latter, sometimes referred to as 'rules of thumb,' are derived from common business knowledge, usually spread by word of mouth. Under most circumstances, formal benchmarks are more precise and more magnitudinally explicit than rules of thumb. For example, an industry-wide average ROI used as a formal benchmark to help qualify performance of a particular company would usually be derived from accurate financial data, and thus would usually be expressed as a magnitudinally precise value. On the other hand, a rule of thumb reflecting well-established and widely accepted norms would tend to be comparatively coarse and slow changing. For example, a common financial rule of thumb suggests that a stock market has a long-term average return of about 10%; another one suggests that one should save about 10–15% of one's take-home income for retirement.

A Closer Look at Outcome Assessment

The preceding brief overview of the commonly used assessment-related approaches touches upon several key considerations that shape the scope and the content of broadly framed means of outcome assessment. The first of those is that organizational outcomes of interest can be evaluated in the context of two abstractly framed contexts: us vs. them contrasts, and now vs. then lookbacks. The former, commonly characterized as *benchmarking*, can be conceptualized as spatial assessments because at their core those contrasts entail point-in-time comparisons of entities that exist in the same abstractly framed space (e.g., a composite of companies comprising a particular industry vs. an individual company), while the latter, built around a comparatively lesser known notion of *baselining*, is tantamount to assessing cross-time change in a particular outcome of interest.

Another foundational assessment-related consideration is the idea of *assessment cadence*, which can be more precisely operationalized in the context recurrence and timing, ranging from episodic to regular, and infrequent to frequent, respectively. It thus follows that assessment cadence is a continuum ranging from ad hoc[1] to real time; the former often taking the form of unplanned, situationally emergent approaches, while the latter manifesting themselves as carefully thought-out and structured mechanisms, usually built into larger processes. *Ad hoc assessment* is commonly used in exploratory learning endeavors, where the goal is to opportunistically examine a wide array of outcomes or states of interest as a part of a larger process of building a more general understanding of a particular situation or a phenomenon. *Real-time assessment*, on the other hand, takes the form of pre-planned, structured, and systemic mechanisms that dynamically update specific points of reference, now commonly computed on-the-fly using data captured on ongoing basis, perhaps best exemplified by the various stock market indices. Filling the large area between those two ends of the assessment contin-

---

[1] From Latin meaning 'for this' or 'for this situation,' a term used to describe something developed or used for a special, typically immediate purpose, and usually without prior planning.

uum is *periodic assessment*, defined here as recurring examinations of outcomes or states of interest conducted using a set assessment mechanism, and in accordance with a predetermined assessment cadence.

A yet another important assessment-related consideration is the idea of *peer group*, which in the context of comparative assessment can be framed as a set of individuals or organizations that share similar characteristics. That notionally simple concept can quickly become surprisingly complex in practice, primarily because of the sheer number of potential characteristics that can be considered and different, in the sense of competing, ways those characteristics can be used in the grouping process. In other words, while the idea of using peers as the basis for comparative assessment is often taken to be intuitively obvious, it is in fact deserving of careful and thoughtful consideration.

To that end, perhaps the most common approach to defining an appropriate peer group is to rely on classification schemas developed by specialized and widely recognized (for their appropriate expertise) public or private entities. Those formal taxonomies are typically built around the general MECE (mutually exclusive and collectively exhaustive) principle, to assure that individual entities – such as business firms – can all be classified into one and only one peer group. Stated differently, peer group framing classification taxonomies aim to encompass all business organizations (i.e., individual classification schemas are meant to be collectively exhaustive), while at the same time assuring classificatory exclusivity (i.e., all groupings are mutually exclusive), meaning that a given company can only belong to a single group. And indeed, industry classification taxonomies yield complete and non-overlapping classification schemas, but there are multiple competing classification schemes that produce materially different structures. That is of pivotal importance to comparative assessment in general, and benchmarking assessments in particular, because as shown later, the choice of industry classification taxonomy can singularly materially impact assessment outcomes.

Also demanding attention is the often-implicit relativity of resultant evaluations, captured in the assessment paradox discussed earlier. Under most circumstances, organizational decision-making requires conclusive determinations, the reaching of which may in turn call for qualitative interpretation of quantitatively expressed assessment outcomes. Though it may seem somewhat counterintuitive at the first glance, there are ample examples of decision contexts where numerically precise outcomes need to be contextualized to become fully informative, as exemplified by many commonly used organizational performance measures such as the overall ROI or more narrowly scoped promotional response rates. The ultimate evaluation of many such outcomes calls for seeing those outcomes as 'good' vs. 'subpar' or 'high' vs. 'low,' but the numerically explicit values alone are simply insufficient to make those determinations. The missing piece is an evaluation standard that can be used to contextualize, and thus give a deeper interpretive meaning to numerically explicit values.

In a very general sense, *evaluation standards* can be either established or derived. Perhaps the most obvious example of the former is the speed of light, which travels at exactly 299,792,458 m/s, or about 186,000 miles/s – everywhere and at any time. In behavioral contexts, however, established assessment standards typically do not take the form of universal constants (it is hard to think of any behavioral characteristics that are universally constant), but rather far more approximate rules of thumb, such as the one positing that the stock market has a long-term average return of 10%. Derived evaluation standards are usually created with a specific purpose in mind, often using composites of like entities, as exemplified by the use of peer group average ROI to assess the efficacy of returns generated by a specific company.

Framing Robust Outcome Assessment

The ability to differentiate between good and subpar outcomes requires thoughtful and deliberate assessment mechanisms that expressly address the core organizational outcome assessment considerations outlined in the previous section. To restate, those considerations include distinguishing between spatial and temporal dimensions of assessment, ad hoc, periodic, and real-time or types of assessment implying static or dynamic cadence, and assessment paradox-implied established or derived evaluation standards.

Spatial vs. Temporal Assessment

In an abstract, if not an ethereal sense, any phenomenon and thus any organizational state or outcome can be conceived as existing in space and time. Taking that philosophical stance, it follows that outcomes of interest can be assessed in the context of two fundamental dimensions: as an element belonging to a larger set (i.e., existing in a particular 'space'), and as a magnitude that can change over time. Stated differently, outcomes can be assessed in spatial and temporal contexts, as graphically summarized in Figure 1.1.

The distinction between *spatial* and *temporal* dimensions suggests that singularly focusing on the 'us vs. others' comparative assessment can lead to narrowing of the scope of organizational assessments to the important but informationally limited question of 'how does our performance compare to that of our peers?' Often left unaccounted for is the related question of performance trending, or 'how does our performance track over time?' That is not to say that cross-time lookback is uncommonly rare, as that is not the case – the point here is that the 'us vs. others' and 'now vs. before' are often considered separately, in response to somewhat different informational needs, rather than as two distinct but informationally interdependent dimensions of the same general assessment. When looked at as two facets of comparative

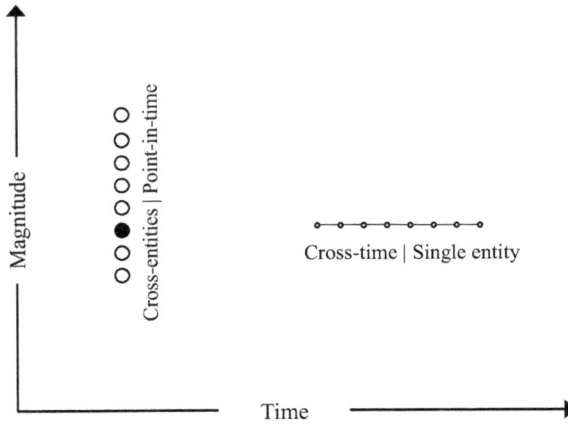

Figure 1.1: Spatial vs. temporal assessment.

assessment, spatial contrasts are framed here as *benchmarks*, and the process of deriving those assessment standards as *benchmarking*; temporal evaluations, on the other hand, are framed here as *baselines*, and the process of deriving those standards as *baselining*.

The general logic of benchmarking is anchored in two core defining characteristics: (1) point-in-time comparisons and (2) relevant and typically external points of reference. Or more explicitly stated, benchmarks represent assessment standards that are valid at a particular point in time, meaning they are themselves subject to change over time, and their validity is tied to being derived from credible, as in objective and unbiased, sources. The core idea embedded in the benchmarking dimension of comparative assessment is graphically depicted in Figure 1.2.

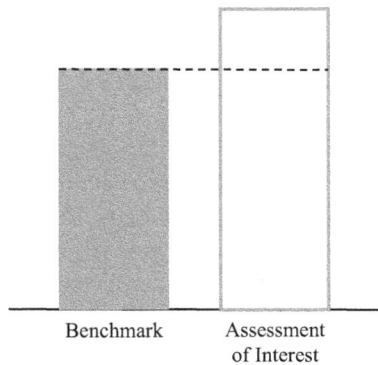

Figure 1.2: Benchmarking: the general idea.

Baselining, on the other hand, is focused on cross-time trending-based comparisons, as graphically summarized in Figure 1.3. As such, baselines contribute to the temporal aspect of comparative assessment, by expressly addressing the 'now vs. before' contrasts; in a more operational sense, baseline can be characterized as appropriately framed (more on that later) long-term trend derived from applicable time series data.

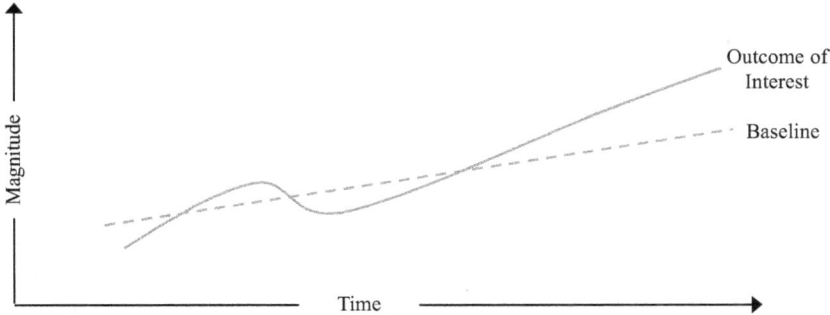

Figure 1.3: Baselining: the general idea.

The key derivation-related difference between the general benchmarking and baselining processes is their character, when looked at from the perspective of being used as assessment frames of reference: The former emphasizes *phenomenological closeness*, which manifests itself in the similarity of meaning of benchmarks and phenomena evaluated in the context of those benchmarks; the latter, on the other hand, emphasizes *informational uniformity*, which manifests itself in cross-time data and methodological consistency, used to assess the same outcome at different points in time. There are numerous, more detailed considerations that comprise phenomenological closeness and informational uniformity; those are explored in more detail in later chapters.

Static vs. Dynamic Estimation

The idea of a fixed point (or line) of reference implies that it is unchanging, at least within a reasonable time horizon. For example, one of the most pragmatic types of benchmarking are experience or practice-based informal 'rules of thumb,[2]' as exemplified by the earlier mentioned generalization of 10% long-term stock market returns. Such broad estimates can remain unchanged (and unchallenged) for extended periods of time; some can even attain the axiomatic status of immovable truths by

---

2 Although there is no agreement among scholars on the exact origin of that phrase, historically, the width of the thumb was used as the equivalent of an inch in cloth trade, and the thumb has also been used to gauge the heat in the process of brewing beer.

virtue of becoming deeply ingrained in what might be considered a commonly accepted body of knowledge. The Pareto principle, also known as the 80/20 rule, falls into that category: It stipulates that roughly 80% of a brand's profits come from 20% of its customer – it is widely used and taught, and rarely, if ever, questioned.

A point of reference, however, does not need to attain the status of immovable truth to remain fixed, at least over some reasonable stretch of time; there are, in fact, numerous examples of benchmarks that are estimated annually, with the intent of remaining fixed for the ensuing 12 months. Erudite Analytics, a risk analytics consultancy, derives a 5-year moving average-based, industry-specific securities class action litigation filing frequencies, geared toward enabling benchmarking of company-specific exposures to the threat of securities litigation. Setting aside practical, procedural, and methodological reasons that point toward the appropriateness of annual – as opposed to more frequent – securities litigation benchmarking, the so-estimated reference values remain unchanged for a year at a time.

As can be expected, there are other situations in which it is far more appropriate for assessment-related points of reference to be updated more frequently – when taken to its logical conclusion, benchmarking values can be *dynamically* updated. In very simple terms (the idea of dynamic benchmarking and baselining is discussed in more detail in later chapters), a dynamically updated point (benchmark) or line (baseline) of reference is computed on-the-fly using the most recent data. In contrast to the earlier mentioned periodic 5-year moving average, which is only updated once every 12 months by replacing the oldest 12 months of data with the newly captured 12 months, dynamic moving average is computed using the most recent 5 years from the timing of the reference, as graphically summarized in Figure 1.4.

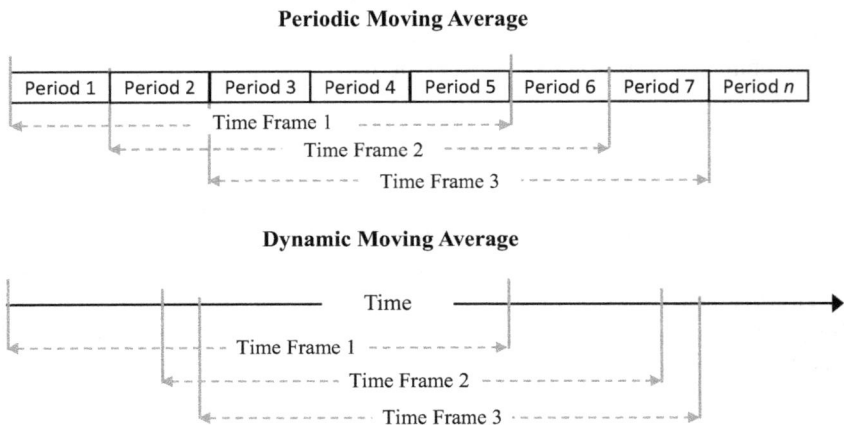

Periodic Moving Average

Dynamic Moving Average

Figure 1.4: Periodic vs. dynamic updates.

The abstract generalization depicted in Figure 1.4 is meant to convey the two key differences: First, periodic moving average illustrated above – and periodic estimates in general – is computed in fixed intervals, which means that so-estimated values remain fixed during successive re-estimation periods – in contrast to that, dynamic estimates are computed as-needed meaning that, in principle, they are ever-changing. Second, periodically estimated references lend themselves to easy and consistent trending, while dynamically estimated ones tend to be more reactive to unexpected changes (more on that later).

Existing vs. Created Origins

Looking beyond the operationally minded considerations of spatial vs. temporal and periodic vs. dynamic basis of assessment standards, derivation of informationally robust benchmarks and baselines also calls for clear and precise framing of their broadly considered origins. In that general sense, the origins of evaluation standards can be seen as either established or derived. *Existing* standards are typically externally determined and are, usually, slow changing; the most obvious examples of those standards are offered by what is known as universal truths in the form of scientific constants such as the speed of light or the π or pi ratio (the circumference of a circle to its diameter). *Created* standards, on the other hand, represent either logical extensions of justified beliefs or mathematical extrapolation underlying facts. The general notion of 'average,' often erroneously seen as synonymous with the arithmetic mean,[3] offers perhaps the most familiar example of a derived standard; the use of evaluation standards such as 'average purchase amount,' 'average age,' or 'average repurchase frequency' is a staple element of basic business analytics.

Implied in the general existing vs. created characterization are several fundamental differences. First, fixed, established standards are uniform across all conceivable contexts and usage situations – light always travels at the speed of exactly 299,792,458 m/s, the ratio of circumference to diameter is exactly 3.14159 for any circle, anywhere, etc. In contrast to that, created standards cannot be ascribed with similar universality, even if those standards are manifestations of the same quantity derived from manifestly the same data, largely due to the combination of data and methods. Without delving into excessive details,[4] two different users of manifestly the same data may end up with

---

3 It is worth noting that the ideas of 'average' and (arithmetic) 'mean' are quite often considered synonymous, which is problematic for a couple of reasons: Firstly, there are three distinct measures of average: mean, median, and mode; secondly, when a distribution of interest is skewed/asymmetrical distributions, median or mode tend to be more appropriate to use as expressions of the idea of average.

4 I discuss those details in several of my earlier books, most recently in *Data Analytic Literacy* (2023); that topic is also addressed in a wide cross section of statistic texts.

somewhat different data-derived estimates, such as the mean, because of random differences in choices relating to sampling and/or any data correction steps (e.g., imputation of missing values and outlier remediation).

It is, however, important to keep in mind that in behavioral contexts the notion of universally fixed standards is elusive – in fact, it is difficult to think of truly universally constant behavioral characteristics or phenomena. In view of that, as used in the context of comparative assessment, existing standards are considered 'fixed' in the sense of being externally sourced, with the intention of being used as given. The perhaps most obvious examples of established standards are the earlier mentioned decision-aiding rule of thumb, which most commonly represent generalized long-term averages or trends; established standards can also manifest themselves as formal statutes or norms, or even codified, legally binding rules, as exemplified by building codes or various manufacturing standards.

Assessment Modalities

Regardless of the target of assessment, outcomes of interest can be usually assessed in one of two ways: absolute or relative. The former tends to be employed in situations where outcomes lend themselves to unambiguous interpretations, perhaps best exemplified by examples in the world of sports – a foot race, for instance, typically has a clear winner, even if the difference between the first- and the second-place finishers is extremely small. That is due to the objectively measurable character of the outcome of interest, which in the case of a foot race is the speed with which competing runners traverse the same distance. Outside the realm of competitive sports, there are numerous organizational contexts that rely heavily on absolute assessments: Sales targets are typically expressed as absolute values, manufacturing firms may set a target of zero defects, banks frequently set explicit performance targets for individual branches, etc.

There are contexts, however, that render absolute assessment practices impractical, if not outright impossible. That is usually the case where outcomes of interest are either nonstandard or lack clearly discernible structural uniformity. For instance, assessing problem-solving abilities of software developers does not lend itself to standardization due to high situational variability; similarly, even overtly similar companies are likely to differ in terms of various structural, cultural, and other characteristics, ultimately rendering direct comparisons – i.e., side-by-side evaluations of absolute outcomes of interest – potentially misleading. In those situations, the task of carrying out analytically sound assessments of interest calls for relative comparisons.

In a general and somewhat abstract sense, the notion of *absolute* entails something, typically a measurable quantity, that is, self-sufficient in its meaning, which in turn means that it is free of any qualifications, conditions, restrictions, or limitations. Within the confines of assessment, an absolute outcome is typically a quantity that has unambiguous meaning, as exemplified by common measures such as total sales or the number of employees. The notion of *relative*, on the other hand, denotes that which has a meaning that is connected to or that depends on something else, or is expressed in relation to another item. Although quite often relative assessments are expressed non-numerically, as exemplified by commonly used terms such as 'high risk' or 'low return,' the earlier discussed assessment paradox points to the fact that numerically expressed outcomes can ultimately be seen as relative, as illustrated by comparison-demanding organizational measures such as ROI or the idea of statistical power[5] in decision-informing analyses. In that sense, when used within the general context of organizational evaluations, relative assessment comes into play when observed outcomes of interest need to be related to something else – typically in the form of a benchmark or a baseline – to yield informative conclusions.

Lastly, it is also important to keep in mind that while in some organizational context the use of absolute vs. relative assessment may be suggested by the outcome itself (e.g., ROI typically invites comparative assessment), in other contexts it may call for carefully considered choice of one over the other. One such context is employee assessment, where either absolute (i.e., evaluating measurable work outcomes as stand-alone quantities) or relative (i.e., comparing an individual's performance to that of peers) performance rating systems can be used. While the choice of one or the other is sometimes dictated by organizational policies or individual managers' preferences, it is worth noting that according to recent research,[6] absolute employee rating systems tend to be more effective when used to assess more routine task-focused performance, whereas relative rating systems tend to be more effective when used to assess more knowledge-intensive tasks.

Focus of Assessment

The earlier discussed *assessment paradox* suggests that numerically precise estimates of narrowly framed outcomes, such as a company-specific likelihood of incurring securities litigation or year-over-year revenue growth, may not be directly informative without some relevant points of comparison. In other words, to become fully informative, an outcome such as, let's say, the 10% chance of incurring shareholder litigation or 10% year-over-year revenue growth may need to be assessed in the context of a relevant evaluation point of reference, such as the overall average likelihood of occurrence of the event of interest or the long-term average revenue growth. Simply put, to

---

5 That technical sounding notion captures the probability of correctly rejecting the null (i.e., no difference, no effect) hypothesis when it is false; it is a component of using statistical analyses to test the efficacy of believed or suspected relationships.
6 Green, C. & Rahmani, M. (2021). 'The implications of rating systems on workforce performance,' *IISE Transactions*, 54(2), 159–172.

become truly meaningful, numerically exact outcomes may need to be properly contextualized.

If, based on past incidence rates, an average company faces, let's say, 5% likelihood of shareholder litigation, the company-specific 10% estimated probability implies comparatively heightened exposure to that particular risk – on the other hand, if the overall average incidence is, let's say, 15%, the same company-specific 10% estimate suggests below average, or comparatively low exposure. Similarly, if the long-term year-over-year revenue growth has been 5%, the 10% outcome suggests strong, i.e., better than expected, performance, but if the long-term growth has been, let's say, 20%, the same 10% outcome would suggest a comparatively poor performance.

Those simple hypothetical examples highlight the often-overlooked fact that the ultimate goal of many, perhaps even most assessments is to draw evaluative conclusions that can be reduced to good vs. bad or below vs. above average evaluation. In view of that, numeric estimates should be seen as necessary but not always sufficient part of the assessment sensemaking process – evaluative frames of reference, typically in the form of appropriate benchmarks or baselines, are needed to interpret outcomes of interest fully and completely.

Another important consideration is the 'what' of assessment, which in organizational management setting could be either *states*, as in the particular condition at a specific time, or *outcomes*, as in consequences of actions of interest, or *processes* used to produce or shape those outcomes. That important distinction is, however, all too often overlooked, as evidenced by often encountered lumping together of the general idea of *standard-based assessment* (i.e., benchmarking and baselining) with the seemingly closely related notion of *best practices*, popularly characterized as identification of procedures or techniques that are accepted or prescribed as being the most effective, or state of the art. The important, in fact, critical distinction between objectively estimable assessment standards, typically encapsulated in the form of an explicit magnitude, and largely subjective assessment of interpretation-prone processes, as in ways of doing something, is – somehow – routinely overlooked by widely used benchmarking classification schemas. More specifically, Camp's internal vs. competitive vs. functional vs. generic,[7] UNESCO's internal vs. external competitive vs. functional vs. trans-institutional vs. implicit vs. generic, and Alstete's international vs. external competitive vs. external collaborative vs. external trans-industry vs. implicit[8] classification schemas all persistently confound assessment approaches focused on tangible (as in countable) outcomes with subjective evaluation-prone processes. Doing so is not only epistemologically unsound – it also leads to methodological fuzziness which in turn leads to lack of application consistency. The importance of drawing a clear line

---

7 Camp, R.C. (1995). *Business Process Benchmarking: Finding and Implementing Best Practices*, Milwaukee: ASQC Quality Press.
8 Alstete, J.W. (1995). 'Benchmarking in higher education: Adapting best practices to improve quality,' ASHE-ERIC Higher Education Report No. 5, ERIC, Washington, DC.

of demarcation between objective standards-focused benchmarking and baselining, and qualitative appraisal-centered delineation of best practices cannot be overstated – that critical distinction is explored in more detail next.

Outcome vs. Process Assessment

Among the many manifestations of the growing embrace of data-driven decision-making mindset is the evermore widespread use of objective assessment standards in the form of benchmarks, along with the growing popularity of the seemingly closely related notion of best practices. However, there is a remarkable lack of definitional and operational consistency in how the notions of 'benchmarking' and 'best practices' are defined, operationalized, and used, resulting in confusion and misuse. In fact, it is common for benchmarking and best practices to be lumped together under a single umbrella of meaning, as illustrated by numerous, popularly referenced framings of benchmarking. For instance, *Business Daily News* sees business benchmarking as 'measuring a company's quality, performance and growth by analyzing the process and procedures of others,[9]' Paychex, a widely used human resources and payroll platform, defines it as 'the process of comparing industry and general business best practices against your own to identify performance gaps and achieve competitive advantages,[10]' and the American Society for Quality, a global association of product and service quality professionals, frames benchmarking as 'the process of measuring products, services, and processes against those of organizations known to be leaders in one or more aspects of their operations.[11]' Somehow, what should be the key distinction between objectively measurable outcomes-focused benchmarking and qualitative appraisal-centered identification of judgment-laden 'best' practices keeps on getting overlooked.

The key culprit here is a persistent failure to expressly differentiate between the very essence of 'processes' and 'outcomes.' Broadly defined, *process* is a series of actions carried out in order to achieve a particular result, whereas *outcome* can be conceptualized as an effect or a result of a particular action. It follows that in many different contexts, processes yield outcomes, which means that processes and outcomes tend to be causally related and thus seen as comprising a single system; that, however, should not be interpreted as implying singularity of assessment. The very essence of outcomes lends itself to fundamentally different assessment mechanisms than those that can be used to comparatively examine the efficacy of processes used to produce those outcomes, which suggests a clear line of demarcation separating benchmarking and identification of best practices. Further underscoring the distinc-

---

9 https://www.businessnewsdaily.com/15960-benchmarking-benefits-small-business.html
10 https://www.paychex.com/articles/payroll-taxes/what-is-benchmarking-for-business
11 https://asq.org/quality-resources/benchmarking

tiveness of those two manifestations of comparative assessment are the differing conceptions of *referencing*, which in the confines of comparative assessment is the identification of relevant evaluative points of comparison. Conceptions of those points of reference range from undefined 'others,' to industry norms, to 'organizations known to be leaders' – it is easy to imagine that the same set of company outcomes may be judged differently depending on the points of comparison, such as industry or peer group average vs. the 'best' in class.

The idea of 'best' warrants some additional reflection. Within the confines of organizational functioning, the genesis of concerted efforts to identify and use emulate superior ways of doing something can be traced to an American mechanical engineer and the father of scientific management, Frederick Taylor. In his influential *Principles of Scientific Management* book, published in 1911, he wrote that 'among the various methods and implements used in each element of each trade there is always one method and one implement which is quicker and better than any of the rest.' Moreover, Taylor went on to also assert that '[the idea of best practice is] applicable to all kinds of human activities, from our simplest individual acts to the work of our great corporations, which call for the most elaborate cooperation.' His ideas were widely embraced; a new, scientific method-centered approach to management was born; and the insatiable thirst for finding and emulating the 'best' began to develop. And while the enthusiasm for scientific management has since waned significantly, the desire to learn from the best shows no signs of abating, in spite of the fact that many modern types of commercial pursuits simply do not lend themselves to singling out the single best approach. An approach that works well for one organization may not work nearly as well for another, overtly similar organization for reasons that can range from organizational culture and philosophy to tactical implementation specifics.

One of the more well-known illustrations of the many pitfalls of the best practice way of thinking is offered by the rise and fall of another, somewhat related and once also hugely influential work *In Search of Excellence*, by Tom Peters and Robert Waterman. Soon after its 1982 release, the book became a bestseller, selling millions of copies; the work's central premise was that the highly structured, number-driven, impersonal approach to management was dead, and the comparatively more humanistic approach defined by more flexible, dynamic, and worker empowerment-focused mindset was destined to produce better results. The authors' captivating conclusions were based on a study of 43 of what they saw as America's best-run companies;[12] the essence of their conclusions was the 'secret sauce' of organizational management, which they summarized in their eight basic principles of successful management. A couple of decades later, nearly two-thirds of Peters and Waterman's 'best' companies have either been acquired by other companies or have gone bankrupt. The point here is that while more

---

12 Peters and Waterman worked for McKinsey & Company, a well-known management consulting firm, at that time.

humanistic, worker empowerment-oriented management approach is clearly preferred, the idea of identifying, and emulating, the 'best' applications of that philosophy may be myopic.

A Closer Look at the Idea of Best Practice

The idea of 'best practice' is synonymous with the notion of 'process,' as in a way of doing something. Even when considered in a comparatively narrow context of organizational management,[13] upon careful consideration it quickly becomes clear that the idea of *process* is unmanageably wide in terms of its implied scope, because of the sheer number of highly dissimilar applications of that overtly simple concept. More specifically, according to the American Productivity and Quality Center (APQC), a nonprofit organization (NPO) focused on process and performance improvement, when considered from the perspective of assessment, the totality of organizational processes can be grouped into 13 distinct operating and management enterprise-level categories, which can be further disaggregated into more than 1,000 processes and associated activities. The number of different types of processes notwithstanding, cutting across those general process types is highly nuanced implementation-specific characteristics, which can be seen as being shaped by a combination of company-specific and industry-wide considerations, in addition to applicable broad environmental and socioeconomic forces. Assessment-wise, that suggests highly interpretive, qualitative information gathering and evaluation mechanisms that go beyond a simple process→outcome relationship, raising an important question: Are the requisite process-describing details readily available? Considering that, at least within for-profit settings the specifics of value producing processes tend to be treated as closely guarded trade secrets, it is doubtful that adequately granular process detailing specifics are publicly available. That is why in the highly competitive business organizational setting, the notion of best practices is primarily advanced by consultants claiming to have the inside knowledge (of other organizations) required to identify best-in-class means of carrying out various organizational tasks; granting that by virtue of past or present engagements with multiple companies' consultants do indeed have insight into some companies' business and operational processes, it is debatable if those insights are adequately representative of the population of interest. A convenience sample of a typically small handful of organizations can rarely justify broad generalizations, as in those claiming to have found the 'best' way of doing something.

Turning back to the challenges stemming from confounding of qualitative process evaluation-focused best practices with benchmarking of overwhelming quantitatively

---

13 The best practice mindset is widely used in a variety of process-oriented activities, such as delivery of medical services or education.

expressed outcomes, that surprising common tendency leads to definitionally ambiguous and methodologically fuzzy framing of both benchmarking and best practices. As suggested by the APQC's taxonomy of organizational processes, process assessment is not only inescapably colored by subjective evaluations – it also requires access to sufficiently granular details needed to substantiate comparative assessments, which in turn are necessary to singling out the best, as in the most efficient or effective, way of doing something. In short, the seductively appealing idea of finding the best ways of doing things is fraught with numerous, difficult-to-surmount obstacles. In a way of a contrast, organizational outcomes tend to be not only objectively measurable, but also fully knowable, which tends not to be the case with state or outcome assessment-minded benchmarking. The main reason for that is that while publicly traded business organizations are not required to disclose how they do what they do (i.e., their processes), they are required to fully, timely, and completely disclose their key outcomes. That means that information needed to benchmark companies' financial results, such as profitability or revenue growth, is readily publicly available, and information detailing the many specific processes that jointly generated those outcomes is, typically, not publicly available.

An even more troubling aspect of the idea of best practices is its implicit uniformity of meaning: What, exactly, are the criteria for determining what constitutes the 'best'? Unlike contexts such as athletics where crowning of the best is usually based on a single, unambiguous outcome (e.g., the best sprinter is someone who in a fair race can traverse 100 m faster than anyone else), in organizational management settings there can be multiple competing framings of what should constitute the best way of doing something, with each typically tied to a different outcome. Hence, a particular business process may deliver outstanding profitability but may underperform in terms of other objectives, such as reaching desired sustainability targets. And while, on the one hand, it could be argued that having multiple 'best' processes that align with different outcomes does not detract from Taylor's idea of 'one method and one implement which is quicker and better than any of the rest,' on the other hand, multiple, context-dependent framings of the notion of best practice inescapably give rise to decision-making ambiguity. It is hard to think of a business or NPO that is motivated by a single goal only, given that modern organizations need to balance interests and priorities of multiple stakeholder groups; under those circumstances, the idea of there being single best process to tackle the various aspects of organizational functioning seems myopic.

Benchmarks and Baselines vs. Best Practices

The preceding line of reasoning is meant to underscore the fundamental conceptual and operational differences separating the ideas of 'best practice' and 'benchmarking' (as well as 'baselining'), as a means of highlighting the importance of expressly differentiating between those informationally distinct notions. Even looking past the above-outlined logical shortcomings of the idea of best practice, the earlier-cited commonly used definitions of benchmarking that frame it as an undertaking that encompasses assessment of outcomes as well as processes that yielded those outcomes confound two distinctly different types of sensemaking efforts, resulting in nonoperationalizable conceptualization. It is intuitively obvious that an analytic approach cannot be both qualitative and quantitative – similarly, to be informationally meaningful, benchmarking cannot be seen as an approach that can be used to assess overwhelmingly numerically expressed (i.e., quantitative) outcomes as well as qualitative interpretation-centered processes. All in all, comparative assessment of organizational states and outcomes calls for definitional and methodological specificity that simply cannot be attained by lumping together assessments of organizational outcomes, and processes used to generate those outcomes.

The essence of benchmarking is encapsulated in two core elements: (1) objective measurement and (2) robust and applicable point(s) of comparison; both of those foundational elements need to be clearly reflected in the definition of benchmarking. The essence of best practices, on the other hand, is encapsulated in comparative dissecting of the logic and specific actions comprising a particular process, seen here as a sensemaking undertaking rooted in subjective appraisal and generally lacking objective points of reference. With that distinction in mind, *benchmarking* is defined here as a process of objective comparative assessment of outcomes of interest, and *best practice identification* is defined as an open-ended set of learning steps aimed at uncovering and describing the most effective or efficient process(es) of doing something, and in a more general sense, a notionally related but definitionally and methodologically distinct (from benchmarking) learning approach.

Thus far, the focus of the overview of the definitional and methodological distinction between outcome and process assessment focused on the difference between benchmarking and best practices, largely because of the widespread tendency to combine those two ideas under a single umbrella of meaning. Ironically, the idea of baseline and the corresponding practice of baselining are rarely discussed jointly with the parallel notion of benchmark and the practice of benchmarking, in spite of the fact that, as discussed earlier, those two approaches represent the two complementary dimensions of outcome assessment (benchmarking captures the spatial dimension and baselining captures the temporal dimension). In view of that, it is important to expand the preceding outcome vs. process overview that was focused on the distinction between benchmarking (outcome) and best practices (process) to also encompass baselining.

Perhaps the most fundamental distinction between the related ideas of benchmarking and baselining, and the distinctly different notions of best practice are their goals: Benchmarking and baselining alike aim to index observed outcome magnitudes to evaluation-enriching comparative contexts of like organizations (benchmarks) and/or past trends (baselines), all while accounting for and adjusting for any pertinent 'us vs.

others' or 'now vs. before' differences. Stated differently, benchmarking and baselining can be seen as mechanisms of objective qualification and contextualizing of observed outcomes or states; the primary benefit offered by those informational tools is that of aiding the task of objectively interpreting numerically precise but meaning-wise uncertain magnitudes (recall the idea of assessment paradox discussed earlier). In contrast to that, the goal of searching for best practices is to discover and describe the most effective or efficient process(es) of doing something. An important characteristic of the idea of best practice is that the very determination of what constitutes the 'best' practice is implicitly substantiated by the perceived credibility of the source, which is typically a service provider with related experience. Two different methods for uncovering two different types of insights rely on fundamentally different criteria.

Applicability and Usages

Summarizing the preceding overview, notionally similar but methodologically distinct (see Figures 1.2 and 1.3) ideas of *benchmarking* and *baselining* are commonly used to assess the relative efficacy of states or outcomes of interest. The former is geared toward peer assessment – i.e., 'how do our results compare to those of similar organizations? (implicitly, at the time of comparison)' – whereas the latter offers a way of assessing cross-time change in an outcome of interest in a way that accounts for the impact of changing situational factors, i.e., 'how does our performance change over time?' Both approaches rely on objective data to yield 'hard,' i.e., rooted in independently verifiable evidence, and unbiased points of reference that can be used to assess the relative efficacy of states or outcomes of interest. In short, benchmarking and baselining offer quantitative means of comparative assessment.

While in a very broad sense of organizational assessment the idea of best practice identification and emulation may appear to be closely related to benchmarking and thus to baselining, it is in fact conceptually and methodologically distinct. Moreover, the idea of best practices lacks meaningful operational framing – it is generally understood to be a loosely defined set of qualitative process assessment efforts, the specifics of which are largely left up to individual investigators, rendering that approach difficult to replicate and its findings equally difficult to validate. The idea itself is seductively appealing, but as discussed earlier, it fails to stand up to closer definitional and methodological scrutiny. To be sure, there can be situations in which identification of what might be deemed the best way of doing something is both viable and appropriate, but that is a long way from assuming that identification of best practices is universally applicable or feasible.

Although all three assessment-focused approaches make important contributions to the larger practice of *evidence-based management*,[14] it is important to be cognizant of fundamental differences separating quantitative outcome assessment-focused benchmarking and baselining, and qualitative process evaluation-focused best practices. Method- and function-wise, the two decision-making tools serve distinctly different goals: Benchmarking and baselining offer methodologically explicit, objective means of categorizing observed outcomes into conclusion-laden evaluations, such as below vs. above average, while best practices offer (largely) qualitative review-derived process recommendations. In view of those fundamental differences, the notion of best practices falls outside the scope of this book.

Developing robust understanding of how organizations can use benchmarking and baselining to carry out comparative assessments of their states and outcomes of interest cannot be achieved without first developing a clear understanding of what constitutes an organization. The reason for that is that while the term 'organization' has a ring of familiarity, the manner in which it is used is not uniform, as there are distinctly different types of organizations, and those differences influence organizational assessment efforts. With that in mind, the next section offers a high-level overview of different types of organizations, framed in the context of organizational assessment.

Organizations and Organizational Assessment

Assessing the effectiveness of prior decisions as the basis of the next set of choices is a staple of modern organizational decision-making practices. While true in principle, that very general characterization can take on different meanings across different organizational settings; consequently, basic *organizational literacy*, or familiarity with basic organizational structures and their innerworkings, is necessary to developing appreciation of the intrinsic value of sound and unbiased, as well as comparatively framed, assessment of organizational states and outcomes.

Organizational Society

At their core, organizations are groups of people joined together in pursuit of shared goals. As it is intuitively obvious from that broad definition, the reason humans tend to 'join together' is because doing so helps with the attainment of goals, which in turn can be seen as manifestations of a wide range of human needs. Within the confines of the

---

14 For a more in-depth overview of evidence-based management, see Banasiewicz, A. (2019). *Evidence-Based Decision-Making*, Routledge.

well-known Maslow's hierarchy of needs, those can range from the most fundamental, namely self-preservation, to those that could be considered refined or evolved, most notably self-actualization. In view of that, organizations are usually formed to facilitate the pursuit of a variety of objectives, and so their influence on the lives of individuals can be expected to grow as those individuals' needs and goals expand. In fact, throughout human history, organizations have been steadily expanding into more spheres of life and have been growing in size and complexity. And so as aptly summarized by a noted organizational scholar Amitai Etzioni, 'our society is organizational society.' Most individuals are born in hospitals, educated in schools, and employed by business, governmental, or other organizations; those individuals then elect to join social, religious, or professional organizations, some for the duration of their lives. From birth through death, at work or at play, life in modern societies is increasingly conducted in organizational settings, so much so that in view of many sociologists, organizations are now the dominant institutions of modern societies.

When considered within the confines of organizational decision-making, the above-suggested general characterization of organization types – i.e., social, religious, service, business, etc. – can be reduced into two very broad categories of commercial and noncommercial organizations. The former encompasses a wide range of business entities that seek to profit from offering goods and services to individuals and other organizations, while the latter instead of seeking to earn a profit aim to further various other goals and objectives.

Commercial vs. Noncommercial Organizations

Commercial organizations exist primarily to generate profit, that is, to earn more money than they spend; quite commonly, those organizations are also described as 'for-profit' or 'business' entities. Under the US law, for-profit companies can be organized as corporations, partnerships, limited liability companies (LLCs), or sole proprietorships; the owners of a corporation are called shareholders, the owners of a partnership are called partners, the owners of an LLC are called members, and the owner (by definition, there is only one) of a sole proprietorship is called, well, the owner. Of those four US-centric (i.e., tied to US laws and regulatory requirements) broad embodiments of commercial organizations, two – corporations and partnerships – can be traded on open stock exchanges such as the New York Stock Exchange or NASDAQ, while the other two cannot. That distinction is important insofar as the so-called public companies, or those traded of open stock exchanges, have a broader set of constituents than non-public[15] (not traded on open stock exchanges) or private

---

15 It is instructive to note that the label of 'public' and 'private'/'non-public' companies have very different meanings in different parts of the world. For example, in North America, a 'public' company

organizations. For instance, being publicly traded on any of the US stock exchanges creates additional performance assessment and disclosure requirements, the specifics of which are outlined by several congressional acts (e.g., the Securities Act of 1933, the Securities Exchange Act of 1934, and the Sarbanes-Oxley Act of 2002), jointly referred to as 'securities laws,' and operationally clarified by numerous regulations issued by the US Securities and Exchange Commission, an independent agency of the federal government charged with enforcing the said securities laws (those considerations are at the center of the case studies in Chapters 9 and 10).

The seemingly endless arrays of noncommercial organizations based or operating in the United States can be grouped into somewhat distinct segments based on the type of their underlying tax exemption and their broadly defined advocacy focus. In terms of tax exemption status, the US Internal Revenue Service recognizes two main types of noncommercial entities: NPOs, and not-for-profit organizations (NFPOs). The former serve the public via goods and services, as exemplified by various social advocacy groups such as American Civil Liberties Union or registered charitable organizations[16] such as Catholic Charities, while the latter typically serve just a specific group, as is the case with professional associations such as the American Bar Association or the American Marketing Association.

While NPOs and NFPOs share some communalities with for-profit business firms, most notably in the sense that both pursue their stated organizational goals, they are separated by distinct differences. Perhaps the most visible of all is their purpose: For-profit commercial companies exist to earn a profit, a goal they pursue by developing products and service aimed at meeting the needs of the broadly defined marketplace; in a way of contrast, noncommercial organizations exist to advance specific causes. The second key difference is the source of capital that is required to operate. Commercial entities' primary source of capital is investment, which is speculative allocation of money by investors with the expectation of future profits, whereas noncommercial organizations' primary source of capital are donations, which are (typically, but not always, monetary) gifts given in support of causes furthered by organizations. Another key difference is the nature of leadership: In a very general sense, for-profit companies are usually managed by select groups of individuals, commonly referred to as executive leaders, who are endowed with legal rights to act on behalf of their organizations, and whose actions are overseen by compensated boards of directors. NPOs, on the other hand, are typically managed more directly by, usually uncompen-

---

is one that is traded on any of the open stock exchanges, whereas in Europe, a 'public' company is a government-owned entity (e.g., a national airline or a public transit organization).

16 In the United States, charities represent by far the largest subset of the noncommercial ecosystem – out of the total of about 1.5 million nonprofits, nearly 1 million are registered charities; foundations are a distant second (a bit more than 100,000), with trade and professional associations (about 63,000) as the third among the most numerous categories.

sated and larger in number,[17] boards of directors; their day-to-day operations are typically directed by (compensated) executive directors who are entrusted with the responsibility of carrying out board of directors' decisions. The combination of those differences manifests themselves in different informational needs, which ultimately call for different modes of assessment.

The type of organization notwithstanding, organizational management requires pooling of diverse types of information that reflect the many different aspects of organizational functioning, which means that organizational decision-making entails varying degrees of collaboration. In fact, collaborative decision-making is now widely seen as not only societally preferred (due to being more inclusive) but also more effective in terms of measurable outcomes; the evidence, however, paints a somewhat different picture.

Collaborative Decision-Making

Implicit in the notion of organization is the idea of collaboration. The term itself has strongly positive overtones, and so not surprisingly, the idea of collaborative decision-making is seductive. It hints of inclusion and equality, and it also promises to circumvent the many challenges inflicting individual sensemaking, as exemplified by cognitive bias precipitated distortions, choice evaluating limitations brought about by human channel capacity, and the unreliable nature of recall, largely attributed to brain plasticity.[18] In addition, collaborative decision-making is also widely believed to offer a forum for critical reviews of individual ideas, which can then be expected to create opportunities for individuals to refine their ideas. All told, it is not surprising that conventional wisdom argues that groups tend to make better decisions than individuals. And yet, while convincing and certainly appealing, there is little-to-no research evidence to back up those commonly held beliefs.

In fact, studies in social cognition and psychology suggest that cognitive and situational influences are generally the strongest determinant of the quality of decision-making, and that when evaluated in the context of objective standards, decisions made by groups do not consistently outshine decisions made by individuals. More on point, research results suggest that while collective decision-making tends to heighten decision confidence, there is no consistent uptick in decision quality. Why? Because just as individual-level sensemaking is affected by cognitive bias and other largely subconscious sensemaking impairments, group sensemaking is subject to different but potentially just as reason-warping influences. Perhaps the most visible of those is

---

17 Typically, 25–30 members, but in some instances as many as 100 members; in the way of a contrast, corporate boards of directors tend to be made up of 8–12 members.
18 See Banasiewicz, A. (2019). *Evidence-Based Decision-Making*, Routledge, for a more in-depth discussion.

biased information search, which manifests itself as strong preference for information that supports the group's view; it could be thought of as a group analog to confirmation bias or bandwagon effect, two somewhat related individual-level cognitive
biases. Often harder to discern is *groupthink*, a dysfunctional pattern of thought and
interaction during group decision-making characterized by closed-mindedness, uniformity expectations, and group bias. At the opposite end of group dynamics from
groupthink is the idea of group conflict. As suggested by social exchange theory,
which views the stability of group interactions through a theoretical lens of negoti-
ated exchange between parties, individual group members are ultimately driven by
the desire to maximize their benefits. When group interactions become more competitive than collaborative conflicts are likely to arise, adversely impacting contributory
participation of individual group members who may see (group) sharing as detrimen-
tal to their self-interest. Simply put, within-group competition reduces the willingness
of individuals to contribute their best to the group effort, which, albeit via a very different underlying set of mechanisms, ultimately has the same cognitive diversity reducing impact as groupthink.

The skepticism that emanates from the preceding overview is not meant to discount the idea of collaborative decision-making – it is merely meant to underscore
the importance of unbiased and objective information. To deliver hoped for benefits,
group collaborations need to be constructed around the review of objective evidence,
and level-setting factual assessment of organizational states and/or outcomes of interest is a key part of such collaboratively shared evidence. The development of formal,
data-driven benchmarking and baselining-based comparative assessment capabilities
that can provide that type of unbiased and valid information is the focus of this book.

Spatiotemporal Assessment

Tacitly implied in the preceding overview is the relationship between benchmarking
and baselining, seen here as two distinct dimensions of organizational assessment. As
noted earlier, the former captures the spatial dimensions of assessment, manifesting
itself in relating to organizational outcomes or features to those other, peer organizations; the latter, on the other hand, embodies the temporal dimension of assessment,
focused on change over time. When used individually, each of the two methods has
some distinct limitations: Starting with benchmarking, by trying to align itself with
their peers, organizations run the risk of losing sight of their own unique strengths
and opportunities; moreover, the very idea of benchmarking organizational outcomes
can lead to excessive proliferation of endless arrays of key performance indicators, in
addition to also implicitly assuming that noted performance indications remain stable
over time. In the case of baselining, the lack of external evaluation standards can lead
to myopic evaluations of change over time, which can lead to distorted conclusions.
Those potential problems, however, can be circumvented by thoughtfully combining

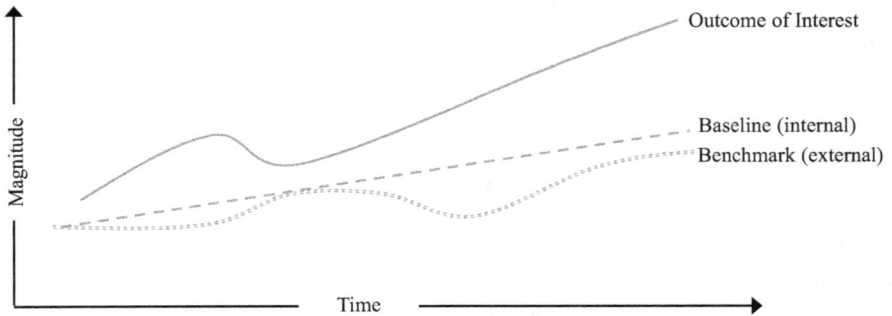

Figure 1.5: Spatiotemporal assessment.

the key elements of benchmarking and baselining into a more complete and more informationally robust ongoing evaluation of organizational outcomes of interest.

Characterized here as *spatiotemporal assessment*, the explicit and deliberate amalgamation of the key elements of benchmarking and baselining offers an informationally complete approach to comparative assessment of key aspects of organizational functioning by framing comparisons with external standards in the longitudinal context. Figure 1.5 shows the graphical illustration of the reasoning imbedded in that idea.

The idea captured in Figure 1.5 is just that – a conceptual point of departure in need of methodological and operational details, which are offered in the ensuing chapters. For now, it is important to emphasize the informational value of framing organizational assessment of outcomes or states of interest in the context that incorporates the spatial (i.e., benchmarking) and temporal (i.e., baselining) dimensions, offering a more motion picture rather than a still image like appraisal capabilities. With that in mind, it is the purpose of this book to describe that more informationally complete approach to comparative assessment.

Structure of the Book

Building on the foundational overview of the scope and focal areas of broadly defined comparative assessment, the ensuing chapters offer a systematic overview of the various aspects of benchmarking and baselining, seen here as the two key mechanisms of comparative assessment. With that in mind, the remainder of this book is organized as follows:

Chapters 2 and 3 offer an overview of key foundational considerations. More specifically, Chapter 2 begins with a brief summarization of the roots of the ideas of benchmarking and baselining, along with a recap of how those ideas are currently used; the second part of Chapter 2 is focused on reframing those ideas to better reflect their intended informational value. Next, Chapter 3 offers an overview of key estimation and parameterization concepts and applications, which are of core importance to crafting unbiased and dependable assessment capabilities.

Building on the general conceptual and methodological foundation laid by Chapters 2 and 3, respectively, the next Chapters 4 and 5 relate those foundational considerations to the two focal comparative assessment mechanisms of interest here. More specifically, Chapter 4 offers an in-depth overview of the key conceptual and methodological details that underpin the development of robust benchmarks, and Chapter 5 offers a parallel overview focusing on baselining.

The goal of the next segment, spanning Chapters 6 through 8, is to expand and 'modernize' the notions of benchmarking and baselining. To that end, Chapter 6 considers the ideas of comparative assessment from the standpoint of static and dynamic perspectives, while Chapter 7 relates the modern machine learning and artificial intelligence capabilities to the idea of standard setting. Chapter 8 takes the next logical step in extending the idea of standard setting by discussing it in the context of predictive analytics.

The last two chapters – Chapters 9 and 10 – are devoted to applied case studies that highlight the key attributes of baselining (Chapter 9) and benchmarking (Chapter 10).

Chapter 2
The Genesis and the Current State

The previous chapter's emphasis on the widely subscribed but conceptually and methodologically unfounded tendency to lump together the ideas of benchmarking and best practices was meant to contribute to the development of the much-needed epistemological (i.e., what it is and what it is not) clarity for the notion of benchmarking, and the related but distinct idea of baselining. By clearly separating the ideas of benchmarking and best practices along the 'what' (states and outcomes vs. processes) and 'how' (quantitative vs. qualitative) dimensions, benchmarking and baselining can be jointly and more clearly framed as spatiotemporal unbiased comparative assessment mechanisms. That narrowing of the definitional scope is now followed by closer examination of the informational essence and utility of benchmarking and baselining, seen here as mechanisms of comparative and objective assessment of organizational states or outcomes of interest. With that in mind, the overall goal of this chapter is to further contribute to epistemological clarity of these two important tools of organizational assessment, starting with an overview of the historical roots of benchmarking and baselining, as a mean of developing better understanding of how the current usages (and misusages) of those ideas emerged over time.

Origins

Nowadays, business and other organizations routinely benchmark their focal states and outcomes such as financial performance or exposure to various threats; though perhaps less often, many of the same organizations also baseline cross-time changes in focal organizational outcomes and states. In a more general sense, the practice of benchmarking is commonly used to comparatively assess the core facets of organizational functioning and well-being by drawing parallels to relevant points of reference, such as peer groups' averages; similarly, the practice of baselining is used to track cross-time changes in organizational measures of interest. Described earlier as spatial (us vs. relevant others) and temporal (now vs. past) facets of assessment, benchmarking and baselining are important tools of evidence-based management, a relatively new approach to management, centered on the use of objective evidence as the basis of organizational decision-making.

However, as outlined in the previous chapter, those two pillars of unbiased comparative assessment are in dire need of definitional and operational clarification. Of particular interest here is to understand how the current conceptions of benchmarking and baselining started and evolved over time, which is not only interesting in a general sense but also potentially instructive to the efforts to bring about the much-needed conceptual and methodological clarity. A natural point of departure in that

https://doi.org/10.1515/9783111001296-002

process is to look back at the origins and subsequent development of the two approaches, with an eye toward understanding the current conceptual framing and usage.

Benchmarking

At its core, the idea of benchmarking can be seen as a manifestation of the appeal of comparative assessment: How do we compare to our peers? To the degree to which, broadly conceived, organizations are collections of individuals joined together in pursuit of shared goals, many aspects of organizational functioning reflect basic human psychological needs. More specifically, the need to compare can be seen as a manifestation of the basic human need to be socially validated; in the organizational context, peer benchmarking is thus analogous to the individual-level need for social validation. Underscoring the strength of that nearly instinctive need for comparative assessment is that, according to established theories[1] and recent empirical studies, as much as 10% of human thoughts involve comparisons of some kind.

The etymology of the term 'benchmark' can be traced to mid-nineteenth-century surveying work and trying to address the critical problem of establishing correct reference *marks* in the ground is a way that assured that placement of a *bench* supporting surveyor's instruments was sufficiently leveled, a key requirement of correctness of subsequent measurements. The general idea of setting a robust point of reference, or benchmarking, was subsequently extended beyond surveying and into a wide array of facets of organizational management. The modern conception of that practice is most directly connected to the emergence of formalized quality management practices in the 1950s in the United States and Japan, perhaps best illustrated by W. Edwards Deming's plan-do-check-act cycle used for the control and continuous improvement of business processes.[2] Around that time, in the United States, the General Electric Company began to experiment with the use of statistical means of evaluating alternative approaches to basic functional activities, while in Japan, Toyota Motor Company began developing its 'kaizen,' or continuous improvement manufacturing processes. However, the practice known today as *benchmarking* is most directly linked to 1980s Xerox Corporation's initiatives geared toward stemming its market share slide by systematically tracking activities of its Japanese competitors and making adjustments based on the resultant

---

1 Social comparison theory, a framework developed in 1954 by psychologist Leon Festinger, captures the idea that individuals determine their own social and personal worth based on how they stack up against others.

2 The term 'benchmark' can be traced back to the emergence of firearms in the nineteenth century, and more specifically, the process that was used to assess the accuracy of firearms: rifles were fixed in a bench to make it possible to fire several identical shots at a target, and the spread in resultant marks was used as the basis for accuracy assessment.

insights; in fact, the first book dedicated expressly to benchmarking was authored by Xerox's head of those competitive tracking initiatives.

Nowadays, the use of the general idea of benchmarking is ubiquitous, but as discussed at length in the previous chapter, there is a considerable degree of variability among the many competing conceptions of that general idea. Many of the widely used framings confound the distinctly different endeavors of quantitative (i.e., unbiased) comparative assessment of organizational states or outcomes, with qualitative (i.e., perspective laden) efforts geared toward identification of the most effective or efficient organizational process approaches, an idea broadly characterized as best practices. Moreover, definitional inconsistencies are apparent even in the manner of how the terms 'benchmark' and 'baseline' are used in practice. For example, in the world of investments, well-known financial indices such as the Dow Jones Industrial Average or the Russell 2000 Index are commonly referred to as 'benchmarks' in spite of their obvious cross-time trend-based orientations. As noted above, the present-day term 'benchmark' is rooted in the idea of a point, i.e., a 'mark,' not a trend(line), that can be used for reference; hence, ontologically speaking, the use of that term should be restricted to standards that do not include the time dimension. The idea of time-dependent standards encapsulated in the notion of 'baselining,' which is discussed next.

Baselining

In a manner that is reminiscent of benchmarking, the present-day concept of *baselining* can also be traced to surveying. Originally conceived as a solution to a related (to setting correct reference marks) problem, baseline was originally 'the line upon which others [could] depend'; in simple terms, it was a defined line between two points on the Earth's surface. As used today, it is a line serving as a basis of comparison of trended change in something – that 'something' can range widely, encompassing physical measurements used in construction or navigation as well as more abstractly framed reference levels used in medical and pharmacological research, educational assessment, financial performance, software development, and numerous other areas where it is beneficial to assess progress in related to a fixed line of reference. It is worth noting that the concept of baselining is particularly popular in the field of psychology and counseling, where it is used to evaluate behavioral and attitudinal change over time. Interestingly, however, in that broad context, baselining is frequently framed as a way of 'benchmarking' some type of a departure from the accepted norm, which muddies, if not altogether disregards, the fundamental conceptual and methodological distinctiveness (see Chapter 1) of those two assessment-aiding approaches. When used in business contexts, however, the idea of baselining is most often used in establishing a level of normalization, which implicitly suggests some degree of distinctiveness from benchmarking. Still, any degree of unwarranted equivocation underscores the importance of establishing clear definitional and methodological lines of demarcation between the ideas and applications of baselining and benchmarking.

Surprisingly, while clearly beneficial in a wide array of assessment-related situations, the general notion of baselining did not attract much attention from social science theoreticians, including those focused on organizational theory and management. A review of related academic literature in which the concept of baselining was used as a part of the research process reveals scant attention to conceptualization and operationalization of that notion. In fact, rarely, if ever, is baselining even expressly and clearly operationally defined; almost as a norm, the discussion is limited to merely mentioning the use of a baseline, without addressing how that baseline was framed. Such in effect dismissive approach to clearly defining how, exactly, a baseline of interest has been derived is a manifestation of failure to recognize the value of that idea, and the larger idea of unbiased comparative assessment. The most direct and highly visible consequence of that lack of conceptual and methodological clarity is the proliferation of plurality of assessment standards, which impinges on organizations' ability to assess the focal aspects of their functioning persistently and consistently. Within the confines of theory building, such ambiguity of meaning and usage can be expected to impede researchers' ability to carry out broader – i.e., norm or theory shaping – comparisons, which are essential to the derivation of sound theoretical structures. More on point, methodologically incongruent assessment baselines can render side-by-side comparisons of similar investigations suspect, even outright implausible, ultimately impeding the development of generalized conclusions.

All in all, much like benchmarking, baselining is a compelling notion that is much in need of clear definitional framing and equally explicit operationalization. Though not as widely used in business contexts as benchmarks, baselines are nonetheless just as fundamental to robust organizational management in general, and evidence-based management practices in particular. In fact, given the complementary character of those two dimensions of organizational assessment – i.e., the earlier discussed benchmarking answering the question of 'how do our outcomes compare to those of our peers' and baselining answering the question of 'how do our outcomes change across time?' – both should be seen as necessary components of holistic organizational performance assessment.

A Call to Action

Recalling the earlier discussed *assessment paradox*, numerically expressed assessments of measurable outcomes, such as return on investment (ROI), a commonly used measure of profitability, can be both precise and vague: Precise because numeric expressions are generally magnitudinally unambiguous, but vague because the meaning implied by those magnitudes may not necessarily be well-defined, in a sense that it does not immediately convey clear interpretation. Is, for instance, 7% ROI a good outcome? In many organizational sensemaking contexts, precisely measured magnitudes ultimately need to be categorized as falling above or below some evaluative standard. Or stated differently, to be meaningful, quantitatively expressed measurements of organizational states or outcomes need to be qualitatively interpretable. Also worth noting is that there is a growing urgency to develop a robust and flexible framework that can serve as a blueprint to develop comprehensive organizational comparative assessment capabilities.

The urgency to develop those capabilities is fueled by ceaseless spread of digitization of evermore facets of organizational functioning, a trend that is rendering more and more of those facets quantifiable and ultimately in need of evaluative assessment. To that end, the central thesis of this book is that thoughtfully and carefully framed, and operationally explicit benchmarking and baselining capabilities are at the center of valid and reliable comparative assessment capabilities. That, however, cannot happen without fundamental redefinition of the notions of benchmarking and baselining, which is made necessary by their manifest lack of *construct*, i.e., does the idea capture what it is intended to capture, and *discriminant validity*, i.e., is the idea of interest separate and distinct from related ideas. As currently used, both of those ideas are not only definitionally and methodologically murky but in fact are confounded with other assessment-related notions, most notably the idea of best practices, an inclination vividly illustrated by one of the more widely cited books on that topic: *Business Process Benchmarking: Finding and Implementing Best Practices.*[17] It is easy to see how that lack of clear and consistent expression results in inconsistent, and ultimately largely unproductive applications of those important ideas.

Diversity of Perspectives or Lack of Focus?

To summarize the preceding arguments, though ubiquitous, as currently used, the notion of benchmarking eludes clear operational specification. It has even been characterized as 'ambiguous, multidimensional and contingent'; in fact, the notion of what, exactly, constitutes benchmarking is seen as so vague that efforts to undertake systematic review of benchmarking-focused literature have been deemed impractical, even undesirable. What tends to be characterized as the 'rich diversity of benchmarking perspectives' is reflected in several competing typologies, with one of the longest standing schemas being one proposed by has been proposed by Camp,[3] the then Xerox Corporation's manager who led the company's 1980s benchmarking initiatives. That framing distinguishes between internal, competitive, functional, and generic forms of benchmarking, but offers scant methodological guidance on how those dif-

---

3 Camp, R.C. (1995). *Business Process Benchmarking: Finding and Implementing Best Practices*, ASQC Quality Press.

ferent benchmarking dimensions should be operationalized. Other classification sche-mas distinguish between results and process dimensions, or between voluntary and compulsory, or between unilateral and cooperative, or between implicit and explicit, or between international, global, external, and collaborative, or between perfor-mance, process, and strategic dimensions. There are two common themes that cut across those competing conceptions of benchmarking: The first is a persistent lack of recognition of critical differences between assessing overwhelmingly quantitatively expressed outcomes, and the largely qualitative process evaluations. The second theme that cuts across those conceptualizations is the lack of meaningful operational-izations – in other words, they offer no concept operationalization-enabling method-ologies, which severely reduces practical usefulness of those classification schemas.

There are, however, several notable exceptions, in the form of methodologically explicit benchmarking approaches that were developed to support specific scientific research efforts. For example, a recent study that investigated the behavior of high-way traffic flows from the perspective of compressible fluid (and expressed through aggregate state variables of flow and density) utilized methodologically rigorous benchmarks to assess the efficacy of competing models' performance in real-world traffic applications; another recent study utilized methodologically robust bench-marking to support taxonomic evaluations of competing artificial intelligence techni-ques used in the detection and classification of COVID-19 medical images. Equally methodologically robust benchmarking approaches have also been proposed to assess the implementation of lean manufacturing principles to healthcare or hotel service quality, to support targeted guidance for individual retail stores, and to assess the overall energy usage and energy efficiency of buildings and air-conditioning systems. By and large, those scientific research supporting benchmarking approaches utilized a combination of physical simulations focused on testing of specific design parame-ters using multivariate statistical estimation techniques such as regression, cluster, data envelopment, or stochastic frontier analyses, or hybrid methods such as Bayes-ian analysis or Monte Carlo simulations. However, a combination of methodological complexity and narrowly defined applications translates into poor transferability of those approaches to applied organizational management contexts, where simpler compare-and-contrast types of assessment techniques are preferred.

In a more general sense, whether it is meant to serve as a mean of assessing per-formance outcomes of business entities or the basis of scientific assessment, the ratio-nale embedded in benchmarking analyses is based on an implicit assumption that assessment benchmarks represent objective norms or standards. And to be sure, there are numerous situations in which that is indeed the case – for instance, the American College of Radiology developed the Breast Imagining Reporting and Data System in the 1980s to serve as a universal standard, which was further solidified by the passage of the Mammography Quality Standards Act by the U.S. Congress in 1992. That, however, is an exception, not the rule. By and large, there are very few such 'natural' evaluation standards – in the vast majority of applied situations, organizational managers need to devise their own comparative assessment standards, which underscores the importance of conceptually and methodologically sound and explicit benchmarking and baselining capabilities.

Rethinking Benchmarking and Baselining

To recap the preceding overview of the current state of benchmarking and baselining practices, the rapid spread of digitization is amplifying the importance of sound assessment, primarily because it offers unparalleled opportunity to objectively measure an ever-expanding array of outcomes and states of interest; at the same time, it is also amplifying assessment paradox-emanating ambiguities. All in all, in the Age of Data, conceptually explicit and operationally specific framings of the general ideas of benchmarking and baselining are of paramount importance.

The key to conceptually sound and operationally clear descriptions of those assessment-critical notions is in framing them in the three-dimensional definitional context discussed in the previous chapter: spatial vs. temporal, static vs. dynamic, and existing vs. created assessments, graphically summarized in Figures 1.1–1.4. The *spatial* vs. *temporal* distinction aims to draw attention to the importance of expressly differentiating between assessments focused on lateral vs. longitudinal comparisons, or between comparing entities' of interest states or outcomes with those of their peers, and evaluating cross-time changes in entity-specific states or outcome of interest, also commonly characterized as trending of key performance indicators (KPIs). In the context of that distinction, *benchmarking* should be seen as a mechanism supporting more meaningful assessment of the spatial comparative dimension, whereas *baselining* should be seen as a mechanism best suited to support the cross-time change dimension.

The meaning of the *static* vs. *dynamic* distinction is nuanced because the idea of 'static' can be taken to mean fixed, as in universally true, or unchanging within somewhat more contained context. The former connotes universally fixed points of reference, such as those used in physical sciences, as exemplified by the speed of light or the ratio of the circumference of a circle to its diameter (commonly known as π); those quantities typically represent discovered features of the observed or observable world. In the way of a contrast, the latter denotes a wide array of comparative points of reference that are derived from observable phenomena, as exemplified by the various economic (e.g., average household income) or behavioral (e.g., average retirement age) point of reference. Within the confines of organizational decision-making, which is the focal context for the overview of benchmarking and baselining offered in this book, the idea of static evaluation standards typically implies reference standards that have been derived from observable and measurable phenomena and are treated as fixed quantities in a particular context and within some period. For instance, average ROI evaluation benchmarks can be derived pooling financial performance data of individual companies that together comprise a particular industry, such as pharmaceuticals; under most circumstances, those benchmarks would be fixed for a period of time, such as a year. It follows that central to the idea of derived static benchmarks is the idea of successive derivation, commonly referred to as re-estimation, which is the process of updating values of interest using either different data (e.g., more recent measurements) or different parameters (e.g., another industry). The idea of re-estimation in turn implies intentionality, framed here as purposeful, reasoned action taken with regard to something, or more specifically in the context of re-estimation, with regard to frequency.

Even though, by and large, behavioral phenomena change over time, estimates of some of those phenomena can be treated as fixed for some period of time, especially if those phenomena are either slow changing, such as buying habits, or are measured infrequently, such as companies' returns (which are typically assessed annually). In view of that, derivation of sound benchmarks and baselines demands addressing the question of how those non-fixed evaluation standards are used and updated, which is at the core of the static vs. dynamic distinction. The former encapsulates standards that are updated at distinct points in time, with update intervals being either fixed, such as every 12 months, or floating (typically driven by some type of material change or updated data becoming available), while the latter describes standards that are updated each time they are accessed or used, i.e., on-the-fly. As could be expected, the on-the-fly dynamic updating is most appropriate for situations characterized by the combination of continuously fluctuating outcomes or states and ongoing access to real-time data.

The third benchmark and baseline framing dimension takes the form of the distinction between existing and created standards. Defined earlier as externally determined and, generally, slow changing, *existing standards* usually manifest themselves as broad generalizations, often taking the form of broad generalizations. *Created standards*, on the other hand, represent situationally determined extensions or modifications of some underlying facts, often taking the form of estimates computed using applicable data. Within the confines of organizational functioning, existing standards can range from rules of thumb, as exemplified by 10% average long-term annual stock market return, to applicable regulations or policies that govern different aspects of organizational functioning, as illustrated by the standard legal definition of what constitutes full-time employment (the U.S. Internal Revenue Service, an agency of the federal government with rulemaking powers, considers, for purposes of employer-shared responsibility provisions, anyone who is employed on average at least 30 h per week or 130 h per month to be a full-time employee). In the way of contract, created standards are often need-based estimates that are derived using mathematically and/ or logically data analytic methods; their exact scope and definition are commonly shaped by informational needs at hand. For instance, average frequency of a particular type of event can be created – meaning, derived – from detailed event tracking data, and those comparative standards are commonly used to inform risk transfer and mitigation decisions.

The General Conceptual Framework

The three sets of dichotomies – spatial vs. temporal, static vs. dynamic, and existing vs. created – can be further reduced into three distinct comparative assessment framing dimensions: focus (spatial vs. temporal), state (static vs. dynamic), and source (existing vs. created). Jointly, those dimensions define the informational scope of the systematic and objective approach to comparative the assessment described here. More specifically, together, they determine both the communality as well as distinctiveness of benchmarking and baselining, the two informationally complementary and methodologically consistent mechanisms of systematic and unbiased comparative assessment.

The focus dimension is the source of distinctiveness, as it expressly addresses the fundamental difference between the two key aspects of comparative assessment: comparing oneself to similar others, i.e., peers (benchmarking) and relating one's current states or outcomes to historical trends. The two other dimensions – state and source – frame the uniqueness of benchmarking and baselining in a way that also maintains linkages to a common conceptual and methodological framing of the general idea of comparative assessment. Figure 2.1 offers a graphic summary of the resultant framework.

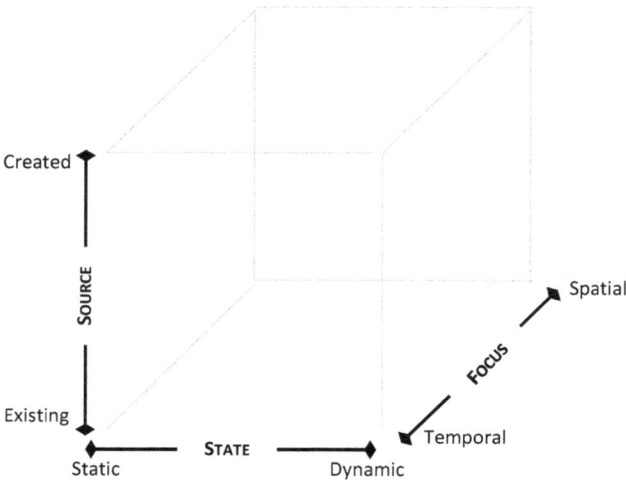

Figure 2.1: The three-dimensional framing of benchmarking and baselining.

The goal of the general conceptual model shown in Figure 2.1 is to offer a clear point of departure that can be used to frame the currently conceptually confusing and methodologically unclear notions of benchmarking and baselining, seen here as two pillars of unbiased comparative assessment. Using that general framework, a more in-depth definitional characterization of benchmarking and baselining is presented next.

Framing the Notion of Benchmarking

Building on the foundation of the three-dimensional framework summarized in Figure 2.1, *benchmarking* can be formally defined as a process of deriving spatial contrast-focused assessment standards that, origin-wise, can be either existing, i.e., drawn from established sources, or derived from applicable data, with magnitudes that either remain fixed within applicable time frames or are derived dynamically. *Spatial contrasting* is a comparative assessment-focused aspect of cross-sectional analysis, or search for insights hidden in patterns of similarities and differences between entities, such as individuals, households, or companies, as seen from the perspective of at a single point in time.[4] In that sense, spatial contrasting, and thus benchmarking, can be seen as a direct outcome of collapsing of the three-dimensional framework in Figure 2.1 along the spatial vs. temporal dimension; as discussed later in this chapter, baselining can be seen as a product of the same general derivation logic, with focus on temporal rather than spatial aspects of assessment. Noting that is important as it highlights both the distinctiveness of benchmarking and baselining, as well as their informationally complementary character.

Figure 2.2 offers a graphical summary of benchmarking-specific conceptual frameset.

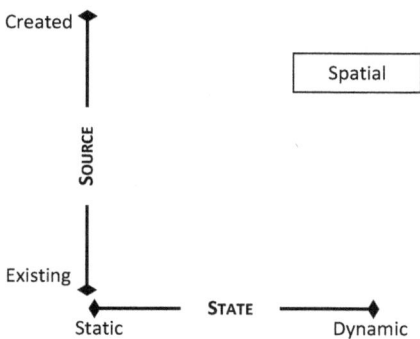

Figure 2.2: The two-dimensional framing of benchmarking.

---

4 The statistical notion of variability, or the spread of entity-specific values, is one of the core manifestations of cross-sectional analysis.

The graphically summarized benchmarking conceptualization implies that benchmarks, as evaluation standards, can be framed as either static or dynamic values, and can be either sourced from existing knowledge or computed using available data. Starting with the state dimension, *static standards* are treated as fixed until modified, whereas *dynamic standards* are updated (i.e., recomputed) each time they are accessed (using most up-to-date data; more on that in Chapter 6). Turning to the source dimension, *existing knowledge*-derived standards are best exemplified by rules of thumb, which are broadly accurate guides, based on experience rather than formally derived from available data or theory; in a more general sense, such known to be true evaluation standards can be thought of as *enduring truths*, which in the context of comparative assessment are established, widely used, and believed to be true standards. *Created* standards, on the other hand, are manifestly probabilistic estimates computed using applicable and available data.

The distinction between 'believed to be true' existing standards and manifestly probabilistic-created standards is at the core of the difference between those two standard types: The former are generally taken as true at face value, leading to unquestioned, and at time misplaced (i.e., once valid insights may simply not keep up with changing times) acceptance, which ultimately raises the specter of relying on invalid standards. The latter requires a more nuanced interpretation, which often runs counter to established practices. More specifically, as discussed in more detail in later chapters, probabilistic estimates of benchmark values need to be expressed as confidence intervals, or statistically framed ranges of values rather than a single value (which is known as point estimate in statistical parlor); doing so, however, complicates the otherwise simple outcome of interest vs. standard type of assessment (more on that later).

It is important to note, however, that not all externally sourced standards take the form of rule of thumb or similar 'tried and true' truisms; some may take the form of applicable laws, regulations, or norms. For instance, in the automotive industry, tire sizes and durability must fall with a predetermined, standardized range; another example of formal standards is offered by norm tables used to estimate project man-hours in offshore and onshore oil exploration-related construction projects, where the goal is to help project planners more accurately estimate completion requirements. Of course, whatever industry norms or standards are used as benchmarking-expressed evaluation standards themselves need to be expressed as measurable quantities rather than qualitative precepts. For example, the key standard used in assessing the extent to which corporate directors and officers of companies fulfill the obligations of their positions is known as duty of care, which is a legal obligation that requires those individuals to make decisions that pursue corporation's interests with reasonable diligence and prudence – while critically important in the context of executive liability (addressed in more detail in case studies in Chapters 9 and 10), the duty of care standard does not lend itself to quantification.

It is also worth noting that while quantitatively expressed by design, derived standards are not conceptually or methodologically homogeneous, even when considered within a relatively narrow context. The peer group average is a case in point. It is commonplace for business organizations to benchmark their KPIs to peer group averages as a way of contextualizing numerically explicit but informationally unclear results (assessment paradox). And while, on the surface, the idea of using industry-wide averages as benchmarks seems almost intuitively conceptually and methodologically singular, there are two sources of ambiguity that make arriving at industry average – e.g., average profitability and ROI – unexpectedly challenging. The first takes the form of competing statistical expressions of the general idea of 'average,' which is commonly, yet unwarrantably equated with the statistical mean. That aspect of derivation of created assessment standards is discussed in more depth in the next chapter; for now: not only are there are three distinct statistical expressions of the general idea of average – the mean, median, and mode – but the use of mean is only warranted once specific data requirements have been met (more on that in Chapter 3). The second source of ambiguity stems from the lack of definitional uniformity of what comprises an 'industry'; simply put, there are numerous competing approaches to industry classification, with each yielding materially different results. It is a relatively unknown problem; thus, an in-depth explanation seems warranted.

Industry Classification Taxonomies

Currently, there are numerous industry classification standards that have been developed over the past several decades by a mix of national governments, transnational bodies, and private organizations. National government-drafted industry classification taxonomies include the Standard Industrial Classification (SIC, the oldest industry classification taxonomy and the source of the ubiquitous SIC codes) created by the US government, the North American Industry Classification System (NAICS) developed by the US, Canadian, and Mexican governments, United Kingdom Standard Industrial Classification of Economic Activities drafted by the UK government, Swedish Standard Industrial Classification developed by the government of Sweden, Australian and New Zealand Standard Industrial Classification created by governments of Australia and New Zealand, and the European Union-developed Statistical Classification of Economic Activities in the European community. Transnational bodies' conceived taxonomies include International Standard Industrial Classification of All Economic Activities and United Nations Standard Products and Services Code, both created by the United Nations. There are numerous private interest-developed taxonomies, a group which is perhaps best exemplified by Standard & Poor's and MSCI codeveloped Global Industry Classification Standard (GICS), and FTSE-developed Industry Classification Benchmark. Table 2.1 offers a summary of the 10 best-known industry classification taxonomies, looked at from the perspective of applied, US-based users.

Table 2.1: Ten Best-Known Industry Classification Taxonomies.

Industry Classification Scheme	Year Introduced	Orientation	Geographic Scope	Classification Units	Hierarchy Levels	Update
Standard Industrial Classification (SIC)	1938–1940	Production and Market	United States	Establishments	4	Last updated* in 1987
International Standard Industrial Classification (ISIC)	1948	Production	Global	Establishments	4	Last updated in 2006
North American Industry Classification System (NAICS)	1997	Production	North America	Establishments	5	Every 5 years
Global Industry Classification Standard (GICS)	1999	Market	Global (120 countries)	Companies; Securities	4	Annual reviews
Morningstar Category Global Equity Classification Structure	2000	Market	Global	Companies; Securities	4	Ad hoc
Industry Classification Benchmark (ICB)	2001	Market	Global (75 countries)	Companies; Securities	4	Biannual reviews
FactSet Revere Business and Industry Classification System (RBICS)	2002	Market	Global (78 countries)	Companies; Securities; Business lines	6	Annual reviews
Thomson Reuters Business Classification (TRBC)	2004	Market	Global (130 countries)	Companies; Securities	5	Ad hoc
Bloomberg Industry Classification System (BICS)	2011	Market	Global	Companies; Securities; Business lines	7	Annual reviews
Sustainable Industry Classification System (SICS)	2012	Sustainability	United States	Companies	2	Ad hoc

*By the US Department of Labor, which maintained the official SIC Code system comprised of 1,514 codes (across the 2, 3, and 4-digit levels); the more granular (6,7, and 8-digit) Extended SIC Codes have since been developed by private companies – those are updated on continuous basis.

The competing taxonomies summarized in Table 2.1 differ, most notably in terms of their orientation, which tends to be either production-centric, i.e., emphasizing process similarities, or market-centric, i.e., emphasizing demand characteristics,[5] geographic scope, classification units (companies, establishments, business lines, and securities), and hierarchy levels. Moreover, there is also a considerable amount of cross-taxonomy update cycle variability, with some like the SIC codes no longer being updated at all, while others, such as GICS, receiving annual updates, and still others, such as TRBC being updated on ad hoc basis.

As can be surmised from the cross-taxonomy differences highlighted in Table 2.1, those competing descriptions of the structure of industrial activities can generate conflicting descriptions of product market competition and firm characteristics across product market competition levels. In fact, different classification systems are seldom consistent for a given firm – for instance, a study by Krishnan and Press[6] found that mapping four-digit SIC codes to five- or six-digit NAICS (which was introduced in 1997 expressly to replace the SIC structure dating back to the 1930s) produced only 41.9% agreement; in a similar study, Bhojraj and colleagues[7] found only 56% agreement between GICS and SIC.

Standard Industry Classification

The genesis of formal industrial classification schemas can be traced back to the 1934 Interdepartmental Conference on Industrial Classification, following which the Central Statistical Board established an Interdepartmental Committee on Industrial Classification 'to develop a plan of classification of various types of statistical data by industries and to promote the general adoption of such classification as the standard classification of the Federal Government.' The focal point of that initiative was to develop universal – in the sense of being usable to various industrial data-collecting agencies of the US government which, until then, used their own classification systems – industry groupings, framed in a way that could apply to all economic activities, both manufacturing and nonmanufacturing. That pioneering undertaking gave rise to SIC, the first comprehensive industry classification taxonomy.

The SIC system was developed in phases, starting with the manufacturing sector, initially completed in 1938 (the full index of products, processes, and establishments, and detailed industry descriptions were finalized in 1939 and 1940, respectively), followed by nonmanufacturing industries, completed in 1939 (the full index and detailed

---

5 The Sustainable Industry Classification System introduced in 2013 uses impact as classification basis, but thus far it is the only taxonomy that is not built around either production or market focus.
6 Krishnan, J., & Press, E. (2003). 'The North American industry classification system and its implications for accounting research,' *Contemporary Accounting Research*, 20(4), 685–717.
7 Bhojraj, S., Lee, C.M., & Oler, D.K. (2003). 'What's my line? A comparison of industry classification schemes for capital market research,' *Journal of Accounting Research*, 41, 745–773.

industry descriptions were finalized in 1940). The new industry classification taxonomy was formally released in 1941 for manufacturing industries, and in 1942 for nonmanufacturing ones. Since then, the full SIC system was revised several times: The first revision, which took place in 1945, reflected technological advances of the Second World War period and produced an updated classification of manufacturing industries, which was followed by the revision of 1949 nonmanufacturing industries. The first revision focused on the combined – manufacturing and nonmanufacturing sectors – system was released in 1958 (prior to that, the manufacturing and nonmanufacturing segments were treated as two separate systems and publications), with subsequent reviews being released in 1963, 1967, 1972, 1977, and 1987. The review process was initially handled by the Bureau of the Budget but the task was eventually taken over by the Office of Management and Budget, following the latter's founding in 1970; input into individual revisions came from key data gathering agencies such as the U.S. Census Bureau and the Bureau of Labor Statistics, appropriate data from the records of the Social Security Administration, Bureau of Labor Statistics, and Bureau of Employment Security, as well as trade associations, businesses, and individuals. In fact, the last, i.e., 1987 SIC system revision, generated over 1,100 individual change proposals from interested parties, which underscored the challenge of applying Industrial Era industry definitions and descriptions to the rapidly emerging Information Age commercial and noncommercial activities (and which was one of the key contributors to the decision to 'retire' the SIC system and develop a completely new industry classification system, the NAICS).

While the SIC system is slowly being replaced by NAICS, the former is deeply ingrained in a large body of historical data. While there is an ongoing transition to NAICS codes from SIC codes in newly captured/developed data sources in the public as well as the private sector (e.g., some government agencies and commercial publishers have developed the so-called bridge tools that cross-reference data in NAICS categories with equivalent SICs), it is now common to simply use both systems side by side, and some high-profile entities – most notably the US Securities and Exchange Commission – continue to rely on SIC codes as the primary classification tool. Moreover, there is no compelling reason to believe that the vast quantities of historical data using SIC codes will be republished in NAICS version. Thus, SICs are unlikely to be eliminated altogether. A more likely scenario is a continuous refinement of the system by adding new, more granular industry definitions, as discussed next.

The SIC Classification Logic

The SIC system uses letters and digits to represent the hierarchy and relation among categories of economic activity, although the former are commonly omitted from SIC codes. Nonetheless, the letters A through K define the broadest categories in the system, called divisions, which are as follows:

A. Agriculture, forestry, and fishing
B. Mining

C. Construction
D. Manufacturing
E. Transportation, communications, and utilities
F. Wholesale trade
G. Retail trade
H. Finance, insurance, and real estate
I. Services
J. Public administration (government)
K. Nonclassifiable establishments

Within these divisions, in descending hierarchical order, are two-digit (known as the major group), three-digit (known as the industry group), and four-digit (known as the industry) classifications that progressively narrow the scope of the category. The four-digit SIC codes are by far the most commonly used in official and private contexts – for instance, the US Securities & Exchange Commission requires individual registrants to select a four-digit SIC code that best describes the registrant's business operations. SIC codes are assigned based on common characteristics shared in the products, services, production, and delivery system of a business. The nested logic of the official SIC system is exemplified below:

E Transportation, communications, and utilities
48 Communications
481 Telephone communications
4812 Radiotelephone communications

The four-digit level is considered the most specific; although some government agencies and private database services have created more elaborate systems detailed to six or eight digits, these are not considered part of the official classification. Another unofficial addition to the SIC classification logic is that trailing zeros can be used at the two- and three-digit levels to round the codes out to four digits – in the above communications example, '4800' four-digit grouping could be created as an 'all other' communications industry.

Currently, the official US SIC system contains about 1,000 unique four-digit industry codes, and a total of roughly 1,500 codes across the two-, three-, and four-digit levels. However, due to the fact that the official SIC Code Manual also stipulates that governmental and private SIC users can further subdivide individual four-digit industries into more narrowly framed subindustries, the total number of SIC codes that are currently available is considerably larger, totaling over 10,000 continually updated individual codes. Known as extended SIC codes, they add up to three additional disaggregation tiers to the original SIC taxonomy (i.e., expressed as six-, seven-, and eight-digit codes), which support evermore specific peer groupings as well as capturing of new and emerging industries. Hence, while the last official update to the SIC took place in 1987 and, nominally, the SIC system was replaced a decade later by the

NAICS; in practice, the use of the SIC taxonomy will likely continue into foreseeable future. Lastly, it is also worthwhile to note that the SIC industry membership is self-ascribed, in the sense of individual companies selecting the specific SIC codes they feel best to capture the essence of their business.

Scope-wise, however, the SIC system is, by design, US-centric, in the sense that its primary aim is to capture the structure of the US commercial ecosystem. A global ana-log to the US SIC system, formally known as the International Standard Industrial Classification of All Economic Activities, or ISIC for short, was developed in 1948 (and released in 1949) under aegis of United Nations to 'to provide a set of activity categories that can be utilized for the collection and reporting of statistics according to such activities.' It is used primarily by public entities to collect and report economic data in a format that lends itself to cross-national economic analysis and policymaking. One of the core limitations of the ISIC system is irregular and relatively infrequent update cycle – since its introduction more than 70 years ago, there have only been four official updates to the system: 1958, 1968, 1989 (that revision was followed by an update in 2002), and 2006. In view of those limitations, private sector-developed, globally oriented taxonomies offer more change-sensing alternatives – of those, the GICS has attracted the widest user base.

Global Industry Classification Standard
In the late 1990s, two of the leading financial services organizations, S&P Dow Jones Indices (formerly Standard & Poor's) and MSCI (formerly Morgan Stanley Capital International), took on the challenge of creating a single, consistent set of global sector and industry definitions to meet the needs of the world financial community. The result was the GICS, which was designed around four core principles of universality (applicable in both developed and developing economies), reliability (to reflect the current state of all industries), flexibility (ability to identify very specialized subindustries), and adaptability (to remain as accurate a reflection of the marketplace as possible). The system is global in its scope, as it accounts for more than 95% of the world's stock exchange listed companies (over 26,000 individual entities); it is one of the two primary industry classification systems used by stock exchanges around the globe.[8]

---

8 The other one is the Industry Classification Benchmark (ICB), owned by the London Stock Exchange and developed by Dow Jones in partnership with Financial Times Stock Exchange (FTSE). Structure and classification logic-wise the two systems are quite similar; the largest difference between ICB and GICS lies in how consumer businesses are classified at the sector level: With the ICB, companies doing business with consumers are divided into providers of goods and providers of services, whereas with the GICS, companies are labeled as cyclical or noncyclical, or between discretionary spending and staples.

The Structure of the GICS Framework

According to S&P Dow Jones Indices and MSCI, 'The primary sources of information used to classify companies are the annual reports, financial statements and investment research reports.' As a general rule, a company is classified in the subindustry, whose definition most closely describes the business activities that generate the majority of the company's revenues. It is worth noting that while company classification is driven primarily by the source of revenue, somewhat more subjective analysis of earnings and market perception also plays a role. Companies that are engaged in more than one significant business activity are classified in the subindustry that generates the majority of revenues and profits, or one which S&P Dow Jones Indices and MSCI together agree best reflects its principal business, and companies participating in different sectors may be classified in industrial conglomerates or multisector holdings. Lastly, the company's subindustry classification automatically determines its industry, industry group, and sector.

In a manner that parallels the SIC system, the GICS structure uses a 4-tier nested logic, starting with 11 aggregate sectors (listed below) organized using 2-digit codes and associated text labels, followed by 24 industry groups coded using 4-digit codes and text descriptions, 68 industries (6-digit codes + text descriptions), and lastly, 157 subindustries (8-digit codes + descriptions). The entire structure is updated annually, with the goal of offering maximally accurate reflection of the structure of the global economy:

10. Communication services
11. Consumer discretionary
12. Consumer staples
13. Energy
14. Financials
15. Health care
16. Industrials
17. Information technology
18. Materials
19. Real estate
20. Utilities

Using a parallel (to the example shown in the section 'Standard Industry Classification') example of Communication:

50 Communication services
5010 Telecommunication services
501010 Diversified telecommunication services
50101020 Integrated telecommunication services

It is important to note that, like other private company-developed industry classification taxonomies summarized in Table 2.1, the GICS system is proprietary, and thus, in contrast to the SIC taxonomy discussed earlier, it is not freely accessible and nonextensible. Moreover, proprietary industry classification systems actively classify individual companies, which is in direct contrast to the earlier discussed public (i.e., typically developed by governmental and other public entities, such as United Nations) SIC system, which leaves it up to individual entities to self-classify into industries they feel best to characterize their business. Stated differently, in contrast to SIC codes that are self-ascribed by individual companies, GICS industry membership is analyst-determined.

Is Product or Market Industry Classification Still Pertinent?

All established industry classification systems start with the original SIC system, including GICS and ICB mentioned earlier, group companies based on either *how* they generate income (production) or *where* they generate income (market), or a combination of both. In recent years, the relevance of the so-derived industry classification taxonomies has been questioned because that classification logic – overtly geared toward identifying focal points of specialization – is rooted Industrial Age economic categories and measurements, which is ill-suited to today's leading business enterprises, many of which cross boundaries between hardware and software and beyond. Apple makes phones and computers, but it also sells entertainment products. Amazon creates hardware, produces entertainment programming, sells cloud services, and delivers just about everything. General Electric manufactures a wide array of industrial and consumer products, and also has interests in NBC, Telemundo, and Universal Pictures. Not surprisingly, critics argue that it is time to move from a vertical industry emphasis to one centered on business models, and considerations that are increasingly more important, such as sustainability. The newest industry classification system, known as Sustainable Industry Classification System (SICS) represents the first widely available attempt at doing just that.

Emerging Perspectives: Sustainable Industry Classification

The SICS system was developed by the Sustainability Accounting Standards Board (SASB),[9] a relatively new (founded in 2011) nonprofit organization focused on developing and dissemination of sustainability accounting standards. The system's primary purpose is to provide a supporting classification taxonomy to help with the larger goal to identify the subset of environmental, social, and governance (now commonly referred to as ESG) issues most relevant to companies' financial performance, and to

---

9 Currently known as Value Reporting Foundation.

unable business organizations to fully and reliably disclose financial material sustainability information to investors.

Starting with the premise that 'a company's market value is determined by more than financial performance . . . [and] as much as 80% of market capitalization is made up of intangibles such as intellectual capital, customer relationships, brand value, and other forms of capital – e.g., environmental, social and human,' the SICS makes use of nonfinancial, impact-focused assessment to categorize business companies 'under a sustainability lens.' The company classification logic groups business entities into thematic sectors, new industries with unique sustainability profiles, and industries classified in different sectors; altogether, the SICS system is composed of 11 sectors (listed below) and 77 industries:

1. Consumer goods
2. Extractives and mineral processing
3. Financials
4. Food and beverage
5. Health care
6. Infrastructure
7. Renewable resources and alternative energy
8. Resource transformation
9. Services
10. Technology and communications
11. Transportation

The resultant schema mixes elements of traditional (e.g., SIC or GICS), meaning production and/or market characteristic-based classification systems, with assessment of business model fundamentals, resource intensity, and sustainability innovation potential. In more operational terms, while guided by a distinctly different classification philosophy, SICS nonetheless builds on established industry taxonomies, onto which it overlays its sustainability assessment, guided by industry-specific standards. In other words, each of the 77 industries is framed by its own set of standards, thus, industries that are deemed to be distinct and different from the perspective of production and/ or market-based evaluation philosophy might be combined into a single industry within the SICS framework, if warranted by sustainability profile similarities. Consequently, SICS focus on less analytically granular sustainability-related considerations can be expected to give rise to a coarser classificatory taxonomy – thus in contrast to four-tier SIC and GICS systems,[10] the SICS system offers only 2 classification tiers of 'sectors' and 'industries,' as exemplified below, using once again an example of a communications organization:

---

10 When the extended – i.e., the six-, seven-, and eight-digit – SIC codes are taken into account, the SIC system can be seen as being a seven-tier taxonomy.

1. Technology and communications
1.1. Telecommunication services

Much like the earlier discussed GICS, and other taxonomies developed by private business interests and summarized in Table 2.1, SICS is a proprietary system owned by a private entity (SASB) which controls the use and access to the system, as well as industry assignments. Given the system's heavy reliance on nonfinancial factors, which tend to pose greater objective assessment challenge, SICS industry assignments can be considerably more interpretation-prone, which can give rise to concerns of appraisal bias, a potential problem clearly recognized by SASB and addressed by the organization's emphasis on evaluative transparency.

All in all, the industry classification taxonomy choice-related considerations outlined above are both profound and difficult to deal with effectively because they represent different solutions to the problem of simplifying the otherwise unintelligible mix of business companies. Choosing one taxonomy over other ones can be expected to yield different, at times quite different, comparative assessment outcomes, something that will be brought to life with several mini-case studies detailed in later chapters.

Benchmarking Definition Revisited

The unexpectedly nuanced definitional framing of what is commonly seen as a straightforward notion of industry is a key contributor to incommensurability of seemingly alike benchmarking efforts. It is not hard to imagine (and it is expressly documented in subsequent chapters) that different definitional framings of industry used in benchmarking can lead to very different conclusions; hence, it is of paramount importance to be deliberate and explicit in that regard. Recalling the earlier outlined definition of benchmarking, which frames it as a process of deriving spatially oriented assessment standards that can be sourced either from existing knowledge or analytically created from objective data, and which can exist in either static or dynamic states, it is important to also include in that general characterization a requirement for explicitly defining the framing of the 'peer group' used in the assessment process. With that in mind, the so-updated definition of benchmarking frames it as a process of deriving spatially oriented and clearly conceptually and operationally defined assessment standards that can be either sourced from existing knowledge or created using objective data, and that exist in either static or dynamic states.

Framing the Notion of Baselining

Building on the general comparative assessment defining framework summarized in Figure 2.1, *baselining* can be formally defined as a process of deriving temporally oriented assessment standards that can be sourced either from existing knowledge or created using objective data, and which can exist in either static or dynamic states, as graphically depicted in Figure 2.3. Other than baselining's focus on temporal, or cross-time contrasts, baselining and benchmarking share a common conceptual framing foundation, as evidenced by comparing Figures 2.2 (benchmarking) and 2.3 (baselining). In view of that, in the broad context of comparative assessment, baselines can be seen as informational complements to benchmarks, as the former capture cross-time variability in states or outcomes of interest, which complements the 'us vs. others' benchmarking contrasts.

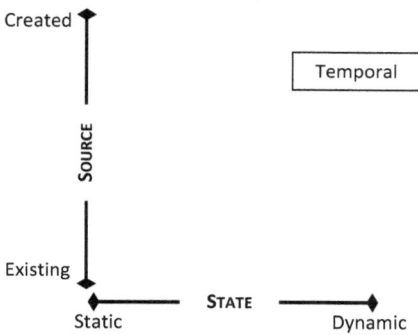

Figure 2.3: The two-dimensional framing of baselining.

It is important to note that the communality of the two defining dimensions, i.e., baselining and benchmarking both being rooted in state and source dimension, does not negate the informational distinctiveness clearly implied by their general descriptions. To that end, although the two expressions of the state dimension (static and dynamic) have essentially the same interpretation in the context of baselining and benchmarking, baselines are rooted in materially different types of existing and created sources of standards. More on point, the source dimension in baselining can either take the form of past experience-based norms (existing knowledge), as exemplified by average historical growth rates, or it can take the form of aspirational goals or targets (created source), such as desired growth rates. Those general differences become far more pronounced at the level of specific baseline-building inputs and related methodological considerations, all of which are discussed at length in Chapter 5.

Implied in the use of benchmarks and baselines is the need to assess the degree of materiality of any deviations from focal standards, which entails numerous, weighty considerations that warrant closer examination. The importance of those considerations is amplified by the rapid proliferation of electronic tracking systems that spew out more and more detailed data that capture a wide range of organizational states and outcomes of interest, and by doing so create ideal conditions for the development of comprehensive automated comparative assessment mechanisms. However, development of those mechanisms, in the form of structured benchmarking and baselining, is contingent on first laying a sound methodological foundation that spells out how materiality of difference should be assessed.

Benchmarks, Baselines, and Materiality of Difference

The core value of benchmarks and baselines is to offer unbiased assessment of the efficacy of outcomes or developments of interest in a way that supports clear conclusions such as 'above average' or 'subpar.' Doing so, however, raises an important question: At what point does an up or down deviation from an applicable standard should be deemed material? The essence of this question is rooted in the problem of drawing unambiguous conclusions from imperfect informational inputs.

To start, even though measurements of various organizational states or outcomes are not always described as estimates, by and large, most are derived from data that are imperfect[11] and thus should be seen as probabilistic estimates. Moreover, it is intuitively obvious that it is unlikely that measurements of phenomena of interest will yield values that are magnitudinally exactly equal to applicable standards; by chance alone some amount of difference can be expected. Together, those two foundational considerations raise a critical question of how much of the overt difference between the magnitude of interest and the appropriate assessment standard should be attributed to factors such as data imperfections, and how much represents the true deviation from the applicable standard. In other words, what amount of the observed differential between the magnitude of the measurement of interest and the applicable standard should be deemed material and interpreted as the amount of up or down deviation? Simply computing the difference between the two observed quantities would be, under most circumstances, tantamount to disregarding the potential impact of data imperfections and estimation imprecision; at the same time, the exact magnitude of those imperfections can be elusive. In very simple terms, the problem of determining the *true* magnitude of the difference between the value of interest and the applicable assessment standard boils down to determining how much of the *observed* difference should be attributed to the contrast of interest, and how much should be

---

11 Data captured by organizations or sourced externally are generally incomplete (e.g., not all purchases of a particular product are electronically captured) and typically contain some missing or inaccurate (typically due to coding, data capture, or entry errors) values.

dismissed as a product of the imperfect nature of the broadly defined estimation process. It is a complex question; for now, let it suffice to say that there is no single, universally accepted solution to that problem – currently, there are two competing statistical mechanisms, and both of those approaches have their proponents and opponents.

The (Not So) Gold Standard: Statistical Significance

The latter twentieth century rise and the subsequent rapid proliferation of an ever-growing array of electronic data capturing systems has had a profound impact on organizational functioning, and more specifically, on the practice of evidence-based management.[12] Granular and near-real-time transactional data now affords previously unattainable ability to assess the efficacy of a wide range of organizational outcomes, on macroscale – e.g., overall profitability – as well as microscale – e.g., effectiveness of individual elements of the market mix. In a sense, it can all be seen as a new chapter in the application of general principles of *empirical learning*, which has long been anchored in the use of the idea and specific applications of *statistical significance*.

The roots of the idea of statistical significance go all the way back to circa seventeenth-century emergence of empirical means of knowledge creation, which have been nothing short of the greatest transformative force in the 8,000 or so years old human civilization, as evidenced by the stunning rate of scientific progress over the last couple or so centuries (especially when put in the context of many centuries leading up to that point). Central to empirical learning has been the idea of the *scientific method*, which frames the creation of knowledge in the context of systematically testing of beliefs and assumptions, formally referred to as hypothesis or conjecture testing. In that evaluative context, to be considered 'true,' a knowledge claim – such as that the outcome of interest is materially larger than the appropriate assessment standard – needs to pass an appropriate empirical test (more on that later), which can then be used as the basis for the conclusion that the difference of interest is 'statistically significant' (failing to pass that test would render that difference 'not statistically significant,' which is typically interpreted as spurious, or due to the earlier mentioned measurement imperfections).

Although, in principle, the idea of *statistical significance testing* has been intended to serve as the mechanism of attesting to generalizability of knowledge claims, i.e., theory building, it has been broadly used in applied business and other analyses, but the manner in which it was used has, at time, been problematic. Perhaps the most obvious reason is that informational needs of organizations tend to be more nuanced

---

12 For a more in-depth discussion of evidence-based management, see Banasiewicz, A. (2019). *Evidence-Based Decision-Making: How to Leverage Available Data and Avoid Cognitive Biases*, Routledge: New York, NY.

than one-size-fits-all-type theoretical generalizations, which means that approaches designed to serve the needs of the latter are not always as well-suited to the needs of the former. On a more practical level, organizational managers are primarily interested in competitively advantageous insights, a need that runs counter to the idea of broad theoretical generalizations. Additionally, organizational managers are usually interested not just in determining if an observed difference is 'real,' but more so in quantifying the magnitude of the difference. For example, when assessing promotion-induced product repurchase, it is simply informationally insufficient to determine if the promotion-induced outcome, such as repurchase rate, is higher than the unpromoted rate – marketing managers and other decision-makers are keenly interested in being able to quantify the magnitude of the increase, because that level of informational specificity is necessary to estimate the return on marketing investment. Tests of statistical significance, however, cannot yield that type of information, because that is not the purpose for which they were designed. Simply put, statistical significance testing offers limited value in applied contexts.

In addition to informational limitations, statistical significance tests (SSTs) are also adversely impacted by data volumes, which is a particularly troubling limitation in view of the widespread practice of utilizing large record counts to compute individual test statistics. The reason for that is that, as noted earlier, the computational mechanics of SSTs predate the modern electronic data infrastructure, and more importantly, do not offer an obvious way of rectifying those shortcomings. That coupled with the widespread, and not always appropriate use of SSTs can create systemic inference validity problems, and thus more in-depth examination of those considerations is warranted.

A Closer Look at Shortcomings of SSTs

Briefly characterized, a key element of the scientific method, tests of statistical significance, known to many as F, t, and χ^2 tests, are established mathematical techniques used to differentiate between spurious and material data analytic outcomes. While originally developed to support theory building efforts, SSTs have also been used extensively in applied analyses, where they are used as tools of single out those data analytic outcomes that should be deemed as meaningful or important. However, what appears to be a communality of goals connecting theoretical and practical pursuits is in fact built on a false premise. The reason for that is that the process of developing new and testing of existing theories calls for assessing generalizability of sample-derived estimates, which requires concurrence of multiple sample-based conclusions; in contrast to that, extraction of applied decision-guiding insights typically only requires a reasonable assessment of a particular set of results' validity. In other words, theory-focused statistical significance testing is ultimately geared toward ascertaining universal repeatability of findings (by attesting to sample-derived estimates being representative of the larger population), whereas practice-focused applications of those tests are used as a part of search for competitive advantage, and thus have far more situationally specific scope (as it is intuitively obvious, the essence of effective organizational management hinges on identification of competitively advantageous, which means unique, insights). It is all a somewhat long way of saying that a result being deemed 'statistically significant' cannot be interpreted as being practically material or significant.

In fact, the idea of *result materiality* points toward an even more disquieting manifestation of tests of statistical significance inapplicability to many applied problems. In the context of comparative assessment, to be deemed 'material,' exact magnitudinal difference between the value of interest (e.g., a specific outcome, such as a particular promotion-induced product repurchase rate) and the standard used as the assessment benchmark would need to be (statistically) significant. Consider Figure 2.4.

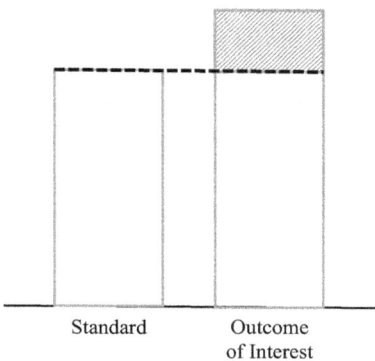

Figure 2.4: Assessing the magnitude of the observed difference.

Let us assume that the shaded area in Figure 2.4 represents the earlier mentioned promotion-induced product repurchase rate. Let us further assume that the standard or the average unpromoted repurchase rate is 15.1% and the 'outcome of interest,' which is here is the promotion-induced repurchase rate, is 16.8%, which suggests the observed 1.7% increase, shown as the shaded area in Figure 2.4. This hypothetical scenario illustrates a common problem of needing to ascertain the validity of the observed outcome vs. applicable standard difference, in situations in which the magnitude of the former is estimated from available (i.e., informationally imperfect) data. Sidestepping for the moment some of the important data and sampling-related considerations, organizational managers are typically interested in being able to determine if the observed, e.g., 1.7%, difference of interest is 'statistically significant,' but doing so outstretches SSTs' methodological limits. More specifically, the finding that there is a difference (without specifying the magnitude of that difference – that is a very important distinction) between the two quantities can be deemed to be statistically significant within the confines of the chosen level of significance,[13] typically 90%, 95%, or 99%, but SSTs cannot be used to attest to the exact 1.7% magnitude being significant, as in material. In short, the test of interest (here, a *t*-test, which as discussed later is the appropriate test to assess the significance of the difference between two means) can be used to determine if there is a statistically significant difference between the two quantities, but not to assess the significance of exact magnitude of that difference.

Still, that is not all. Tests of statistical significance also become progressively less and less discriminating as the number of data records used to compute their test statistics increases. What is commonly known as SSTs' sample size dependence presents a formidable obstacle to the use of those tests nowadays, given the frequency with which large data volumes used in most modern applied settings. To that end, it can be easily shown that as the number of records used to compute the individual test statistic (i.e., F, t, or χ^2) increases, the likelihood of detecting statistical significance also increases, more or less in proportion to sample size; perhaps even more alarming is the fact that the effect of interest starts to become visible at a relatively low, by modern-day standards, record counts. More specifically, a given estimate might be deemed not statistically significant when computed using a small but adequate sample size, such as 200 cases, only to become significant if the underlying record count was increased severalfold, which by present-day standards would still amount to a modest record count, everything else being the same.[14] To be clear, that means that the number of data records used to compute the appropriate test statistics can singularly determine the credibility of statistical estimates. In the context of the hypothetical example shown in Figure 2.4, using smaller number of records could yield a conclusion of the difference not being statistically significant, but repeating the same test using a larger record count would likely yield the opposite conclusion.

That peculiar situation raises some uncomfortable questions: If analytic outcomes based on a smaller, but once again statistically adequate, meaning sufficiently large to produce unbiased estimates, record counts are deemed to not be statistically significant, how is one to make sense of a contradictory conclusion stemming from identical except

---

13 The role of which is to expressly specify the probability that the conclusion of statistical significance is incorrect; in that sense, the commonly used 95% level of significance means 95% probability of reaching correct conclusion. Of course, the higher-level significance would be generally preferred, but there is a trade-off between the level of significance and a corollary statistical notion of *power*, which is the sensitivity of the test itself, or its ability to detect the difference in the first place – the higher the level of significance, the lower the power of the test (one of the reasons that 95% is the most commonly chosen threshold is that it balances that trade-off).

14 Central to the estimation of many statistical parameters is the notion of 'standard error' (SE), which is an estimated standard deviation of a particular statistic (it is computed by dividing the standard deviation by the square root of the sample size). Abstracting away from technical details, given that SE is a quotient of standard deviation and sample size, as the magnitude of sample size increases the value of standard error decreases, resulting in the ever-smaller, eventually trivial, differences being deemed 'statistically significant.'

for the sample size analysis? And then, what happens when in the age of massive data-sets, the determination of statistical significance is routinely made using large record counts, something that is becoming the norm? Even trivially small differences can be deemed statistically significant. Not surprisingly, analysts oftentimes feel compelled to group statistically significant findings into those that are 'practically significant' and those that are not. While the impulse to do so is, on the one hand, understandable, on the other hand, such practice nullifies the benefits of objective estimate validation standards by opening the door to biased result interpretation. As is well-known, intui-tion-based evaluation of empirical results is often fraught with numerous cognitive and behavioral traps, in view of which the core benefit of objective analyses is to help deci-sion-makers to surmount or circumvent those reason-warping effects. All in all, subjecti-fying initially objective results runs counter to that goal, and thus the idea of subjective reassessment of initially objective results is clearly counterproductive.

Still, there is more bad news for habitual applied users of tests of statistical signif-icance. Diving a bit deeper into SSTs' methodological foundations brings into focus additional, frequently overlooked considerations. Being rooted in normal distribu-tion-derived probability estimation, the interpretation of statistical significance can-not be divorced from the underlying symmetric distribution, which is not in keeping with many real-life scenarios. In fact, many, perhaps even most real-life phenomena are not normally distributed: brands have fewer high-spending than low-spending buyers, banks have far fewer high net worth account holders than low net worth ones, insurance companies incur far more low-cost than high-cost claims, nonprofit organizations have far fewer large than small donors, schools tend to have more struggling than high-performing students, the list goes on and on. There are innumer-able examples of measurable states and outcomes that, in aggregate, are not normally distributed; some of those can be mathematically transformed to become approxi-mately normal but others cannot, and when used with such persistently non-normal data, tests of statistical significance become even more suspect in applied settings.

The preceding overview statistical significance testing is strongly suggestive of considering alternative means of determining materiality of observed vs. benchmark or baseline differences; the best available option here is to use what is commonly re-ferred to as *effect size*-based assessment.

The Alternative: Effect Size

Within the realm of statistical analyses, *effect* is an expression of bivariate association; when considered in the context of comparative assessments, *effect size* is simply a quantitative assessment of the magnitude of the contrast of interest, expressed in re-lation to the degree of imprecision stemming from the earlier discussed data imper-fections. When looked at as a mechanism for assessing the validity of benchmarking and baselining-expressed comparisons of magnitudes of interest with appropriate

standards, the effect size approach offers an alternative to tests of statistical significance, and it is sometimes used in parallel with SSTs, to offer a different evaluation
perspective. Doing so, however, is not recommended because it is quite possible for
the two approaches to yield contradictory findings (which is particularly likely when
using larger, i.e., a few thousand or higher, record counts); pragmatically speaking,
such conflicting conclusions would do more to confuse than to inform by creating difficult to resolve result interpretation ambiguities (i.e., which of the two conclusions is
correct, and why?). It is more appropriate to view effect size-based assessment as a
way of circumventing the limitations of statistical significance testing, a stance which
strongly suggests that effect size be used as a replacement of, rather than a supple-
ment to tests of statistical significance.

Application-wise, effect size estimates most commonly manifest themselves as
magnitudes of the strength of relationships between measured quantities of interest,
which means that the underlying computational mechanics are tied to the implied
measurement scale, which in turn manifests itself in distinct types of data (i.e., variables). In the most general sense, any measured quantity can be expressed as either a
continuous or a *categorical*[15] quantity or variable,[16] which suggests three possible
types of interactions: continuous vs. continuous, categorical vs. categorical, and continuous vs. categorical; those three distinct types of contrasts translate into three distinct types of estimation procedures: correlation (continuous vs. continuous), odds
ratio (categorical vs. categorical), and mean difference (continuous vs. categorical).

Correlation analysis captures the direction and the magnitude of an association between two normally distributed continuous variables,[17] as such, it yields probably the
most straightforward assessment of the effect size. That is because the standardized correlation coefficient, which ranges in value from −1 (perfect negative or inverse association) to +1 (perfect positive or direct association) is intuitively obvious to most users.
Within the confines of correlation, effect size is simply the absolute value of the correlation coefficient, where larger values indicate stronger effect. One often noted source of
interpretational ambiguity is discerning a point at which observed associations can be
interpreted as 'strong' – here, *Cohen's standard* is an often-recommended interpretation guide. Using that as a guide, correlations smaller than 0.1 (disregarding the sign)
should be considered spurious or informationally immaterial, correlations between 0.1

---

15 Categorical variables can be further subdivided into nominal (e.g., gender or race) and ordinal
(e.g., educational level: 'high school,' 'BS,' and 'PhD'); the former are unordered, meaning, they lack
intrinsic ordering, labels while the latter or intrinsically ordered; the nominal-ordinal distinction,
however, is not important in the context of effect size as it has no bearing on effect size calculations.
16 A continuous variable can take on any value within a range, thus in principle can assume an infinite number of values (e.g., speed, distance, and age); a categorical variable can take on one of limited,
and typically fixed, number of values (e.g., gender, state, and marital status).
17 For Pearson r correlation, which is the most widely used correlation statistic; the lesser-known
Spearman ρ (rho) rank correlation and Kendall τ (tau) rank correlation can accommodate rank-order
(i.e., not continuous) data.

and 0.3 should be interpreted as 'weak,' correlations between 0.3 and 0.5 should be interpreted as 'moderate,' and those 0.5 or greater as 'strong.'

The second effect size estimation procedure is *odds ratio*. The notion of *odds* is defined as the probability that the event of interest will occur, divided by the probability
that it will not occur. In a binary, success-failure context, it is the ratio of successes to
failures (in contrast to the notionally similar idea of *probability*, which expresses the
chances of outcome of interest, e.g., success, as a fraction of the total, i.e., successes + failures). Odds ratio captures the association between two categorical measures, as in two
sets of counts; more specifically, it quantifies the impact of the presence or absence of A
on the presence or absence of B, under the assumption of A – B independence. The
computational logic of odds ratio-expressed effect size assessment is framed in the context of a 2 × 2 contingency table, summarized in Figure 2.5.

	Present	Absent
Present	A	B
Absent	C	D

$$\text{Effect Size}_{\text{Odds Ratio}} = \frac{AD}{BC}$$

Figure 2.5: Calculating effect size for odds ratio.

Interpretation of odds ratio-expressed effect size is as follows: When the effect size
equals 1.0, the two events are considered independent (the odds of one event are the
same, whether the other event is present or absent); when the effect size is greater
than 1.0, the odds of one event increase when the other event is present (it is analogous to positive correlation), and lastly, when the effect size is smaller than 1.0, the
odds of one event decrease when the other event is present (which is analogous to
negative correlation).

The third and final of the three effect size estimation procedures is *mean difference*. Effect size evaluation of mean difference can be characterized as standard deviation-adjusted assessment of the magnitude of statistical effects; computation-wise,
the best-known approach is *standardized mean difference*, with the most widely used
formulation known as Cohen's *d*, which is computed as follows:

$$\text{Effect size}_{\text{mean difference}} = \frac{\text{Mean}_1 - \text{Mean}_2}{\text{Std deviation}_{\text{diff}}}$$

As clearly visible in the above computational formula, mean difference expressly
takes into account variability of estimated effects, which here is meant to capture the
degree of imprecision of the estimate(s) of interest. Overall, the larger the standard
deviation in relation to the mean, the less precise the estimate in question, which in
turn means smaller effect size. A commonly used interpretation logic of standardized
mean difference-expressed effect size classifies the effect size of less than 0.2 as spuri-

ous or 'trivial,' 0.2–0.5 as 'small,' 0.5–0.8 as 'medium,' and those greater than 0.8 as 'large.' It is worth noting that Cohen's *d* formulation assumes that the underlying distributions are normal (i.e., symmetrical) and homoscedastic (i.e., exhibit comparable error[18] variability); moreover, the computational logic makes no allowances for the impact of outliers, all of which suggests that more computationally involved approaches that relax the said assumptions and rely on trimmed mean-based comparisons might be more appropriate,[19] though those considerations fall outside the scope of this overview.

The type of effect notwithstanding, it is important to be mindful of the impact of method-specific assumptions on the interpretation of results. For example, Pearson's *r* correlation-expressed effect size reflects the degree to which two continuous, symmetrically distributed variables are linearly associated, as graphically illustrated in Figure 2.6. Keeping those result framing considerations in mind is critical not only to assuring the validity of results (i.e., input data are expected to meet the normality and related assumptions) – it is also critical to correctly interpreting those results. In the case of Pearson's *r* correlation, the effect estimate only captures the extent to which two data features (e.g., the value of outcome or state of interest, and the value of the relevant assessment standard) are linearly related; if the underlying association is nonlinear, which as can be expected is common, the underlying relationship will likely not be captured, thus both the presence and absence of correlation need to be interpreted in the narrow context of linear associations.

Similarly, the mean difference-expressed effect size assessment imposes specific requirements on data to be used in estimation, namely normality of the underlying distributions, equality of error variances, and independence of individual records (meaning that the value of a given variable does not depend on the value of the same variable in the preceding record). Consequently, interpretation of mean difference-expressed effect size should be couched in the extent to which data features of interest meet those requirements.

Lastly, while somewhat less bound by assumptions (largely because count-based categorical data permit fewer operations), the interpretation of odds ratio-expressed effect size needs to clearly differentiate between the meaning of odds and the notionally similar but mathematically different probability. The distinction between the two can be confusing, especially given that odds are defined in terms of probability of occurrence, but there can be material differences in estimated magnitudes. Starting with basic operational definitions, the notion of odds relates the chances of event A

---

18 As noted earlier, in the context of statistical analyses, the notion of 'error' is used to denote deviation, as in the difference between an estimated mean and individual actual values.

19 Those interested in additional details and alternative formulations are encouraged to consult more in-depth overviews, such as Wilcox, R. (2022). 'One-way and two-way ANOVA: Inferences about a robust, heteroscedastic measure of effect size,' *Methodology: European Journal of Research Methods for the Behavioral and Social Sciences*, 18(1), 58–73.

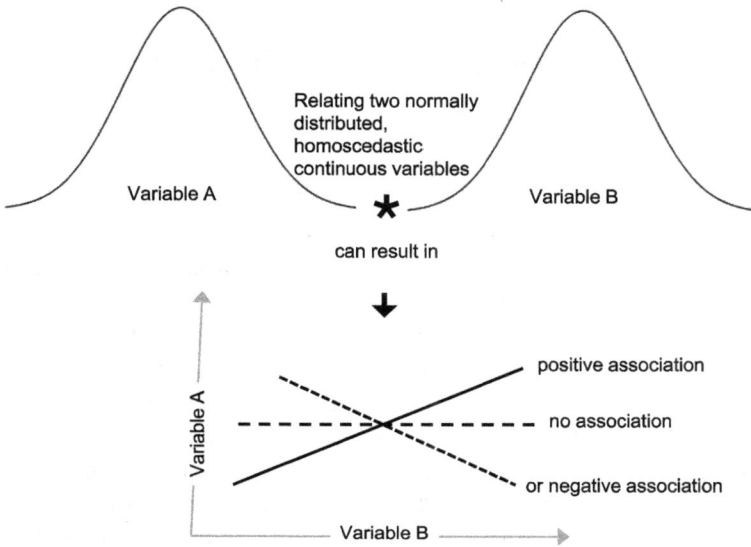

Figure 2.6: Graphical representation of the logic of Pearson's correlation.

occurring to chances of event B occurring, whereas probability relates the chances of event A to the overall total. So, for instance, the odds of rolling '5' using a standard dice are 1-in-5 (since there are five other outcomes that are possible), or 20%, whereas the probability of rolling '5' is 1-in-6 (since there are a total of 6 outcomes that are possible), or 16.6%.

The overview of the origins and the current state of benchmarking and baselining, along with the brief summary of the key statistical notions that underpin those two comparative assessment approaches is meant to serve as the point of departure in what is the central premise of this book: Benchmarking and baselining can be a source valid, reliable, and persistent decision-shaping insights, but both are in need of clear definitional and operational framing. Starting with the former, this and the previous chapter offered a conceptual overview of the core meaning and definitional scope of those two similar but distinct dimensions of assessment, and building on that foundation, Chapter 3 delves into general standard estimation considerations.

Chapter 3
Foundational Estimation and Parameterization Considerations

The preceding two chapters were focused on the key elements of benchmarking and baselining processes, at the heart of which is a contrast between a set evaluation standard and a magnitude of interest. Within the confines of benchmarking, that standard can take on a wide array of different forms, ranging from general rules of thumb to highly situationally tailored estimates derived from available data. Within the confines of baselining, however, evaluation standards predominantly take the form of data-derived estimates. The type of standard notwithstanding, however, central to benchmarking and baselining alike is the idea of evaluation standards being 'set' or 'fixed,' which implies being seen as a true, singular value. For example, the widely used average stock market return of about 10% per year is a general benchmark derived from about a century's worth of returns, as measured by the S&P 500 Index. When considered from the perspective of technical estimation, since the S&P 500 Index, which tracks the stock performance of 500 of largest companies listed on the US stock exchanges, that 10% value is a sample-based estimate, and so as all sample-derived estimates, it is subject to *sampling error*, or estimation imprecision arising from unrepresentativeness of the sample used to compute it (more on that later). Recognizing that the 10% S&P 500-derived benchmark and many other benchmarks are often characterized using qualifiers such as 'about' or 'approximately,' but such sampling error-implying qualifiers cannot be used in benchmarking contrasts that call for exact numeric values. All in all, comparative assessments are often carried out using rough approximations as exact, set standards, which can undermine the validity of those efforts.

Moreover, both benchmarking and baselining evaluation standards are nowadays commonly derived from transactional and other applicable types of readily available data, which further underscores the importance of more explicitly and thoughtfully considering magnitudinal values of standards used in comparative assessments. More specifically, benchmarks and baselines tend to take the form of estimated values computed from data, which brings into the spotlight numerous critical estimation-related considerations. It is widely held (and can be easily demonstrated) that virtually all data used in organizational settings are somewhat structurally and/or informationally imperfect, which is reflected in estimation techniques used to analyze those data being geared toward arriving at approximately correct values. Simply put, using data-derived estimates as benchmarks and baselines effectively transforms benchmarking and baselining into probabilistic processes. As can be expected, it adds additional layers of complexity that comes with framing evaluation standards as probabilistic

https://doi.org/10.1515/9783111001296-003

estimates, but at the same time, the more formal embrace of the key tenets of probability theory also infuses the much-needed element of mathematical rigor.

With the preceding considerations in mind, it is the goal of this chapter to take a closer look at the key considerations at the heart of estimating maximally valid and reliable evaluation standards, a broad topic approached from two distinct but ultimately interrelated perspectives: the impact of data imperfections, and the key elements of estimation and parameterization.

Probabilistic Estimates

Few mathematical concepts have as profound an impact on decision-making as the idea of *probability*. Interestingly, the development of a comprehensive theory of probability had relatively inglorious origins in the form of a 1654 gambling dispute[1] which compelled two accomplished French mathematicians, Blaise Pascal and Pierre de Fermat, to engage in an intellectual discourse that ultimately laid the foundations of what is today known as the theory of probability. For the next 150 or so years, however, further developments of the notion of probability were solely concerned with mathematical analysis of games of chance, until another renowned mathematician, Pierre-Simon Laplace, began to apply probabilistic ideas to diverse scientific and practical problems, ultimately leading to formalization of the theory of errors, actuarial mathematics, and statistical mechanics. More than a century later, in 1933, noted Russian mathematician Andrey Kolmogorov outlined the axioms that form the basis for the modern theory of probability.[2] Today it is hard to think of a domain of modern science that does not make extensive use of the ideas and mechanics of probabilistic estimation; in fact, more and more aspects of everyday life are also being framed in probabilistic perspectives. It might even be reasonable to go as far as saying that nowadays, rational decision-making and probabilistic thinking are inseparable.

And yet, structured *probabilistic decision-making* is not as common as might be expected, largely because what could be characterized as organic subjectivity, which is at the core of intuitive decision-making. Many individual and group decisions alike are 'personal' in the sense of being based on or influenced by individual-level feelings, tastes, or opinions, and alternatives that more closely align with those subjective states of mind tend to be preferred to other choices, such as those that might be suggested by objective analyses of available evidence. The problem here is that intuitive and probabilistic or data-driven decision-making modalities are often seen as either-

---

1 In fact, the earliest known contribution to the study of probability goes even further back, and it is attributed to an accomplished Italian Renaissance mathematician, astrologer, and gambler, Gerolamo Cardano (1501–1576).

2 Kolmogorov, A. N., *Foundations of the Theory of Probability*, 1950 (originally published in German in 1933).

or – either one trusts one's instincts, or one trusts objective evidence. That perspective, however, is myopic. Silencing of one's subjective states of mind is neither realistic nor necessary. It is not realistic because instinctive sensemaking is evolutionarily hard-coded into human cognitive processing, and it is not necessary because the ultimate goal of data-driven decision-making is to eliminate or at least diminish the impact of cognitive bias. It is hard to deny that some subjective feelings or beliefs turn out to be correct, while others turn out to be incorrect, but within the confines of intuitive decision-making those conclusions can only be drawn retroactively, at which point the damage may have already been done or the opportunities might already be lost. But what if subjective beliefs could be evaluated in the context of probability of being correct, prior to committing to a particular choice? That is the very essence of probabilistic decision-making.

Although the general notion of probability might be familiar to most, the notion of probabilistic decision-making is comparatively more complex as it combines the general idea of probability, and the comparatively far less known idea of multisource evidence amalgamation, evaluation, and synthesis. In addition, when looked at from a more practical or operational perspective, to be meaningful, the practice of probabilistic decision-making needs to be explicit in terms of the general rationale and the how-to mechanics, the latter detailing the process that can be used to conclusively summarize the totality of dissimilar and divergent evidence. The ensuing overview is focused on those considerations.

The Question of Believability

Organizational decision-making commonly entails making choices under conditions of *uncertainty*; broadly characterized as reflection of the general state of ambiguity regarding the future, connoting a nonspecific opacity or insecurity that accompanies not knowing. Not surprisingly, in the context of decision-making, the core value of any credible information lies in reducing choice-related uncertainty; however, the value of data-derived insights can, at times, be more nuanced, especially when it contradicts long-standing beliefs, a state that psychologists refer to as cognitive dissonance.

A decision-maker's uncertainty can be a result of being unaware of decision-pertinent information or being unwilling to believe the available evidence. Interestingly, not believing objective evidence should not be dismissed as simple closed mindedness – sometimes, mathematically correct information can be very difficult to accept. One of the better-known examples of difficult to accept but true information is offered by paper folding illustration: Using an ordinary sheet of paper, roughly about 0.1 mm in thickness, and folding it several dozen times (theoretically, since, in practice it is only possible to fold an appropriately sized sheet of paper some dozens of times or so), the resultant stack would reach astounding, as in unbelievable height. Assuming an appropriately sized sheet of paper (to allow many successive folds), folding it seven times will result in a stack approximately equal in height to the thickness of an average notebook, and adding extra three folds will result in the stack height about the width of a hand (thumb included). At this point it should be noted that, in practice, it is not possible to go far beyond 10 folds,[3] but due to the fact that the paper folding exercise is a manifestation of a well-known mathematical property known as *exponential growth* (according to which the rate of growth can increase at an accelerating rate as the quantity, here the number of folds, gets larger), the size of the resultant stack can be determined mathematically. Using the basic computational logic of exponential growth,[4] additional 4 (for a total of 14) folds would push the height of the stack to be roughly that of an average person; then adding extra 3 folds (for the total of 17) would produce a stack the height of an average two-story house, and just 3 more folds (for a total of 20) would yield a stack reaching approximately a quarter of the way up the Willis Tower (formerly known as the Sears Tower), the landmark Chicago skyscraper. But that's just the beginning: If folded over 30 times, the resultant stack would reach past the outer limits of Earth's atmosphere, and lastly, if folded over 50 times, an ordinarily thin sheet would produce a stack of paper reaching all the way to the Sun, which is roughly 94 million miles away. And if that was not hard enough to accept, a little more than doubling the number of folds, for a total of 103 total folds, would result in a stack of paper larger than the observable Universe, which, by the way, measures 93 billion light-years (and given the speed of light of approximately 186,000 miles per second, that translates into an unimaginably large value of 5.4671216×10^{23} miles). For most, the idea that an ordinary sheet of paper about 0.1 mm thick folded a few dozen times would result in such staggeringly high stack is extremely difficult to accept, even if the underlying mathematical principles and mechanics are well-known and readily accepted.

This somewhat far-out example speaks to the believability of mathematically, or otherwise abstractly derived knowledge – it simply cannot be taken for granted that just because a claim can be shown – using mathematical logic or other abstract methods – to be true, it will be believable. To help overcome potential cognitive resistance brought about by information that contradicts one's current beliefs, a phenomenon known as cognitive dissonance, sound communication strategy, is needed. Such strategy ought to be anchored in deeper understanding of the mechanics of *probabilistic reasoning*, a general sensemaking approach triggered by the sense of uncertainty and rooted in degrees of belief and leading to conclusions of varying degrees of likelihood. As currently understood, probabilistic reasoning encompasses three distinct dimensions: computational, inferential (or statistical), and evidentiary. The computational

---

3 The 12-fold threshold was reached using a very long stretch of thin paper, resembling toilet paper, using what is known as single direction folding; that approach, however, has been questioned by those believing that a proper folding approach entailed folding a sheet in half, turning it 90° and then folding it again. Using that approach, a single sheet of thin paper can be folded no more than 11 times.
4 Thickness$*2^{\wedge(n \text{ folds})}$.

dimension of probabilistic reasoning can be seen as a reflection of one's understanding of data types and sources used as input into deriving standards used in deriving the estimates of interest; it includes general understanding of data feature engineering steps needed to make data usable.[5] Stated differently, the process of overcoming cognitive resistance begins with conveying familiarity with what 'raw materials' were used to produce the contradictory knowledge, and how those materials were prepared to assure valid outcomes. The next step is to tackle the *inferential* dimension of probabilistic reasoning, which encapsulates conveyance of basic familiarity with scientific means of deriving insights from data. This step can be particularly challenging because it calls for distilling methodological complexities into easy-to-grasp yet adequately complete summarization of the mechanics of new knowledge creation. And lastly, the evidentiary dimension captures the intended meaning aspect of probabilistic reasoning; in other words, how should the information be interpreted. Here, it is important to make a compelling argument that while the new, data-derived benchmarks or baselines may contradict prior beliefs, they offer a more dependable basis for dealing decision-making uncertainty. All in all, the goal is to thoughtfully and systematically overcome the instinctive impulses to reject information that contradicts prior beliefs in a way that minimizes cognitive distress, which typically triggers defensive reactions in the form of questioning the accuracy of data or correctness of inferences drawn from data.

Probability as Uncertainty-Reducing Tool

Prior to the seventeenth century, the term 'probable' was synonymous with 'approvable' and was used in reference to opinions or actions reasonable individuals would hold or undertake. In a sense, that general sentiment is still true of the modern conception of probability: The most probable outcome is one that a reasonable – as in rational – individual would hold or undertake. However, probability is ultimately a notion that is framed in precise mathematical treatment of estimating the chances of distinct outcomes materializing; to that end, there are two competing philosophies – the frequentist and Bayesian – of probability estimation, each promoting logically and mathematically distinct approaches.

The frequentist approach, as implied in the name, is strictly empirical, or objective data based. Relying on objective data, nowadays largely captured by the endless arrays of transaction processing and communication systems, the probability of ran-

---

5 By and large, data used in benchmarking and baselining analyses are generated by automated transaction processing systems in a manner that emphasizes capture and storage efficiency; those data typically require substantial preprocessing to make them analytically usable; for more details, see Banasiewicz, A. (2021). *Organizational Learning in the Age of Data*, Springer Nature: Cham, Switzerland.

dom variable reflects the relative frequency of occurrence of the observed outcome. For instance, there are more than 6,000 companies traded on the two major US stock exchanges (New York and NASDAQ), and more than 12,000 companies traded over-the-counter, or via a broker-dealer network; of those 18,000 or so companies, in an average year about 200 or so are sued by their shareholders alleging incomplete, untimely, or incorrect disclosure of performance-related information. Given that information and using the frequentist approach to probability estimation, an average publicly traded company faces approximately 0.011% chance of being sued by its shareholders. As suggested by that example, the frequentist approach is particularly well suited to problems characterized by abundant historical outcome data and relatively stable longitudinal trends, as exemplified by automotive accidents.

The *Bayesian* approach to probability estimation, named after Thomas Bayes, an English clergyman and statistician who developed what is now known as Bayes' theorem, treats likelihood as measure of the state of knowledge, known and available to the decision-maker at decision time. To a Bayesian statistician, probability is a function of (1) largely subjective prior beliefs (of the decision-maker and/or decision-influencers) and (2) of past outcomes, or objective data. As such, it is particularly well suited to problems characterized by sparse or otherwise undependable or poorly projectable historical outcome data. Consequently, when considering the above scenario of forecasting average future probability of shareholder litigation, a Bayesian would expressly take into account expectations regarding the future, which could be shaped by factors such as new laws expected to either hamstring or galvanize shareholder activism, and combine those expectations with historical trends; all considered, an analogous (to the aforementioned frequentist projection) Bayesian estimate of expected average future probability of shareholder litigation would be a product of past frequency and expected future changes, and thus would likely be somewhat higher or lower.

In general, the frequentist approach is recommended for situations characterized by relatively stable trends and readily available, robust (meaning maximally accurate and complete) data. Of course, abstracting away from somewhat extreme cases of wars or pandemics, it is not always easy to draw a meaningful line of demarcation between 'sparse' and 'robust' data. In view of some, the above example of some 200 occurrences (of securities litigation) out of more than 18,000 possible cases constitutes poorly projectable trend, especially considering the impact of factors such as considerable amount of year-over-year volatility (over the most recent 25 years, the lowest annual number of shareholder lawsuits was 121 and the highest was 411), differences across industry sectors (e.g., firms in the information technology and life sciences sectors tend to sued noticeably more often than those in other sectors), and evolving legal and regulatory environment (i.e., changing laws and regulations). Others may insist that while those factors are indeed important, sticking strictly to empirical trends is nonetheless preferred, because it eliminates the possibility of biased interpretations. In the end, the two logically and mathematically distinct probability estimation approaches have their proponents and detractors, and often which approach is used is determined more by the preference and intellectual learning of a particular analyst than by careful side-by-side comparisons of strengths and weaknesses of those two distinct schools of probability estimation. Unfortunately, those personal preferences may have a nontrivial impact on resultant estimates, something that should not be overlooked when considering the efficacy of data analysis-derived benchmarks or baselines.

Interestingly, it is indeed rare for probability estimates to expressly disclose which of the two approaches were used to produce the forecast of interest. A case in point: Which of the two approaches is typically used to prepare the ubiquitous weather forecasts? (Weather forecasters use elements of both the frequentist and Bayesian statistics). How about the equally widely used survival probabilities used in medical diagnosis? (Typically, frequentist). All in all, while the technical details of probability forecasts might be prohibitively complex, it is nonetheless critical to understand if a particular data-derived standard, e.g., a benchmark, was estimated strictly adhering to past frequencies (a frequentist approach) or if its estimation process also factored in subjective informative priors (Bayesian approach).

Lastly, no information should be assumed to be correct without proper validation. Data can be incomplete, outright inaccurate, or corrupted by malfunctioning data capture systems; separately, analyses of valid data can be flawed, or interpretation of outcomes may not accurately capture the informational content. The next section takes a closer look at potential challenges in extracting valid and reliable evaluation standards out of available data.

Dependability of Probabilistic Estimates

'Chance favors the prepared mind' wrote Louis Pasteur, nineteenth-century biologist and chemist renowned for discovering the principles of vaccination and pasteurization (the latter named after him). His words are timeless, although what constitutes the 'prepared mind' continues to change. Early in the evolution of human civilizations, prepared mind was informed by the description of natural phenomena, as exemplified by writings of Aristotle, which eventually (circa seventeenth century) gave rise to theoretical scientific knowledge, such as Newton's laws, following which the prepared mind started to be informed by experimentally derived insights, best exemplified by the Large Hadron Collider experiments, and most recently data-intensive science where mining of vast quantities of multisourced data is the source of bulk of the new knowledge. The growing importance of data, however, underscores the significance of remembering that data should be seen as mixture-informative signal and noninformative noise, and thus inferences drawn from data should be seen as approximately correct, even if expressed and used as comparative assessment standards.

As suggested earlier in the context of overcoming cognitive resistance, there are three potential reasons for why new information might be hard to accept, and so it follows that new information might in fact be incorrect for the same three general reasons: data, data analytic methods, and result interpretation. Data capture processes or mechanisms can be flawed or may malfunction, data may be retrieved and/or curated improperly or it may be analyzed in logically or methodologically unsound manner, and lastly, inferences drawn from analyses may be unsound. It follows that each of those distinct elements that jointly form the process of extracting sound insights out of data requires explicit and committed due diligence, the importance of which cannot be overstated – to use the long-standing computer science's GIGO concept: 'garbage in, garbage out.'

While the issue of data due diligence tends to receive a lot of attention, further heightened by the recent rise of interest in artificial intelligence-based data analytic systems, an aspect of general analytic due diligence that is often overlooked is the use of inappropriate (in view of data and desired outcomes) estimation methodologies or using an overtly appropriate method incorrectly. Perhaps the most telling example here is one of the simplest ones: estimation of average values. Even though there are three distinct methods of estimating average – the mean, median, and mode – many data users instinctively associate the general notion of 'average' with the arithmetic mean, without carefully considering the distributional properties of data. Consider Figure 3.1.

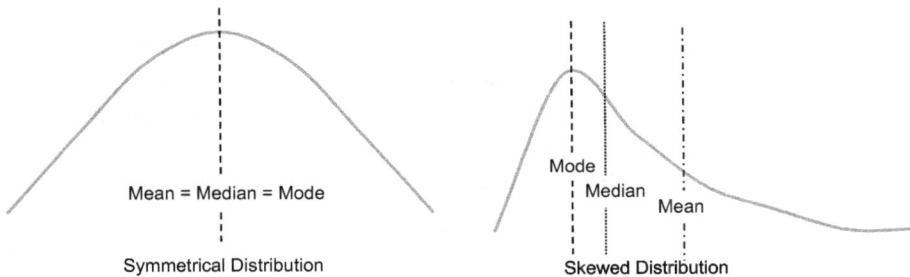

Figure 3.1: Mean vs. median vs. mode.

When the distribution of a particular variable, such as 'purchase amount' is symmetrical (left-hand side drawing in Figure 3.1), the arithmetic mean will indeed be an appropriate expression of average, but if the distribution is not symmetrical (commonly referred to as skewed), the arithmetic mean does not validly capture the idea of average, as in 'typical,' because its value is influenced by the outlying values; in that situation, median tends to be a better representation of average. Depending on the degree of skewness of a particular data element, the magnitudinal difference between the estimated mean and median can be substantial – for instance, the mean securities class action settlement is $52.4 million, while the median settlement value is 'only'

$8.5 million. It is intuitively obvious that choosing one over the other will have a profound impact not only on the general interpretation of the typical cost of shareholder litigation, but also on any benchmarking analyses that use average as a comparative assessment standard.

An even more nuanced aspect of efficacy of data-derived probabilistic estimates is generalizability. For example, is the average return on investment (ROI) of S&P 500 companies a sound assessment standard to be used to benchmark a specific company's ROI? The short answer is that it depends. The S&P 500 is composed of 500 largest (in terms of market capitalization) companies traded on public stock exchanges in the United States – with that in mind, if the company of interest is an established, comparably sized entity, the S&P 500 average will offer a sound assessment standard, but likely not if it is a relatively young, much smaller organization.

A Note on Probability vs. Likelihood

The concepts of 'probability' and 'likelihood' are quite often used interchangeably, as notionally they can be seen as synonymous. In the common usage sense, the two terms indeed point toward the general idea of chances of some future event materializing (i.e., as used in the preceding general overview); in a more technically rigorous sense, however, probability and likelihood differ in ways that are subtle, but nonetheless worth mentioning, in the spirit of clarity.

Likelihood represents a direct interpretation of the underlying data, meaning that it can be thought of as being fixed in relation to data from which it is derived. The earlier mentioned example of about 200 annual shareholder lawsuits filed annually against one of about 18,000 companies traded on public US stock exchanges gives rise to an average likelihood of 0.011%. In contrast to that, probability represents expectations regarding the future, in which sense it is not expressly tied to any specific and fixed data (thought probability estimation certainly uses data, but it is not fixed with regard to what data to use and how those data should be interpreted). The two distinctly different approaches to probability estimation discussed earlier – frequentist and Bayesian – underscore the distinction between probability and likelihood in the sense that both use fixed likelihood estimates (e.g., 0.011% derived from past occurrences), while at the same time each espouses manifestly conceptually and mathematically different views of how the probability of outcomes of interest should be estimated.

Key Estimation and Parameterization Considerations

The idea of probabilistic estimates is a composite of two separate concepts: the notion of probability discussed in the previous section, and the comparatively less intuitively obvious notion of *estimation*, commonly defined as the process of finding an approximate value using imperfect information. The two general probability estimation approaches – frequentist and Bayesian – can be expected to, under most circumstances, yield numerically different values, but they are nonetheless both rooted in the common conception of *variability*, or spread of individual values in a set of data, characterized as statistical dispersion in the confines of data analytics. The notion of variability is just that – a general idea, which is operationalized with the help of another technical concept: variance, a mathematical expression of the spread of values in a set of data. Variance, however, is not directly interpretable and so interpretive assessment of variability of a set of data is typically undertaken with the help of another technical concept, the *standard deviation*, which is a standardized measure of the amount of variation (and a direct derivative of variance; more on that later). Moreover, the idea of variability is usually encapsulated in the broader notion of *statistical distribution*, or a cumulative representation of all values, and their relative frequency of a measured quantity of interest, and understanding of which calls for a yet another idea, the *average*, which is the statistical summary of a set of numbers and expressed as a single value, often incorrectly equated with the arithmetic mean. In short, developing sound understanding of key estimation-related considerations calls for robust grounding in elementary statistical concepts, which are discussed in this chapter.

Within the confines of standard-defining analytics of interest here, also of interest is the notionally related but otherwise distinct idea of *parameterization*, which is the process of selecting measurable quantities – here, data-derived estimates – that best describe factors of interest. So, while the process of estimation yields approximations of quantities of interest, the related process of parameterization guides the selection of specific estimates deemed to be most appropriate in a particular context. The distinctiveness of estimation and parameterization is perhaps best illustrated in the context of the difference between frequentist and Bayesian estimation: Here, the goal of parameterization is to discern which of the two separately computed and likely numerically dissimilar estimates of the same quantity of interest is more appropriate in a particular context. In the confines of comparative assessment built around numerically expressed standards, the interplay between estimation and parameterization is critically important.

In the somewhat narrower context of comparative assessment mechanisms, i.e., benchmarks and baselines, also critical is the difference between broad types of data, as seen from the perspective of structural and informational characteristics. What types of data can be used to support 'us vs. others' benchmarks, and what data can be used to support 'now vs. then' baselines? That distinction is of fundamental importance as it directly impacts core methodological choices; in view of that, its overview kicks off a deeper dive into the key estimation and parameterization considerations.

Spatial vs. Temporal Data

The notion of variability is commonly thought of in the context of statistical distributions, most notably the bell-shaped standard normal distribution, which offers an elegant background for conveying the otherwise mathematically abstract statistical concepts. In that sense, the idea of variability tends to be implicitly tied to data pooled across multiple entities, such as customers, households, or companies, at an implicitly single point in time; those data are sometimes referred to as cross-sectional but in the context of comparative assessment are better characterized as *spatial data* (which also better aligns that data characterization with the general comparative assessment framework discussed in the previous chapter). In the context of spatial data, variability captures the spread of values of a phenomenon of interest across different entities, at a point in time.

The concept of variability is just as applicable to time-focused data, which are data that track values of interest measured/captured at different, typically fixed and equally spaced, points in time. Commonly known as *time series*, those data can be framed here as *temporal*, a label seen as more appropriate in the context of the spatiotemporal comparative assessment framework outlined in Chapter 2. When considered in the context of temporal data, variance captures the spread of values of a phenomenon of interest – which could be entity-specific values, such as the stock price of a single company, or an aggregate, such as S&P 500 – across time. Strongly suggested by that general characterization of spatial and temporal data is the alignment of those two broad data types with the two general mechanisms of comparative assessment: benchmarking and baselining, a distinction that is at the core of the difference between those two informational tools.

In both spatial and temporal data contexts, the idea of variability is operationalized using the statistical concept of *variance*, which is a measure of the spread between numbers in a dataset in relation to the average in the form of arithmetic mean. Figure 3.2 offers a graphical representation of the difference between variance expressed in terms of spatial and temporal data.

The most noticeable feature depicted in Figure 3.2 is that, but for the difference in the horizontal dimension (commonly known as the x-axis), the two graphs are identical, which is intended to underscore that outside of 'what' is being measured, and the general interpretation of the idea of variability is the same for spatial and temporal data. That said, however, the distinction between 'entity' and 'time' highlighted in Figure 3.2 is critical to clearly differentiating between statistical foundations of benchmarking and baselining. That seemingly small difference cascades into numerous, critical methodological differences, understanding of which is essential to development of valid and reliable comparative assessment capabilities; given that, a more indepth exploration of the key spatial and temporal data-related analytic considerations follows.

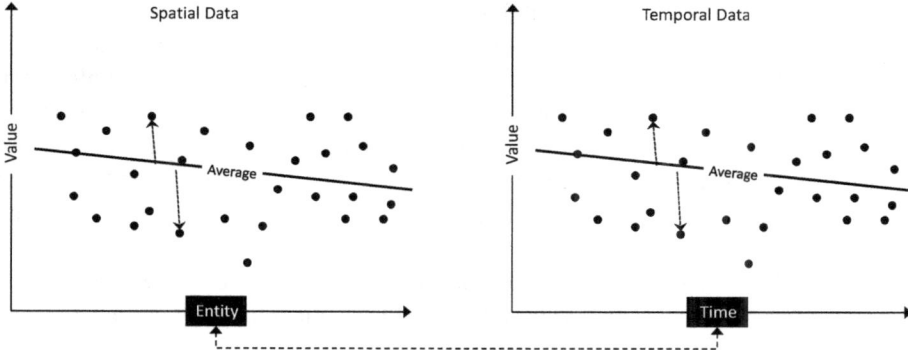

Figure 3.2: Graphical representation of variance in spatial and temporal data.

Estimating Spatial Average and Variance

Meaningful understanding of the idea of variability of spatial data is rooted in understanding of broader notion of *statistical distribution*, which is a cumulative representation of all values of a particular variable in a set of data; a distribution of, for instance, 'purchase amount' variable shows all distinct purchase amount values along with their relative frequencies. Given that the same value can appear more than once, e.g., multiple customers may have the same exact 'purchase amount,' statistical distributions are commonly represented by what is known as *density function*, which forms the basis for estimating the likelihood[6] of a specific value of a continuous variable. The familiar bell-shaped *standard normal distribution*, shown in Figure 3.3, is perhaps the best-known example of a probability density function, and thus of a statistical distribution in general.

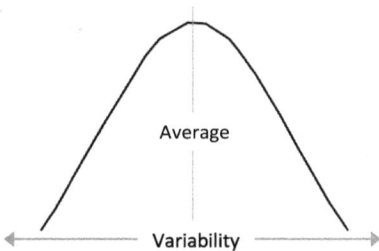

Figure 3.3: Standard normal distribution.

As graphically depicted in Figure 3.3, the two main characteristics, or to use more technical language, two main parameters of the normal distribution are the mean

---

6 Recall the distinction between likelihood, which represents a direct interpretation of the underlying data, and probability, which represents more generally framed expectations regarding the future.

and a measure of variability around that mean, known as *standard deviation*,[7] which as noted earlier is the standardized expression of variance. In a general sense, the mean captures what is considered most 'typical' value of a normally distributed variable, while standard deviation captures the typical degree of up and down deviations from the mean. In that sense, it is appropriate to think of standard deviation as a complement to the mean – in other words, a metric that captures information lost during in the process of collapsing individual values into a single summary expression of the average.

Implied in the preceding overview is a computational progression where the first computed (arithmetic) mean is then used as the basis for estimating variance, which is then used to derive the standard deviation:

$$\text{Mean} = \frac{1}{n} \sum_{i=1}^{n} x_i$$

where x_i is an individual observation and n is the number of cases.

With the estimated mean as the starting point, variability is simply expressed as

$$\text{Variability} = \sum_{i=1}^{n} (\text{Observed} - \text{mean})$$

It is important to note that since the mean falls more or less in the middle of the distribution, roughly half the values can be expected to be larger than it and half can be expected to be smaller; if simply added together, the positive and negative deviations from the mean would largely cancel each other out, resulting in zero (0), or close to zero variability estimate. That undesirable consequence can be avoided by simply squaring both the positive and negative values to eliminate the canceling effect. It is also worth noting, however, that this mathematically necessary step yields a mathematically abstract value, one that is not directly interpretable (more on that below). The statistical measure of variance is computed as follows:[8]

$$\text{Variance} = \frac{\sum_{i=1}^{n} (x_i - \overline{x})^2}{n - 1}$$

where x_i is an individual value, $\overline{x}$ is the mean, and n is the number of cases.

The squaring and summing of individual deviations from the estimated mean produces an abstract and practically not useful value, which does not lend itself to direct interpretation or comparisons (everything else being the same, a larger number

---

7 For completeness, there are two other additional parameters that complete the description of the standard normal distribution – skewness (a measure of symmetry) and kurtosis (a measure of flatness or peakedness) – but for the purposes of framing analytically robust benchmarks and baselines, the mean and standard deviation are of primary interest.

8 Assumes it is computed in a sample (as opposed to the population).

of records will yield larger variance). For that reason, estimated variance is usually seen as a throughput used to estimate a more informative expression of variability, the standard deviation (SD), which is simply the square root of variance, computed as follows:[9]

$$SD = \sqrt{\dfrac{\sum\limits_{i=1}^{n} (x_i - \bar{x})^2}{n-1}}$$

where x_i is an individual value, $\bar{x}$ is the mean, and n is the number of cases.

Standard deviation is an important metric because it illustrates the amount of variability contained in a particular variable – the larger the standard deviation, the more variability there is in a particular variable across individual cases. The interpretation of the size of standard deviation, however, is nuanced: When considered from the perspective of estimation, measures with very small standard deviations are usually seen as informationally poor because they contribute little to the cross-case differentiation; at the same time, when considered from the perspective of parameterization, small standard deviation is desirable as it is an indication of stable estimates.

Estimating Temporal Average and Variance

Time series or temporal data capture the value of states or outcomes of interest at fixed, usually equally spaced intervals. Assuming some degree of cross-time change in values of interest, the general notion of variability is equally applicable to temporal data, where it encapsulates cross-time spread of individual values around an estimated average, as graphically depicted in Figure 3.2. However, the core 'entity' vs. 'time' distinction, also highlighted in Figure 3.2, draws attention to more nuanced differences embedded in that dissimilarity. One of the more consequential differences manifests itself in the statistical concept of *autocorrelation* (also known as serial correlation), which in the information processing sense is the correlation of a signal with a delayed copy of itself as a function of delay. In other words, individual values of time series, i.e., records in a set of data, are linked by the implied commonality of a single phenomenon being measured at different points in time; that general provision stands in a sharp contrast with the basic design logic of spatial data discussed earlier, where individual data records are expected to be independent of one another. In more statistically explicit terms, temporal data are assumed to be autocorrelated, which has a direct impact on how the idea of variability is operationalized.

Firstly, in the context of temporal or time series data, the idea of 'average' is commonly operationalized with the help of notionally analogous but statistically distinct measure known as *moving average*, which is the arithmetic mean of a given set of values over a specific number of time units. In the manner that loosely parallels mul-

---

9 Sample standard deviation; it can also be expressed as a square root of variance.

tiple manifestations of the idea of average in spatial data (i.e., the mean, median, and the mode), there are also multiple manifestations of idea in temporal data, with the best known being simple moving average (SMA) and exponential moving average (EMA). *SMA* is called 'simple' because it is based on computing a straight or simple average using the following basic formula:

$$\text{SMA} = \frac{V_1 + V_2 + V_3 + \cdots + V_n}{n}$$

where *V* is the time period-specific value and *n* is the number of distinct time periods.

Implicit in the general framing of SMA is equal weighting of all individual values, which may be appropriate in some contexts but not others. For instance, when computing SMA for certain types of behavioral patterns, such as the repurchase value for a particular product, the question of recency or newness of data might arise, as in many behavioral contexts, more recent behaviors are more indicative of future behaviors. In those situations, a more refined variant of moving average, known as *EMA* might be more appropriate. EMA weighs recent values more heavily to make the computed average more responsive to newer information. That means that the core difference between SMA and EMA is the latter's use of a weighting factor, known as *smoothing factor*, typically computed using a simple formula: 2/(number of time periods + 1).[10] Expanding the smoothing factor computation to encompass the entirety of EMA yields the following formulation:

$$\text{EMA} = \left[V_{t-0} \times \left(\frac{\text{SF}}{1+n}\right)\right] + V_{t-1} \times \left[1 - \left(\frac{\text{SF}}{1+n}\right)\right] \cdots$$

where V_t is value recency (V_{t-0} is most recent, V_{t-1} second most recent, etc.), SF is the smoothing factor, and *N* is the number of distinct time periods.

The 'moving' aspect of temporal data-specific estimates of the average carries over to the associated derivation of variability. Using SMA as the point of departure (and the expression of the average needed as the basis for estimation of variance), estimation of *temporal variance* is largely analogous to the computational logic used with spatial data: For each time period, the difference is between that value and the SMA calculated, then squared, summed up, and divided by the number of records, as formulaically summarized below:

$$\text{Temporal variance} = \frac{\sum_{i=1}^{n}(x_i - \bar{x})^2}{n-1}$$

where x_i is an individual, period-specific value, $\bar{x}$ is SMA, and *n* is the number of cases.

Strongly implied in the above reasoning is that the general idea time series variability can be ultimately expressed in the formed of standard deviation, computed

---

10 For example, to compute a 7-day moving average, the smoothing factor would be 2/(7 + 1), or 0.25.

simply as the square root of temporal variance ($\sqrt{\text{Temporal variance}}$). All considered, when considered from the perspective of deriving evaluative standards to be used in comparative assessment, the general temporal estimate derivation logic parallels the spatial estimate derivation rationale.

Statistical Aspects of Benchmarking and Baselining

The preceding brief methodological overview was meant to lay the necessary foundation of basic statistical knowledge that is necessary to correctly frame data analysis-derived benchmarks and baselines. With that in mind and recalling the general outline of benchmarking and baselining processes outlined in Chapters 1 and 2, statistically expressed evaluative norms or standards need to be operationalized in the manner that expressly accounts for data imperfections, by factoring-in the imprecision in parameter estimates. In simple terms, that means that both benchmarks and baselines need to be expressed as ranges rather than exact values (also known as point estimates in statistical analysis). Operationalizing that idea, however, entails going a step deeper into some underlying technical considerations.

First and foremost, the denotational meaning of the idea of variability needs to be broadened to encompass two distinct interpretations: The first of those is the earlier discussed extent of spread of actual values around an estimated mean; the secondary or expanded meaning of variability is the relative imprecision of the estimate of the mean itself.[11] In other words, under most circumstances, the estimated mean should be viewed as approximately rather than absolutely true, which in turn calls for explicitly factoring-in the degree of imprecision into estimated value of the mean. The statistical concept that captures that imprecision is known as the *standard error of the mean*, or simply the standard error, and it measures the variability of the estimated mean around the generally unknown true mean. Mathematically, the standard error of the mean (SE_{Mean}) is a derivative of the earlier discussed standard deviation, and it is computed as follows:

$$SE_{Mean} = \frac{SD}{\sqrt{n}}$$

where SD is the standard deviation and n is the number of cases.

Using the so-computed standard error, the mean-expressed point estimate can be re-expressed as a so-called *confidence interval*, which is a range that has a defined probability of containing the true but unknown (because of imperfect data) parame-

---

11 The idea of imprecise mean estimation can be seen as a direct consequence of informationally imperfect data, as discussed earlier. In that sense, any parameter estimate is subject to some degree of imprecision, which is typically encapsulated in the idea of *random error*, which is a chance difference between the estimated and true values of something.

ter estimate. While in principle a confidence interval can be framed using any proba-bility level ranging from slightly over 0% to just under 100%, customarily three dis-tinct probability levels are used – 90%, 95%, and 99% – with 95% by far being the most commonly used.[12] Keeping in mind the symmetrical character of standard nor-mal distribution that frames the idea of confidence intervals, each probability level corresponds to a specific number of *standard units* away from the mean, where the 'standard unit' can be either the standard deviation, if the goal is to define the proba-bility of a specific value occurring in the overall scattering of values, or it can be the standard error, if the goal is to define the range of possible values that the estimated mean can assume (which is the case here), as graphically depicted in Figure 3.4.

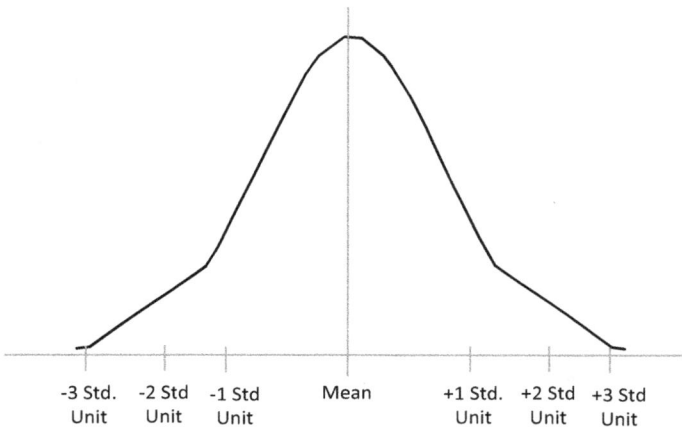

| -3 Std. Unit | -2 Std Unit | -1 Std Unit | Mean | +1 Std. Unit | +2 Std Unit | +3 Std Unit |

Figure 3.4: Standard normal distribution and standard units.

The abstract standard units shown in Figure 3.4 are jointly a manifestation of the *empir-ical rule*, according to which 99.7% of normally distributed data lies within ±3 standard deviation of the mean. Using that general rationale and the supporting mathematical procedures, probable ranges of estimated mean values can be computed using as inputs the value of the mean, the estimated standard error of the mean, and the desired level of precision, expressed in terms of the number of standard units (i.e., standard errors) that correspond to the chosen level of significance, which as noted earlier are typically 90%, 95%, or 99%. Given the well-defined mathematical properties of standard normal distribution, those values are fixed at 1.65, 1.96, and 2.58 for 90%, 95%, and 99% levels of

---

12 Though often seen as a convenient middle-ground between 90% and 99% levels, the more funda-mental reason for the popularity of the 95% threshold is that it offers the optimum trade-off between significance, which is the probability of rejecting (as false) true estimate, and power, which is the probability of rejecting false estimate.

significance, respectively. Consequently, confidence intervals are computed as up (>mean) and down (<mean) deviation from the estimated mean, or mean ± probability level*standard error. For example, assuming the mean of 2.45, standard error of 0.2, and 95% probability, the resultant confidence interval is computed as follows:

$$\text{Lower confidence level} = 2.45 - 1.96 * 0.2, \text{ or } 2.058$$

$$\text{Upper confidence level} = 2.45 + 1.96 * 0.2, \text{ or } 2.842$$

Assuming that the above computed confidence intervals represent the benchmark (as in evaluative standard) promotional response rates, observed rates falling below 2.058 could be considered subpar, and those falling above 2.842 could be considered to be above the norm.

It is important to note, however, that the about outlined reasoning is couched in the context of standard normal distribution, which means that the underlying data are expected to be normally distributed, i.e., approximately follow the symmetrical, bell-shaped distribution depicted in Figures 3.3 and 3.4. However, in many, perhaps even most real-life scenarios data are not normally distributed – in those situations, it is usually recommended to use one of the two distinct and well-established remedies: mathematical transformations or bootstrapping.

Transformations. Data transformations entail re-expressing of original values in different units with the goal of bringing about desired data qualities, in this case, correcting for departures from normality. There are multiple types of mathematical transformations available, and transformed values are thus a function of original values and a type of a transformation used. In a very broad sense, transformations can be either linear or nonlinear. A linear transformation changes the scale, but not the shape of the distribution, while a nonlinear transformation changes the shape of the distribution. In terms of purpose, linear transformations are typically used to standardize variables, which entails converting values expressed in original units of measurement to standard deviations from the mean (more on that later). It is important to note that standardization does not normalize a distribution; hence, a skewed distribution will remain skewed following variable standardization. Nonlinear transformations, on the other hand, are focused on changing the shape of the underlying distribution, most notably, on recasting of originally non-normally distributed variables into normally distributed ones. In general, non-normality can manifest itself in the form of skewness (lack of symmetry) and/or kurtosis (excessive flatness or peakedness). Depending on whether the problems manifests itself as skewness or as kurtosis, and also on the strength of non-normality, different types of transformations can be used, all of which falling under two broad categories of logarithmic and power transformations. For example, logarithmic transformations using either natural or base-10 logarithms tend to be an effective remedy for positively skewed data; however, if the degree of skewness is relatively mild, a logarithmic transformation may overcorrect, in effect replacing positive with negative skewness, and in those situations, power transformations. Many statistic texts offer more specific guidelines for what types of transformations are most appropriate to use with specific types of non-normality, but it is important to keep in mind that no transformation can produce desired outcomes, in which case it might be appropriate to consider bootstrapping.

Bootstrapping. Although the term 'bootstrapping' conveys multiple meanings,[13] within the realm of data analytics that term is used to describe a method for estimating basic distribution statistics, most notably the mean and variance, in the absence of normality. Process-wise, it uses serial resampling of (non-normally distributed) datasets to produce unbiased estimates, that are generally accepted as being unaffected by the underlying non-normality. While conceptually straightforward, bootstrapping is computationally intense but many of the most used data analytic languages (e.g., R or Python) and systems (e.g., SAS or SPSS) have standardized built-in bootstrapping algorithms; more extensive discussion of methodological and operational aspects of that method are offered in many popular statistic texts.

The two 'tried and true' approaches outlined above do not exhaust the possible solutions to extracting valid and reliable estimates out of non-normal data. Realizing that becomes particularly important in some organizational management contexts, as exemplified by risk management-focused comparative assessments (discussed at length in the context of case studies in Chapters 9 and 10), in which non-normality is in itself highly informative. More on that next.

Positive vs. Negative Variability

The two established approaches to dealing with the problem of non-normally distributed data – data transformations and bootstrapping – are rooted in the general idea of reshaping actual data to fit the underlying theoretical construct, in the form of normal distribution. Implicitly, that line of reasoning frames non-normal data as being in some sense aberrant (as evident even in the term 'non-normal'), which is hard to reconcile with preponderance of so-distributed data. Even more importantly, such reshaping of data can lead to loss of information in situations in which values seen as outlying are particularly informative, as readily illustrated by many facets of risk management.

Expressly focused on just those types of situations is the third, and comparatively unconventional approach to dealing with the problem of statistical non-normality, one that is built around the idea of *nonsymmetric variability*. Recalling the earlier dis-

---

13 For example, entrepreneurs are bootstrapping when they attempt to build a new company without external help, relying instead on personal finances or on operating revenues.

cussion of the computational progression from variance to standard deviation to standard error of the mean, the ultimate end goal of that computational sequence is to recast the initial point estimate-expressed value of an evaluative standard of interest into a more analytically sound confidence interval-expressed form. Implicit in that progression is the assumption that negative (i.e., smaller than the mean) and positive (i.e., greater than the mean) variance is the same, as graphically illustrated in Figure 3.4. But what if that foundational assumption was set aside, and instead of trying to make non-normal data normal, the overall variability was broken down into *positive variability*, or upward deviations from the mean, and *negative variability*, or downward deviations from the mean? Figure 3.5 offers a graphical summary of that idea.

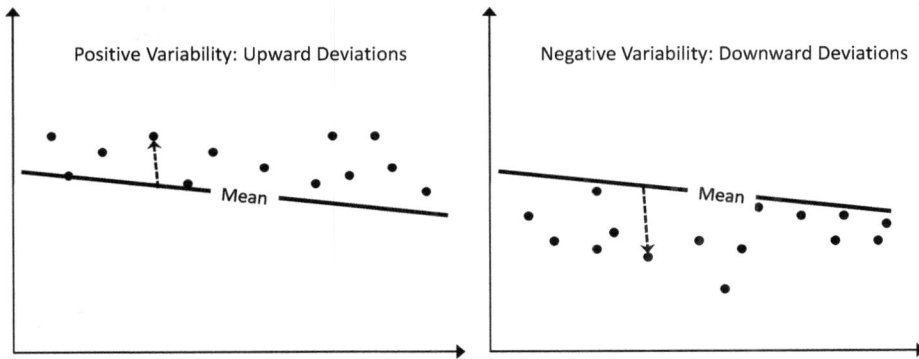

Figure 3.5: Positive vs. negative variability.

There are numerous real-life instances where such an approach might be appropriate, even preferred. Consider the example of hydroelectric generation, where power output is highly dependent on the level of water in a particular river, but it is particularly impacted by declining flows, as recently illustrated by the example of drought-stricken Lake Mead in Nevada, the main reservoir serving the Hoover Dam Hydroelectric Plant. Prior to the 2023 and 2024 winter seasons that saw blockbuster snowfall in the mountains surrounding the Colorado River (the key determinant of water level in the Colorado; in fact, Lake Meade was created by the damming of the Colorado River), greatly diminished flows in the river caused by multiple low precipitation years resulted in steady decrease in the level of Lake Meade, which ultimately manifested itself in 22% decline in annual generation from Hoover Dam.[14] On a larger

---

14 To complete this line of reasoning, the opposite – an increase in hydroelectric flows – does not have proportional impact because the excess water tends to be released or otherwise redirected to prevent overpowering of the generation systems. In short, in that particular scenario there is a comparatively narrower upside variance.

scale, the State of California normally derives about 13% of its electricity from hydro-power, but during a drought that decreases by more than a half, to about 6%; the high-flow precipitated increase in output is generally less than half of low-flow caused declines, underscoring the need for separate upward and downward variability estimation.

As illustrated by the above example, there are recurring, important situations that call for addressing the idea of variability in a way that preserves, rather than masks, the underlying systemic asymmetry. In such situations, even if non-normality can be remedied with the help of mathematical transformations or bootstrapping, doing so may result in estimates that are not robust; in those situations, it is more analytically sound to replace the distributional symmetry-focused conception of variance with one that expressly differentiates between upward and downward variability, known as *positive* and *negative semivariance*, and computed as follows:

$$\text{Positive semivariance} = \frac{1}{n_a}\left(\sum_{\substack{x_i > \bar{x}}}^{n_p}(x_i - \bar{x})^2\right)$$

$$\text{Negative semivariance} = \frac{1}{n_b}\left(\sum_{\substack{x_i < \bar{x}}}^{n_n}(x_i - \bar{x})^2\right)$$

where n_a is the number of cases with values greater than the mean, n_b is the number of cases with values smaller than the mean, x_i is an observed value i, and $\bar{x}$ is the mean value.

Following the earlier outlined computational logic, positive and negative semivariances are next used to derive positive and negative semi-standard deviation, and positive and negative semi-standard error of the mean. The respective computational formulas are as follows:

$$\text{Positive semi–standard deviation} = \sqrt{\frac{1}{n_a}\left(\sum_{\substack{x_i > \bar{x}}}^{n_a}(x_i - \bar{x})^2\right)}$$

$$\text{Negative semi–standard deviation} = \sqrt{\frac{1}{n_b}\left(\sum_{\substack{x_i < \bar{x}}}^{n_b}(x_i - \bar{x})^2\right)}$$

where n_a is the number of cases with values greater than the mean, n_b is the number of cases with values smaller than the mean, x_i is an observed value i, and $\bar{x}$ is the mean value

$$\text{Positive semi–standard error} = \frac{SD}{\sqrt{n_a}}$$

$$\text{Negative semi–standard error} = \frac{\text{SD}}{\sqrt{n_b}}$$

where SD is the standard deviation, n_a is the number of cases greater than the mean, and n_b is the number of cases smaller than the mean.

The ideas of upward and downward, or positive and negative variability and their operational implementations in the form of positive and negative semi-standard deviation and semi-standard error form the conceptual and methodological basis for what is characterized here as *nonsymmetric confidence intervals*. That somewhat non-traditional (once again) application of the long-standing idea of confidence intervals warrants a closer explanation.

Nonsymmetric Confidence Intervals

As evidenced by the earlier example of hydroelectric power, there are contexts in which approaching variance as a composite of separately estimated positive and negative deviations from the mean more accurately captures the essence of the phenomenon of interest. The domain of risk management, a broadly framed facet or organizational management focused on identification, assessment, and response to distinct threats facing organizations[15] offers an example of such a context. The heart of modern risk management practices is an objective assessment of individual threats, centered on estimation of organization-specific exposure to those threats, with the overall process rooted in analyses of threat-type specific data. By and large, risk outcome data are non-normally distributed, as illustrated in Figure 3.6.

Figure 3.6 shows the aggregate distribution of shareholder litigation settlements; what looks like a long, flat line that closely parallels the x-axis is in fact a very long tail of an extremely right-skewed distribution, as evidenced by the imbedded table. The extreme skew of shareholder litigation outcomes poses an analytic dilemma; the 'standard' approach is to either eliminate or trim the outlying-most values, but de-marking those values can be challenging because those values are not clearly de-marked by magnitudinal discontinuities (i.e., the values just keep on getting larger without clearly identifiable jumps). In view of that, the approach that is commonly used in applied analytics is to magnitudinally trim (i.e., recode) 5% of values – 2.5% on both ends of the distribution – to 2.5th and 97.5th percentiles, respectively. Taking that step here yields the following outcome:

Somewhat better, but still far from normal. On the one hand, magnitudinal trimming clearly had large impact on the key parameters (e.g., the mean and the associated standard deviation, and, of course, the maximum value) as evidenced by comparing the

---

15 For a more in-depth discussion of organizational risk management scope and practice, see Banasie-wicz, A. (2016). *Threat Exposure Management: Risk, Resilience, Change*, Lightning Source: La Vergne, TN.

Settlement Amount

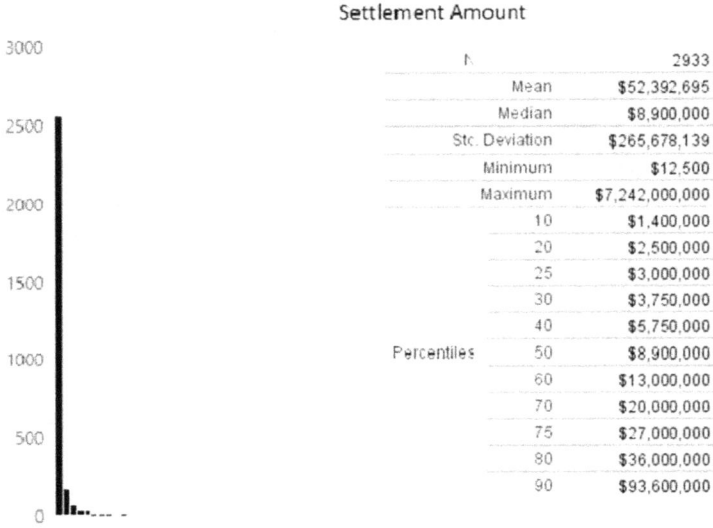

	N	2933
	Mean	$52,392,695
	Median	$8,900,000
	Std. Deviation	$265,678,139
	Minimum	$12,500
	Maximum	$7,242,000,000
	10	$1,400,000
	20	$2,500,000
	25	$3,000,000
	30	$3,750,000
	40	$5,750,000
Percentiles	50	$8,900,000
	60	$13,000,000
	70	$20,000,000
	75	$27,000,000
	80	$36,000,000
	90	$93,600,000

Figure 3.6: Distribution of shareholder litigation settlements.

Trimmed Settlement Amount

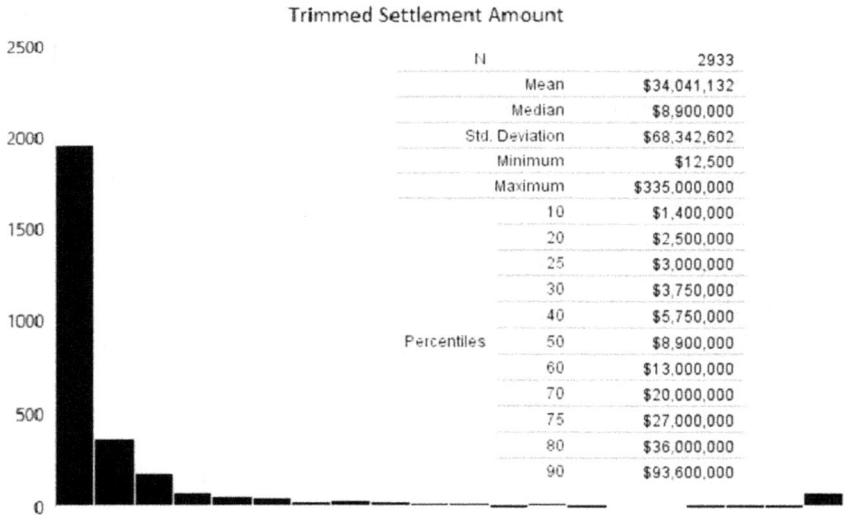

	N	2933
	Mean	$34,041,132
	Median	$8,900,000
	Std. Deviation	$68,342,602
	Minimum	$12,500
	Maximum	$335,000,000
	10	$1,400,000
	20	$2,500,000
	25	$3,000,000
	30	$3,750,000
	40	$5,750,000
Percentiles	50	$8,900,000
	60	$13,000,000
	70	$20,000,000
	75	$27,000,000
	80	$36,000,000
	90	$93,600,000

Figure 3.7: Trimmed distribution of shareholder litigation settlements.

tabular values in Figures 3.6 and 3.7; however, it had a comparatively trivial impact on the shape of the overall distribution. The aggregate distribution in Figure 3.7 is still very positively skewed; moreover, now it is also showing a hint of bimodality, an inescapable consequence of recording of the largest values into the value that represents the 97.5th percentile. An even more practically troubling consequence of magnitudinal trimming is the artificial shrinking of what in the context of risk assessment is commonly seen as the worst-case scenario, in the form of the eliminated outlying-most values. In short, the standard remedy produced minimal statistical gains at the expense of disproportionately large informational cost in the form of underestimation of, in this case, the extent of the economic threat posed by shareholder litigation.

The preceding illustration was meant to shine a light on the fact that, particularly in applied data analytic contexts, 'tried and true' remedies might – at times – need to be reconsidered. It may be possible to use various mathematical operations to mold manifestly and strongly non-normal data into some approximately normal shape, but it is important to be open to the possibility that the resultant overtly 'statistically sound' parameter estimates may lack what ultimately matters the most: informational validity. In a more general sense, it is instructive to keep in mind that while statistical efficacy is, of course, essential, it is a mean to the end and not the end goal, and so if the latter is not being served adequately well by a particular approach, an alternative solution to the problem at hand might need to be considered. The idea of nonsymmetric confidence intervals is a case in point here. Some real-life data simply cannot be made to fit established data analytic approaches, and subjecting such 'non-compliant' data to corrective mathematical manipulations may be counterproductive, yielding mathematical artifacts rather informative insights. With that in mind, nonsymmetric confidence intervals offer a more rational solution to the problem of developing robust comparative assessment benchmarks using strongly skewed data.

Standardization and Normalization

The general overview of foundational estimation and parameterization-related benchmarking and baselining considerations would be incomplete without expressly addressing two often confused ideas of normalization and standardization. Somewhat indirectly alluded to in the earlier discussion of distributional characteristics, *normalization* entails bringing about cross-data elements uniformity in the sense of making (actual or implied) measurement scales comparable, whereas *standardization* entails rescaling of individual data elements to a mean of 0 and standard deviation of 1, which effectively replaces original values with an idealized notion of the number of standard units away from the mean of 0.

The core benefit of normalization is that it enables direct comparisons of effects measured on different scales – for instance, the originally not directly comparable 'household income' (typically measured in thousands of dollars) and 'age' (typically measured in years) magnitudes, once normalized can be compared to one another (e.g., average Brand X customer may have household income that falls in the 60th percentile overall, and that customer may fall into 80th percentile age-wise). Standardization also contributes to making comparative assessments easier, but the primary benefit of standardization is cross-record (e.g., across customers or companies) rather than cross-data feature comparisons. Given their notional similarity and the resultant usage and methodological fuzziness, it is worthwhile to consider their distinctiveness in the context of their respective computational formulas, which are as follows:

$$\text{Standardization: } \frac{x - \bar{x}}{\text{SD}}$$

$$\text{Normalization: } \frac{(x - \min)}{(\max - \min)}$$

where x is the actual value, $\bar{x}$ is the mean, SD is the standard deviation, min is the minimum value, and max is the maximum value.

The topics discussed in this chapter were meant to contribute to forming of a robust methodological foundation, seen here as a critical element of knowledge needed to be able to derive analytically robust assessment standards from available and applicable data. Framed in the context of the two related but nonetheless distinct ideas of estimation, or finding of approximations, and parameterization, or selecting the most situationally appropriate estimates (under the assumption of multiple competing estimates), the statistical details were meant to guide the process of computing valid and reliable assessment benchmarks and baselines. Building on that general foundation, the next section takes a closer look at benchmark- and baseline-setting, and related considerations.

Part II: **Framing the Ideas of Benchmarking
and Baselining**

Chapter 4
Benchmark-Setting

Despite widespread usage in organizational management, and even though it is also used in theoretical research, the general idea of benchmarking received surprisingly little methodological attention from academic researchers. By and large, benchmarking is often seen as a tool of opportunity, and it tends to be framed and operationalized in whatever way seems to fit a particular situation. Even when used in typically methodologically rigorous academic research studies, conceptual and methodological treatment of that important, comparative assessment tool is largely dismissive of the specifics of norm, i.e., benchmark-setting, and methodological validity of benchmarking evaluations. Needless to say, the typically not as methodology-centric applied research studies tend to be even less explicit regarding their framing and operationalization of the idea of benchmarking. All in all, it seems as if there is a prevailing sentiment suggesting that it is acceptable to assume that given the seemingly intuitively obvious meaning of the idea of benchmarking, no clarifying specifications are needed.

That mindset, however, is simply myopic. In just about any comparative assessment situation, definitional and methodological efficacy of the standard used in the evaluation process – here, an applicable benchmark – is as critical to assuring the validity of results as the measurement of the phenomenon of interest. Relying on conceptually and methodologically vague assessment standards is tantamount to allowing random chance to play an unnecessarily outsized role in shaping answers to important business or research questions. With that in mind, it is the goal of this chapter to subject the idea of benchmarking to the much needed conceptual and methodological scrutiny.

One of the key aspects of the ensuing overview is an explicit differentiation between two distinct elements of benchmark-based comparative assessment process: The process of deriving benchmarks, framed here as *benchmark-setting*, and the process of carrying out standard-based comparative assessments, framed here simply as *benchmarking*. This commonly overlooked distinction is one of the manifestations of the general conceptual and methodological fuzziness that characterizes the general notion of benchmarking, and benchmark-setting in particular, given which, the focus of this chapter is on detailing an explicit benchmark-setting process.

Benchmarking and Benchmark-Setting

Benchmarking's lack of robust ontological foundations manifests itself in, among other things, inconsistent definitional scoping and methodological framing. Not only that, but the idea of benchmarking is also commonly used in tandem with the conceptually and methodologically distinct notion of best practices, even though the two

https://doi.org/10.1515/9783111001296-004

comparative assessments focused approaches are more different than they are alike. And lastly, though somewhat less obvious, there is also a persistent lack of attention to benchmark-setting, or how evaluative standards used in spatial aspects of comparative assessment are derived and formalized.

First thing first, some basic definitions: *Benchmark-setting* is defined here as a process of deriving and parameterizing spatial (i.e., in relation to peers) evaluation standards, and *benchmarking* is defined as a process of using those standards to carry out unbiased comparative assessment of outcomes or states of interest. It follows that benchmark-setting efforts can be seen as a precondition of the benchmarking process, in the sense that sound comparative assessment (here, benchmarking) requires the existence of valid and reliable assessment standards in the form of benchmarks.

The distinction between benchmarking and benchmark-setting processes is important because while ultimately interrelated, the two processes have distinct functional roles that translate into distinct sets of methodological considerations. To that end, the earlier discussed concepts of statistical distribution, normality, estimation, and parameterization all play an important role in deriving valid and reliable assessment standards, i.e., benchmark-setting, while the mechanisms for assessing the materiality of difference between an outcome of interest and the appropriate assessment standard, in the form of statistical significance tests and effect size evaluations, play a critical role in benchmarking.

While important, methodological considerations need to be grounded in a rational and purposeful procedural logic if their application is to yield the desired outcomes. To that end, benchmark-setting is particularly in need of such conceptual fabric, which is summarized next in the form of explicit benchmark-setting criteria.

Benchmark-Setting Criteria

Examination of different aspects of benchmark-setting and the broader benchmarking process offered in the previous chapters is suggestive of general principles that should guide derivation of definitionally clear, methodologically sound, and application-friendly assessment standards. It is important to note that, given the explicit focus on objective data as the source of assessment standards, benchmark-setting principles need to encompass a wide range of considerations, ranging from definitional framing to derivation and deployment guidelines. With that in mind, benchmark-setting criteria are as follows:

1. Definitional clarity:
    a. Explicit conceptual definition of the standard
    b. Appropriateness of the standard
2. Data and methodological soundness:
    a. Data due diligence
    b. Estimation and parameterization

  c. Reliability and generalizability
  d. Stability and consistency
3. Usability:
  a. Refresh cycle
  b. Relevance
  c. Ease of administration and interpretation

The above-summarized benchmark-setting typology casts a purposefully wide net, the goal of which is to assure the maximum degree of validity and reliability of assessment standards, which are seen here as critically important to comparative assessment. It is intuitively obvious that the value of a standard used to evaluate the efficacy of an outcome of interest can singularly shape the resultant conclusions, with standard magnitudes set unjustifiably low or high, subsequently leading to artificially inflated or deflated evaluations (those challenges can be further amplified by overlooking inherent imprecisions in data derived standards, as discussed in more detail later in this chapter). The above-outlined typology was developed expressly for the purpose of avoiding those types of pitfalls.

 Anchored in three broad categories of definitional clarity, data and methodological soundness, and usability, the nine conceptually and operationally distinct criteria are meant to serve as a general guide to careful and deliberate benchmark derivation. Of those three broad categories, the data and methodological soundness considerations are perhaps the most complex part of the overall process, in part because they call for careful and informed review of numerous technical (i.e., statistical) standard-setting related details, while also challenging some of the longstanding approaches to extracting insights out of data. It is worth noting, however, that the initial investment in developing a robust understanding of those methodological foundations can pay significant long-term benefits in the form of significant future time and effort savings stemming from reusable processes and templates.

 The remainder of this chapter delves into the above-outlined benchmark-setting criteria, starting with the two-part definitional clarity, followed by the four-part data and methodological soundness, and ending with the two-part usability.

Definitional Clarity

The well-known 'say what you mean and mean what you say' expression offers perhaps the most concise summarization of the idea behind clearly and expressly defining the informational essence of benchmarks. Embedded in that idea are two more narrowly framed considerations: First, providing a clear definition of the standard of interest, and second, equally clearly spelling out the applicability of that standard to usage contexts of interest. Within the confines of measurement theory, which encompasses the general thought process and interrelated body of knowledge that form the basis of valid measurement, the former can be thought of in the context of construct validity, and the latter in the context of discriminant validity.

The notion of construct validity concerns how well-observable indicators represent a latent, or not directly observable idea (i.e., a construct); in an applied sense, it manifests itself as a relationship between the intended and the actual facets of measurement. For example, are measures that capture the proportion of companies' assets that are physically located in areas that face heightened incidence of natural disasters, such as earthquakes, floods, or tornadoes, good indicators of exposure to climate change-related risk? The notion of discriminant validity is an expression of uniqueness or distinctiveness of latent constructs, by means of assuring that indicators used to operationalize a particular concept are unrelated to other concepts. For instance, are indicators associated with climate change largely (meaning, in the sense of statistically valid associations) unrelated to other, similar ideas such as sustainability?

Keeping the preceding general ideas in mind, the two key aspects of definitional clarity are discussed in more detail next.

Conceptual Definition

Explicit and clear conceptual framing is the first step in the benchmark-setting process. The primary goal of that important first step is to clearly communicate what something is, and what it is not, in a way that acknowledges the difference between a *definition* of something and a *description* of that something. A good definition should be as concise as possible, which means it should exclude any descriptive nonessentials, whereas a description can be expected to be lengthier, more narrative, and include implications, interpretations, and other supporting rationale. In a more technical sense, a formal definition generally consists of three parts: (1) the term (i.e., a word or a phrase) that is being defined; (2) the class of ideas or concepts to which the term belongs; and (3) the specific characteristics that distinguish it from others in its class.

An example of setting a benchmark that captures the average cost of securities litigation might make those general ideas more meaningful. The term that is being defined here is the 'average cost of securities litigation,' the class of concepts into which that term falls is 'executive risk,' and the specific characteristics that set it apart from other notions that also fall under 'executive risk' is that it 'represents shareholder litigation alleging violations of securities laws' (as opposed to other organizational stakeholders, such as employees or creditors taking legal action alleging violations of other laws or regulations). In addition, to be unambiguous, the definition of 'average cost of securities litigation' also needs to address the idea of 'average,' given that it can be operationalized in more than one way.[1] All considered, the following definition meets the requirements outlined here: 'Average cost of securities litigation is a subset of a broader domain of executive risk, and it represents the median value of settled and/or adjudicated shareholder lawsuits alleging violations of the Securities Act of 1933 or the Securities Exchange Act of 1934.' Framed that way, the definition of the average cost of securities litigation addresses all three parts required for a robust definition, and it also clearly addresses the potentially ambiguous notion of the average.

Although a sound definition needs to be as succinct as possible, it is usually beneficial to also include with it more in-depth description, though care should be taken to make sure that the two are structured and clearly communicated as complementary, but distinct. The overriding objective here is for the definition (and any associated descriptions) to create uniformity of understanding of the concept of interest.

Appropriateness of Standard

Why this conceptualization, why not a different one? While that may not always be the case, in situations in which there is a plurality of potential framings of a standard of interest it is important to expressly address the appropriateness – really, the advantage – of the chosen one. It is common for benchmarks to be chosen for reasons such as tradition, convenience, or familiarity – it is important to make sure that those and similar reasons of habit do not overshadow other, potentially more appropriate or applicable options. Given that most individuals are risk-averse, it is natural to gravitate toward familiar and established solutions, and readily available standards are generally easier to access; in fact, those tried-and-true approaches might have been the best possible solutions in the past. However, much as is the case with scientific instruments that continue to evolve to offer previously inaccessible precision or granularity of measurement, informational resources also continue to evolve to offer previously inaccessible ways of knowing. Moreover, informational needs tend to evolve over time, even in overtly similar contexts. All told, the appropriateness of assessment standards of interest needs to be assessed at the time at which the standard is being considered and in the context in which individual standards are to be used, and the

---

1 As discussed in Chapters 2 and 3, while the notion of 'average' is, in the minds and habits of many, synonymous with the arithmetic mean, there are three different expressions of average – mean, median, and mode – which under conditions other than perfectly symmetrical distribution (which is exceedingly rare in practice) will yield often starkly different values. In that sense, the goal of explicitly defining which of the three available expressions of the general idea of average is used is not only to remove any potential ambiguity but also to be methodologically thoughtful (i.e., not making an inappropriate, in view of the underlying distribution, choice) and deliberate.

final appropriateness determination should reflect the present state of knowledge and contributing resources.

Data and Methodological Soundness

Once the foundation of robust conceptual framing has been set, the work of operationalizing those abstract ideas begins; by and large, turning ideas into clear, outcome-producing steps is the heart and the most involved aspect of benchmark-setting. Each of the four distinct subsets of the data and methodological soundness benchmark-setting dimension – data due diligence, estimation, and parameterization; reliability and generalizability; and stability and consistency assessment – is itself a composite of numerous data usage and analysis-related considerations. Although specifics of individual data processing and analysis steps need to be tailored to uniqueness of individual informational contexts, there is nonetheless a distinct set of recurring data preparation and analysis considerations that cut across otherwise distinct informational contexts.

Given the combination of expected and situationally determined data analytic steps, starting with an explicit data analytic plan is highly recommended. As famously verbalized by Dwight D. Eisenhower, the WWII five-star General of the Army (and the Supreme Commander of the Allied Force in Europe), and later the 34th president of the United States, 'plans are useless, but planning is indispensable.' An analytic plan is just what it sounds like: An explicit detailing of what and how needs to be done. The key benefit of a plan, as astutely observed by Eisenhower, is the process of planning, which entails focused thinking through what, and in what sequence, needs to be completed to achieve a desired goal. Engaging in an explicit planning process brings about the type of discipline that is needed to avoid, or at least greatly reduce potential missteps, and while plans can be expected to change as work progresses, the process of planning is an invaluable part of the overall data analytic process.

The general structure of analytic planning processes is framed in the context of the interplay between expected outcomes and known inputs. Within the confines of benchmark-setting, expected outcomes are the benchmarks that are to be derived from available and applicable data, which are the known inputs. In that context, the essence of analytic planning can be reduced to identifying specific data preparation and analysis steps that are necessary to transform the available inputs into desired outcomes. With that in mind, an effective analytic plan needs to be mapped out at the lowest possible level of detail because that is where some of the most potentially consequential pitfalls are often hidden. The earlier discussed challenge of dealing with highly skewed data offers a good example here: A robust analytic plan will expressly address that possibility, and it will do so in the context of outlining alternative pathways for addressing that problem, in the context of the specifics of informational needs at hand.

Data Due Diligence

Assuming the existence of a clear and appropriate (given the informational need at hand) conceptual foundation, a review of available data is typically the next logical step in the benchmark-setting process. That review process is commonly referred to as "data due diligence"; it is an open-ended undertaking that entails review of data's validity and reliability, and it also includes any necessary data corrections or amendments falling under the broad umbrella of data feature engineering.

Validity of data can be broadly characterized as truthfulness, an idea that encompasses factual accuracy of individual values, as well as their logical correctness; the former most often refers to derived data elements, which are values computed using other values (e.g., classifying a household as 'middle class' based on several other characteristics). Reliability, on the other hand, is an expression of dependability or stability of data, or the extent to which individual variables can give rise to stable and consistent insights. When interpreted jointly, the combination of validity and reliability attests to informational legitimacy of data to be used in benchmark-setting (and other contexts, of course). In a general sense, those two dimensions are equally important, but that is not necessarily so in all contexts. For instance, product purchase data used to predict the probability of an outcome of interest, such as product choice, must be reliable to be valid, but does not have to be valid to be reliable. More specifically, consistent mischaracterization of purchaser characteristics can be expected to result in invalid causal explanations, but if those misrepresented characteristics, or variables, are stable, the prediction based on those variables will likely be dependable. What could be characterized as empirical validity-reliability asymmetry is often overlooked in spite of the fact that working with imperfect data may, at times, entail choosing one over the other.

In a more operational sense, data due diligence entails review of each individual data element, or variable, from the perspective of implied unit of measurement,[2] the degree of completeness, and reasonableness of values. The *implied measurement* unit is a conjoint measurement scale, which can be either categorical, further broken down into nominal or ordinal, or continuous, and variable encoding, the most common of which include numeric (digits only), string (text or alphanumeric, or a combination of letters and digits), date, or some form of restricted value, such integers with leading zeros. The degree of completeness reflects the presence, and if so, the extent of missing values, and the reasonableness of values captures the extent to which the range of values for a particular variable can be deemed correct.[3] Framed by those

---

2 Since data are defined as measurements of events or states, the term 'measurement,' as used here, is meant to communicate that basic characterization of data, rather than the act of measuring, as in quantifying the size, length, or amount of something.

3 It is important to draw an explicit distinction between the *accuracy* of individual values and *reasonableness* of the range of values for a particular variable – for example, a person's age showing as '56'

three core data considerations, data due diligence aims to assure the validity of data to be used in analyses.

An important, and not always considered, aspect of data due diligence is *metadata* preparation. Somewhat tautologically defined, metadata is data about data. In more operationally specific terms, it is a summary view of the individual variables contained in the dataset of interest, and expressed in terms of the key statistical descriptors, such as value ranges, and summaries of basic distributional properties such as frequencies, measures of central tendencies, and variability, as well as coverage and accuracy summarizations. Although historically more familiar to academicians than to practitioners, the concept of metadata is gaining popularity among the latter as the sheer volume and diversity of data contained in organizational repositories continue to grow. The ballooning of organizational data holdings means that organizational databases, even those supported by clear data model descriptions and comprehensive data dictionaries, are often hodgepodges of well-populated as well as sparsely populated data elements, and those data elements can run the gamut that includes fully populated and true values, as well as mixtures of inconsistent, redundant, definitionally amended, and discontinued metrics. The idea behind metadata is to offer a concise and complete summarization of what data (in the sense of individual data elements) are available, and how usable those data are, as seen from the perspective of a multipoint assessment. To state the obvious, when confronted with large, distributed data resources such summarizations are simply invaluable, especially to those with limited familiarity with those data.

Data Feature Engineering: Spatial Focus

Broadly defined, data feature engineering is the process of manipulating and transforming raw data into analytically usable data. Recalling the distinction between spatial or 'us vs. others' contrasts that characterize benchmarking, and temporal or 'now vs. then' contrasts that typify baselining, the general domain of data feature[4] engineering takes on somewhat different forms in context of those two different types of data. That distinction becomes more evident when the key features that frame spatial and temporal data are considered in the context of a typical two-dimensional, structured (i.e., fixed layout) data format: In the simplest of terms, spatial data file is a collection of measurements of states or outcomes of interest, i.e., variables, where each set of measurements is associated with a particular entity, such as an individual or a

---

may ultimately be incorrect (due to data entry or other errors), but if the range of age values falls within a typical human lifespan it would nonetheless be considered reasonable.

4 In a very general sense, the terms 'data feature' and 'variable' can be thought of as being synonymous with both denoting a single data element; the former tends to be preferred in the context of computer and data sciences, while the latter tends to be more widely used in the context of general business analytics.

company, and is structured as a distinct record (typically a row in a two-dimensional data matrix). In that type of organizational structure individual records demark distinct entities, which means that spatial data is a collection of records that capture the same type of information for individual entities, at a point in time; implied here is that each record is independent of other records, meaning that values of record 1 do not determine values of record 2, etc. Temporal data file, on the one hand, is also a collection of records typically arranged into rows, but on the other hand it is different in that each individual record represents measurement of states or outcomes of interest of a single entity, captured at different points in time (typically in fixed intervals). Using familiar to many stock data as a backdrop, an example of spatial data is offered by a dataset that captures today's stock prices of companies that comprise a particular sector, while a dataset that captures daily stock prices for Company X for the past 12 months offers an example of temporal data. That is a fundamental difference, and it translates into material differences in how raw cross-sectional and longitudinal data are transformed into usable data.

Type of data notwithstanding, the core purpose of data due diligence is to transform 'what is' into 'what could be,' using appropriate data processing operations. It is an almost unavoidable step in the process of extracting insights out of data because the way the vast majority of data are captured and subsequently stored emphasizes efficiency, not ease of usage. An even more fundamental challenge is posed by structural incommensurability in units of measurement, a problem commonly encountered in analyses of transactional data, as exemplified by the point-of-sales (POS) scanner data captured in retail settings. Given that POS scanners record individual items' attributes, such as the unique product identification, item price, time of sale, etc., data captured by those systems can be expected to be organized around items, not purchasers of those items (for the purposes of this illustration we assume that purchaser information is also captured, as is typically the case for purchasers who are identified members of retailers' loyalty programs). That, however, poses a problem for purchaser-focused analysis, in the form of structural incommensurability of units of measurement, as graphically illustrated in Figure 4.1.

Item	Price	Purchaser		Purchaser	Item 1	Item 2	Item 3	Item Price 1	Item Price 2	Item Price 3
8439263692	$ 5.99	John Doe	→	John Doe	8439263692	4339211549	2992201013	$ 5.99	$ 12.50	$ 34.99
4339211549	$ 12.50	John Doe								
2992201013	$ 34.99	John Doe								
1100235234	$ 12.00	Jane Doe	→	Jane Doe	1100235234	7000923774	9923128831	$ 12.00	$ 40.99	$ 2.95
7000923774	$ 40.99	Jane Doe								
9923128831	$ 2.95	Jane Doe								

Figure 4.1: Data file layout restructuring: a transactional data example.

The left-hand side of Figure 4.1 shows an abbreviated layout of POS scanner-captured data, and the right-hand side shows the structural changes that are necessary for those data to support purchaser-focused analyses. The focal difference here, as captured by the notion of structural incommensurability of units of measurement, is that POS-captured data are organized around 'items,' but the analysis of interest calls for those data to be organized around 'purchasers,' which calls for fundamental restructuring of that data file. Discussion of computational specifics of such rearranging of the basic organizational structure of data falls outside the scope of this overview; let it suffice to say that it can be computationally challenging, and so not surprisingly it requires proficiency with at least one general-purpose data manipulation applications (e.g., SAS or SPSS) or open-source languages[5] (e.g., Python or R).

Although specifics of preparing data for analyses are inescapably situational, there are nonetheless recurring general data feature engineering considerations that cut across otherwise distinct contexts. Those can be grouped into several broad categories: *Data correction*, best exemplified by missing value (if there are missing values) imputation, and outlier identification and resolution; *data enhancements*, typically taking the form of recoding of existing into desired values or creation of specific indicators,[6] *data aggregation*, which entails computing of higher-order summaries, as in rolling up item-level (e.g., individual items in Figure 4.1) data up to brand-level, and *file amalgamation*, or combining all or select contents of two or more separate data files. As could be expected, each of those general data feature engineering activities entails numerous steps that typically require the ability to manipulate data and the ability to correctly interpret coding and meaning of individual elements of data. Again, while those technical details fall outside of the scope of this overview,[7] it is essential to never lose sight of the fact that time and effort invested in thoughtful and thorough data feature engineering will pay dividends in the form of enhanced validity and reliability of data analytic outcomes.

Estimation and Parameterization

Recalling the nuanced character of basic statistical estimate derivation processes discussed at length in Chapter 3, data analysis rooted in benchmark-setting entails nu-

---

[5] The relatively rapid emergence of one of the newest professions of *data science* can be traced back to the type of problem illustrated here: As businesses and other organizations began to realize the value and the power of data, they also began to realize that making those data (which includes structured numeric as well as unstructured text and symbolic) usable required a unique set of technical skills that combined elements of several domains, most notably computer science and statistics, which ultimately gave rise to the new discipline of data science.

[6] An example of recoding of existing into new value could be the creation of tiered 'customer value' categories (such as 'high,' 'average,' and 'developing' groupings) out of a continuous 'customer spending' variable; an example of indicator creation (which commonly take the form of binary, yes vs. no values) could be derivation of an event indicator, such as 'litigation' from a field containing a date when a lawsuit was filed.

[7] For more details, see Banasiewicz, A. (2023). *Data Analytic Literacy*, De Gruyter: Berlin, Germany.

merous technical considerations, largely tied to distributional characteristics of focal data. All those details need to be examined and decided on, and ultimately clearly described and communicated, in the form of a detailed analytic plan. Keeping in mind the analytically limited scope of benchmark-setting, where the focus is on identification of a standard to be used in comparative assessment, of central interest are specifics of summarizing individual variables as standalone values, technically known as univariate analyses. Building on the earlier overview of the basic statistical distribution-related concepts while also taking into account data element (i.e., variable) type-related differences, a broader discussion of the logic of univariate analysis is outlined next.

Univariate Analyses

Univariate analysis is an umbrella term used to characterize exploration of properties of individual variables, manifesting itself in descriptive summarization of key characteristics that defined and describe aggregate (i.e., all records combined) their distributional properties. The specifics of univariate analysis are tied to variable-specific *measurement scale*, which define and categorize individual data elements, under the assumption that they represent measurements of states (e.g., gender, location, age) or outcomes (e.g., purchase amount, income) of interest; at the most general level, a variable can be either categorical or continuous.

Categorical variables assume only values that represent discrete and distinct categories, and can be either nominal (i.e., unranked labels, such as 'male' and 'female' values for gender) or rank-ordered (i.e., relative magnitude or position implying designations such as 'small,' 'medium,' and 'large' for size). From data analytical standpoint, it makes no difference if the actual values are encoded as numbers, such as '1,' '2,' and '3,' or as so-called 'strings' (words or alphanumeric values, which represent a combination of letters and digits), such as 'high,' 'medium,' and 'low' – either set of values is ultimately treated as labels for individual categories comprising a particular categorical variable. Also worth noting is that while in principle there are no limits on how many categories a categorical variable can encompass, in most applied business situations, categorical variables have a finite, often relatively small number of values. In short, categorical data elements can be seen as enumerations of distinct types of states or outcomes of interest, which contrasts with *continuous* variables, which capture values of states or outcomes that can be characterized as uninterrupted or continual. Given that, though usually bounded by the upper and lower extremes, continuous variables can assume any of an infinite number of possible values.[8] Hence in contrast to categorical variables that place

---

8 Being bounded by two extremes does not contradict the idea of infinite number of values because the distance between those two extremes can be infinitely divided into ever smaller number of units.

phenomena into one of finite categories, continuous variables capture specific values that can take on any magnitude framed only by the upper and lower limits.

Implied in the very brief overview of the two general variable types is the fundamental difference in their mathematical properties: the 'label-only' or 'ordered-group' encompassing categorical values permit far fewer numeric operations than the 'any value between the two extremes is possible' continuous variables. In an informational sense, categorical variables are informationally poorer than continuous variables, which manifest itself in fewer descriptive statistics (this is also why continuous metrics can always be recoded into categorical ones, but the reverse is not possible). It follows that the impermissibility of some basic algebraic operations, such as division required to compute the average, can place rather severe limitations on the informational value of categorical data. More specifically, description of categorical variables is limited to simple counts, i.e., the number of data records associated with each delineated category, and frequencies, i.e., the relative proportion of data records associated with each category. In contrast to that, continuous variables can be described using much wider arrays of statistical outcomes, most notably, measures of central tendency (i.e., the mean, median, and mode), variability (i.e., variance or its derivatives, the standard deviation, and the standard error of the mean), and spread (i.e., the range). It should be noted, however, that the multiplicity of available descriptors can lead to confusion or even misuse, as evidenced by the earlier example of inappropriate equating of the general notion of average with the arithmetic mean.

Approach-wise, being composed of finite number of groups, categorical variables naturally lend themselves to visual descriptions, with basic tools such as histograms offering an easy-to-interpret way of conveying relative frequency counts of individual categories. However, just because the number of categories is finite does not mean that it is small. For instance, descriptors such as 'address' or 'location' can yield a very large number of distinct values, which when graphed might produce visually and otherwise incoherent representation (it should be noted that when summarized statistically, with help of a numerically expressed frequency distribution table, the results might be equally difficult to interpret). An easy corrective step is to create meta-groupings of categories; though taking that step can be expected to reduce the specificity of results, it can also be expected to make those outcomes more meaningful. Taking that step can also help to reduce the amount of noise, since low-frequency categories tend to contribute disproportionately more to noninformative parts of data analytic outcomes.

Delving into continuous variables' informational content is almost always more involved. In theory, a variable measured on a continuous scale can assume a different value for each individual data record, and though that rarely happens in practice, almost always the number of different values is quite high, which necessitates the use of different statistical approach: Rather than focusing on absolute and relative frequencies of individual values, univariate analyses of continuous variables focus on defined characteristics of aggregate distributions, or summaries of values pooled across all data records for each individual data element. The resultant statistical distributions are described with the help of three related but distinct measures: (1) the typical, or *average*, value; (2) the expected *deviation* from the average or typical value; and (3) the observed *range* of values, which is the difference between the smallest and the largest value.

The three core descriptors of continuous variables – the average, deviation, and range – call for additional, more methodologically explicit clarification. As discussed in Chapter 3, even though there are three distinct mathematical expressions of the general notion of 'average,' the mean, median, and mode, in everyday business vernacular, the idea of average is nearly synonymous with the arithmetic mean.[9] That seemingly small oversight can have disproportionately large impact on validity of statistical estimates, if the underlying distribution of values of interest is skewed – in fact, the more skewed the distribution, the greater the potential distortion. That warping of statistical estimates is particularly important in the context of benchmark-setting, given the importance of robust evaluation standards to comparative assessments; thus, a more in-depth exploration of that often-overlooked consideration is warranted.

The almost instinctive inclination to use the arithmetic mean when describing the average tendency of continuous states or outcomes of interest is likely due to the combination of the statistic's simplicity and general familiarity with it. Under some very specific circumstances, i.e., when the distribution of the variable of interest is symmetrical (i.e., follows the so-called standard normal distribution), it is indeed warranted; in fact, as discussed in Chapter 3 and graphically depicted in Figure 3.1, under those conditions all three estimates of central tendency can be expected yield approximately the same value. However, in applied organizational analyses and many other real-life contexts, those instances are quite rare, simply because many – perhaps even most – real-life phenomena are not normally distributed. For instance, considering customer value to a brand, virtually all brands have a lot more 'low' than they do 'high' value customers; similarly, there are significantly more trivial than severe automotive accidents, there are a lot smaller than large companies, there are considerably more people living in poverty than those living in opulence, and the list goes on and on. In fact, it is hard to think of a practical business outcome measure that is symmetrically distributed – revenues, earnings, growth, and other key business outcomes are skewed; all in all, the elegant standard normal distribution makes for a handy statistical concept teaching aid, but that is where its usefulness ends. So, in most practical situations the values of the mean, the median and the mode will diverge, often quite

---

9 The prefix 'arithmetic' is usually required for specificity because there are several types of mean: arithmetic, weighted, geometric, and harmonic, with the first two used frequently in various business applications.

considerably,[10] gives rise to a dilemma: Which of those numerically different estimates of the average offers the most robust approximation of the 'typical' value? Under most circumstances, when describing either positively or negatively skewed variables,[11] median tends to yield the most dependable portrayal of the typical value. The reason for that is rather simple: Median is the center-most value in a sorted distribution, with exactly half of all records falling above and below it;[12] it is also unaffected by outliers, since it is an actual, rather than computed value. On the other hand, when computed using skewed data, mean-based estimates can be expected to be upwardly (positive skew) or downwardly (negative skew) biased, because the mean is a computed by summing all values and dividing the total by the number of cases; thus, it is directly impacted by outlying magnitudes. Lastly, in theory the mode can also yield reliable depiction of the average (like median, it is also an actual, rather than a computed value), but in practice there are often multiple modes, especially in larger datasets, which tends to reduce the practical utility of that statistic.

The second of the three continuous variable descriptors is the measure of variance or *deviation*, which complements the earlier discussed average by capturing the amount of dispersion or spread of values around the estimated center of the distribution. In other words, while the idea of average captures the typical value that can be used to characterize an entire set of data, the idea of deviation captures the typical departure from that average value. In a sense, it can be seen as a measure of heterogeneity of individual records with respect to the estimated mid-point of the distribution – the higher the deviation, the more diverse (in terms of values) a dataset.

While conceptually a bit more abstract than the notion of the average, operationally it is more straightforward as it is operationalized using a single metric of *standard deviation*. There is a caveat, however: Standard deviation is a property of the mean (as it measures the spread of value around the mean); thus, it can only be used with the mean, not with the median or the mode. Given the inappropriateness of using the mean as a measure of the average for nonsymmetrical distributions, the practical utility of standard deviation is thus considerably reduced. A methodologically sound alternative is offered by a comparatively lesser-known statistic of *average absolute deviation* (also referred to as *mean absolute deviation*), which is a generalized summary measure of statistical dispersion that can be used in any measure of central tendency – the mean, the median, as well as the mode.

---

10 For instance, the untrimmed (i.e., including all values) mean settlement of securities class action, discussed in Chapters 9 and 10, is $52,421,324, while the median settlement is $8,874,048.

11 A distribution is skewed if one of its tails is longer than the other; a positive skew means that the distribution has a long tail in the positive direction (i.e., higher values), while a negative skew means that the distribution has a long tail in the negative direction (i.e., negative values).

12 In situations in which there are an even number of data records (in which case there is no actual value that falls symmetrically in the center of the distribution), the median is computed by taking the average of the two values closest to the middle of the distribution.

The third and final continuous variable descriptor is the *range*, which is also a measure of dispersion of values, but expressed in terms of the difference between the two extremes: the largest and smallest values. While, on the one hand, it can be useful as an indication of how spread out the data are, on the other hand, the range statistic can yield inflated estimates of dispersion when outliers are present. A seemingly obvious remedy is to simply filter out extreme values, but doing so can be both difficult and problematic. It is difficult because there are no standard, objective outlier lines of demarcation, and while it might be relatively easy to pinpoint some outliers in some situations (e.g., Bill Gates or Warren Buffett would certainly stand out if compared to others in their respective high school graduating classes in terms of income), it is quite a bit more difficult to do so in other situations in which values of interest keep on getting larger, but where there are no natural outlier-suggesting discontinuities. It is also problematic because, after all, in many real-life situations outliers are valid data points, which suggests that excluding them from analyses can introduce downward bias. For instance, when measured in terms of economic damage, hurricanes Harvey (2017), Katrina (2005), and Sandy (2012) are three of the costliest storms in US history; when compared to a median cost of hurricane-caused damage, Harvey, Katrina, and Sandy were each more than 50 times costlier, which clearly renders those storms outliers. But is it appropriate to exclude those storms from forward-looking hurricane forecasts? It is a difficult question to answer because while those are real and important data points (the argument against exclusion), the sheer magnitude of just those three data points can be expected to exert disproportionately large, and potentially distorting influence on at least some of the estimates (the argument for exclusion). All told, explicit and careful consideration of the trade-off between informational completeness and statistical soundness should be an important part of benchmark-setting.

Dealing with Outliers

From the standpoint of benchmark-setting, outlier identification and remediation is one of the most important data cleansing steps, because of the direct and potentially highly consequential impact abnormally large or small values can have on magnitudes of comparative assessment standards. To start with, *outlier* is a value that falls outside of what is considered, in a particular context, an acceptable range; in that sense, some outliers might be products of data errors, but others could represent actual and accurate, though abnormally large or small values. Depending on the size of the dataset, i.e., the number of data records, outliers can be visually identified by means of simple two-dimensional scatterplots or can be singled out by means of distribution scoring, which is the process of 'flagging' individual records with values that fall outside of the statistically defined norm, such as ±3 standard deviations away from the mean. The goal here is to identify individual values that could potentially exert excessive and analytically undesirable degrees of influence. In the context of outlier detection, that undesirable degree of influence is usually characterized as *leverage*, which is an expression of 'outlyingness' of a particular value. In more operationally clear terms, it is the distance away from the typical, i.e., average value – the further away from the average a particular value is located, the more leverage it has.

While the general idea of leverage might sound nearly formulaic, in practice, outlier identification is a vexing undertaking that can yield imperfect outcomes, unless approached with care. More specifically, while relying on statistical leverage as the basis of detection might sound reasonable, the approach can potentially mask some outliers. The reason for that is that the approach is rooted in standard deviation as an expression of outlyingness, which in turn necessitates the use of the arithmetic mean as a measure of average (as a point of reference in determining the degree of outlyingness). Since the mean and the standard deviation are computed to support subsequent outlier detection, their values are typically derived using all data points, including any outliers; consequently, magnitudes of the mean and the standard deviation are likely impacted by the very values they are to detect. Those challenges, however, can be overcome using a relatively easy fix: Prior to computing the mean of a variable, all data records to be used should be rank-ordered, following which the lower and upper 5–10% of the records should be excluded, prior to calculating the mean. Doing so will prevent any potential outliers from affecting the mean and thus eliminate the masking problem outlined above.

What remains is the setting of an outlier threshold – at what point an otherwise large value becomes an outlier? In thinking about this issue, consider the goals of the planned analysis and the general inner-workings of statistical methods to be used. Statistical parameters are commonly evaluated in terms of their level of statistical significance. The commonly used 95% significance level expresses the validity of an estimated parameter in terms of the likelihood of it falling within ±2 standard deviations away from the mean. Why not calibrate the acceptable value range to the anticipated level of precision? Using such a simple yet objective threshold only records falling outside the standard deviation-expressed range of allowable departures from the mean should be flagged as abnormal. This rationale can be translated into a simple four-step process:

Step 1: Compute the mean and the standard deviation of the variable of interest.

Step 2: Select the desired allowable limits; i.e., ~2 standard deviations away from the mean = 95% of the values, ~3 standard deviations away from the mean = 99% of the values, etc.

Step 3: Compute the maximum allowable upper values: mean + upper allowable limit and the maximum allowable lower values: mean − lower allowable limit.

Step 4: Flag abnormal records falling outside the allowable range, both above and below.

***

The overtly straightforward descriptive univariate analysis can be surprisingly nuanced, underscoring the need for thoughtful planning and execution. The above-outlined considerations, together with the more technical overview offered in Chapter 3, were meant to draw attention to the most critical aspects of benchmark-setting focused univariate analyses.

Reliability and Generalizability

Under most circumstances, to be deemed valid and reliable, an estimated benchmark needs to be unbiased as well as adequately generalizable. Starting with the former, broadly defined, *bias* is a disproportionate preference for or against an idea or a thing; those preferences can be either explicit or implicit, and it is the latter is of particular interest here because it is often unintended and as such, can easily fall outside of one's conscious awareness and control. Within the confines of benchmark-setting, involuntary unconscious preferences can manifest themselves as either cognitive bias, or as somewhat lesser-known statistical bias.

Cognitive Bias

Defined as a systematic pattern of deviations from norm or rationality in judgment, *cognitive bias* can lead to logically or factually faulty inferences, ultimately resulting in irrational choices. It commonly manifests itself in otherwise competent individuals reaching factually unfounded or logically irrational conclusions, brought about by factors such as peer influence, the desirability of options under consideration, or illusory associations. It is important to note that to be considered biased, one's conclusion has to be a product of a *persistent* departure from what an informed and objective observer would deem to be rational or factually sound; simply espousing a different perspective does not automatically render a viewpoint biased. Moreover, there are numerous situations in which a person may draw an irrational or otherwise unfounded conclusion because of nonsystematic situational factors such as time pressure, but given another chance (or more time, as in the case of time-constricted decision-making) would likely reach a different conclusion – in other words, care must be taken to not confuse an error in judgment with biased judgment. Still, given the somewhat elusive character of those ideas, the distinction between biased and simply different opinions is not always clear; in fact, because of that fuzzy distinction between alternative and biased points of view or between errors in judgment and biased judgment, the idea of cognitive bias was met with some skepticism when it was first suggested in the early 1970s. However, hundreds of cognitive experiments carried out over the past four or so decades by dozens of independent researchers not only led to widespread acceptance of the existence of subconscious reasoning-related predispositions, but also produced a deluge of scientifically valid and documented manifestations of those proclivities.[13]

Still, there is no agreement on the source of cognitive bias. Numerous origin explanations have been suggested over the years, and those can be grouped into two broad categories: reasoning and emotions. The former attributes cognitive bias to brain's cognitive limits, or more specifically the need to counteract brain's finite information processing capabilities, especially when presented with an overwhelming volume of stimuli or alternatives (recall the earlier discussed 'ends-and-means' heuristic utilized by expert chess players). According to that school of thought, bias-causing heuristics are permanently ingrained into human cognitive processes through evolution or learning and can be seen as natural countermeasures to the brain's finite information processing capabilities.

A noticeably different explanation is offered by the latter of the two cognitive bias origin explanations, which attributes those predispositions to the impact of emotions on cognitive processes. On the one hand, that explanation appears to be supported by research suggesting that reasoning and emotions are indeed closely interconnected,[14] but on the other hand it is widely held that brain processes underlying emotions are distinct and separate from those responsible for cognitive functions. Not surprisingly, that is the main counterpoint made by the critics of the 'emotional' explanation. All considered, while it is tempting to conclude that cognitive processes that are responsible for rational reasoning give rise to cognitive bias, and emotional processes give rise to emotional bias, it would be a mistake to ignore the well-established connection between reason and emotions and thus unwise to entirely dismiss the role of emotions in the formation of cognitive bias. More on that shortly.

While interesting, the origins of cognitive bias are of secondary importance to the recognition of the potentially profound impact those predispositions can exert on an individual's decision-making. But to truly understand and, more importantly, to remedy the potentially disadvantageous consequences of those mental processes, it is essential to develop a more substantive understanding of the manner in which the otherwise dependable reasoning processes can lead us astray. It is not an easy task – the earlier mentioned 40 or so years of cognitive sense-making research produced quite an array of cognitive bias manifestations, with some of the better known including the availability heuristic, base rate fallacy, confirmation bias, omission bias, or gambler's fallacy. According to some sources, there are dozens of distinct manifesta-

---

13 For instance, a Wikipedia page devoted to that topic lists nearly 200 different cognitive biases, and the list keeps growing.

14 For more details, see a recent research study by N. Jung, C. Wranke, K. Hamburger, and M. Knauff titled 'How emotions affect logical reasoning: evidence from experiments with mood-manipulated participants, spider phobics, and people with exam anxiety.'

tions of cognitive bias; in fact, a Wikipedia-hosted page[15] dedicated to this topic lists nearly 200 distinct types of cognitive bias.

Statistical Bias

'Statistics don't lie, but liars use statistics.' This frequently cited assertion, likely derived from the famed sentiment of W. Churchill, a British World War II era statesman, 'there are lies, there are dammed lies, and there are statistics,' underscores the potential pitfalls of systematic distortions of statistical results. It is important, however, to emphasize the 'systematic' part of the characterization of statistical bias. As discussed earlier, all statistical analyses contain some degree of imprecision, which is due to the combination of imperfect data and probabilistic nature of statistical techniques. In fact, the bulk of statistical reasoning and methods expressly acknowledge the distorting impact of what is broadly characterized as *random error*, which is simply a chance difference between the estimated and true values of something. With that in mind, statistical bias is a manifestation of a persistent leaning in favor of a particular outcome or conclusion, and as such it is distinctly different from random error, which is a chance-caused – thus not persistently leaning in any one direction – deviation from some unknown true value. All in all, statistical bias is a manifestation of systematic inclination, and as such it undermines the value of objective analysis of available (and presumably unbiased) data. Not surprisingly, assuring the absence of statistical bias is of key importance to benchmark-setting.

Within the confines of univariate analysis-minded benchmark-setting context, there are two general types of statistical bias: selection and measurement. Broadly framed, *selection bias* occurs when the subset of data used in the analysis is not representative of a larger universe; for example, analysis of customer repurchase behavior that uses loyalty card data would likely be systematically biased, because customers who chose to sign up for a loyalty card are likely not representative of all customers. The second type of systematic error, *measurement bias*, occurs when the manner in which data are used is incongruent with what informational outcomes of interest.

A quick methodological note: The common depiction of selection bias frames it as a problem of sample (as in the subset of data selected for the analysis) representativeness, or the extent to which sample-derived estimates can be generalized onto a larger population. However, in a narrower context of benchmark-setting, the general notion of *representativeness* needs to be couched in the context of benchmark appropriateness, which can be more challenging in view of the earlier (Chapter 2) discussed peer group framing plurality stemming from competing industry classification schemas. In other words, it is not simply a matter of assuring that benchmark values derived from

---

15 https://en.wikipedia.org/wiki/List_of_cognitive_biases

a subset of data can be generalized onto a larger population – assuring benchmark representativeness also demands making sure that the subset of data used to estimate a benchmark of interest is the 'right' subset of data. In other words, when selecting an industry-defined peer group, which of the several different industry classification schemas should be utilized, keeping in mind that different schemas will likely result in compositionally and otherwise dissimilar peer groups? Given that the competing industry classification schemas represent different and equally valid perspectives, the choice is far from obvious; in most situations, the most widely used schema might be the most defensible choice, but it warrants careful consideration.

The second of the two general types of statistical bias, measurement error, draws attention to the importance of developing a sound understanding of data to be used in setting benchmarks: Is what is believed to be the informational content of data indeed the informational content? That might seem to be an oddly obvious question to ask, but the ever-greater diversity of data sources can easily lead to data confusion, with data users struggling to keep up with new and changing data sources and types. Feeling overwhelmed by data variety and volumes, data users are not always able to commit adequate time and attention that are needed to develop sound understanding of the informational context of individual datasets, instead relying on snap judgments in answering that important question. Not surprisingly, one of the more predictable consequences of data overabundance is ascribing biased, and often incorrect informational properties to individual data types and sources.

Generalizability

The idea of generalizability can be confusing: On the one hand, it alludes to the earlier discussed representativeness, a manifestation of statistical bias, while on the other hand it also hints of the more usage-related idea of appropriateness, or the extent to which a particular standard is applicable to specific situations. The latter aspect of generalizability can be illustrated using ROI (return on investment) metric across different parts of a particular industry sector, such as retail. Here, the problem manifests itself in a fundamental question: Is a single ROI standard equally applicable to all facets of the retail sector? To start with, 'retail' is a very broad designation; a standard definition of retail frames that sector as a collection of companies engaged in selling of goods and services to consumers. Hence, it encompasses not only physical retail outlets but also direct sales via vending machines, door-to-door sales, as well as online sales; moreover, it also encompasses a wide range of different types of products, such as food, clothing, or automobiles, and services, such as dining, hospitality, or transportation. Given the considerable market dynamics and operational differences separating, for instance, food retailing and transportation, it is unlikely that a single 'retail ROI' would be appropriate to use across the numerous and dissimilar retail subsectors. And the question of generalizability may reach even deeper – the transportation subsector, for example, encompasses air, railways, roadways, and marine, all of which could likely warrant a separately estimated ROI benchmark.

While the preceding discussion of generalizability looked at that concept from the perspective of applicability of a particular benchmark to specific usage contexts, a yet different potential manifestation of the generalizability problem arises in situations in which a benchmark is created by pooling data from multiple sources. Continuing with the example of retail, the data pooling aspect of the generalizability problem is exemplified by a retail company that operates across multiple physical locations and wishes to benchmark its retail shrinkage (inventory losses from causes other than sales). To start, there are multiple contributors to retail shrinkage, with shoplifting as the most obvious contributor but other factors such as employee theft or outright fraud also playing significant roles; in view of that, shrinkage assessment is error-prone due to the difficulty of attributing losses to a specific cause. Consequently, each location specific assessment of shrinkage can be expressed using the longstanding measurement approximation:

$$X = T + e$$

where X is a measurement instance, such as location-specific shrinkage estimate; T is the true and generally unknown value of estimate; and e is the random estimation error.

The above is a formalized way of capturing the idea that individual measurements, such as location-specific estimates of retail shrinkage, contain some degree of random error[16] that needs to be expressly factored into benchmark-setting. To that end, while at the level of individual measurements the values of T and e are generally unknown, the earlier outlined standard error estimation logic can be used to approximate the most likely average degree of imprecision, ultimately offering methodologically sound basis for expressing the appropriate benchmarks as probabilistic confidence intervals (more on that later). Moreover, focusing on the lowest level of measurement, e.g., shoplifting or employee theft, it is worth considering computing benchmarks at the most disaggregate measurable level of analysis. In terms of the example used here, that means employee theft-related shrinkage, shoplifting related shrinkage, etc., rather than the more aggregate total amount of shrinkage. Recalling the variance → standard deviation → standard error computational logic, the following is the step-by-step procedure:

$$\text{Variance} = \frac{\sum_{i=1}^{n}(x_i - \bar{x})^2}{n-1}$$

$$\text{Std deviation} = \sqrt{\text{Variance}}$$

---

16 It is worth noting that contrary to the everyday usage of the term 'error,' as used here, as well as in statistical analysis in general, it is meant to denote imprecision rather than a mistake.

$$\text{Std error} = \frac{\text{Std deviation}}{\sqrt{n}}$$

where x_i is an individual measurement (e.g., location- and type-specific shrinkage); $\bar{x}$ is mean; n is conjoint-specific number of cases (e.g., location- and type-specific).

Within the confines of benchmarking, the so-estimated standard error becomes an important *unit of uncertainty*, encapsulating the expected amount of imprecision in the estimated evaluation standard. In an operational sense, it enables unbiased and robust transforming of inherently somewhat inaccurate exact value-based estimates into more informationally robust ranges. Computation-wise, the process uses a simple formula of *mean ± standard error x multiplier*, where the multiplier is the number of standard errors, which could be 1 or higher (typically 2 or 3, depending on the desired degree of informational precision of the resultant interval).

Stability and Consistency

Endemic to the idea of benchmarking is a reasonable degree of permanence of standards used in comparative assessment. In science, there are numerous fixed norms, such as the speed of light or Planck's constant, that are used to study natural phenomena; in behavioral realms, however, true permanence is elusive. It is, in fact, hard to think of behavioral standards that are not subject to at least some time or context variability. Further compounding that lack of truly fixed standards is measurement imprecision, which necessitates expressing standards as range-contained approximations rather than as exact values. In view of those challenges, it is important to frame the idea of *validity of standards* in a way that both acknowledges those limitations while also offering a meaningful way of carrying out comparative assessments of interest. That general rationale is rooted in explicit recognition of uncertainty associated with discerning the 'true value,' as graphically summarized in Figure 4.2.

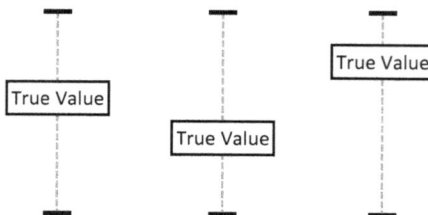

Figure 4.2: True value uncertainty.

Let us assume that the 'true value' shown in Figure 4.2 is the magnitude of the standard to be used to benchmark multiple instances of the same type of outcome, such as different promotional offers meant to stimulate product sales. Let us further assume that the evaluative standard of interest is Average Purchase $, where 'average' is computed as the arithmetic mean. In that context, using all available (i.e., stored in an accessible data repository) purchase records would generally not be deemed appropriate due to recency and other factors, which would then necessitate selection of an appropriate *sampling frame*, or a list of all purchases from which a sample to be used to compute the average is to be taken; the use of a sample would in turn necessitate repeated mean re-estimation in view of the earlier discussed sampling error. The result of that cascading logic is the true value uncertainty graphically captured in Figure 4.2; multiple, sample-based mean estimates can be expected (due to sampling error) to yield somewhat different values, which begs the question: what is the true value of the mean? Sidestepping that question for a moment, the repeated mean re-estimation idea is critically important in the context of benchmark-setting because it offers the only plausible way of circumventing the inherent imprecision of values of standards derived from data in applied settings, but it comes at a cost: It necessitates reframing of assessment standards as ranges, rather than exact values (known as point estimates in statistical jargon).

What if it made sense to use all available data to compute the Average Purchase $? The short answer is that – most likely – it would still be appropriate to treat the estimated mean as an imperfect reflection of the (unknown) true mean. Recalling the overview of the various aspects of estimation imprecision (see Chapter 3), in applied organizational settings, 'all available purchase data' is generally not synonymous with 'all purchases' (because not all transactions are electronically captured and properly attributed[17]), in addition to which available data tend to be noisy (contain some incorrect or missing values). All in all, benchmarks derived from imperfect data are themselves imperfect, meaning that their magnitudes are only approximately correct. Hence once again, true value uncertainty needs to be dealt with, and expressing data-derived estimates as ranges offers the most methodologically and informationally robust solution to that problem.

A direct consequence of that line of reasoning is that stability of data derived assessment standards ought to be framed in the context of statistically sound ranges, an idea characterized here as *interval stability*. In a more operationally explicit sense, this means that magnitudes of individual assessment standards need to be expressed as confidence intervals, with the upper and lower limits delimited by separately estimated positive and negative, respectively, variability about the grand mean of successively re-estimated sample means. The general reason for that requirement is graphically illustrated in Figure 4.3.

The logic encapsulated in Figure 4.3 harkens back to the basic statistical considerations discussed in the previous chapters, and once again underscores the importance

---

17 As exemplified by soft drink sales, such as Coca-Cola; given the practically uncountable types of outlets through which one can purchase a can or a bottle of that drink, using electronic (credit card) or nonelectronic (cash) forms of payment, the true population of all Coca-Cola buyers cannot be precisely determined.

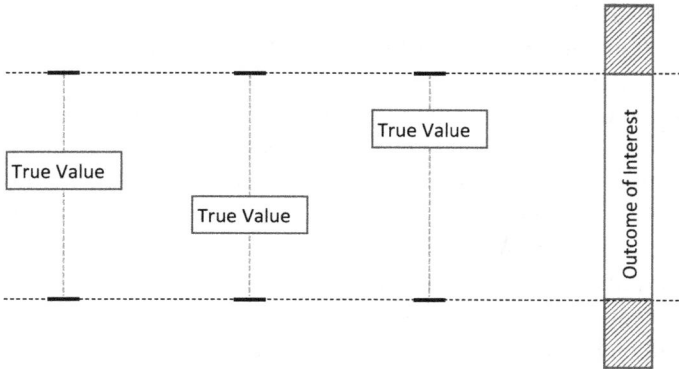

Figure 4.3: Impact of relative stability of true value estimation.

of benchmark reliability. To serve their intended purpose, benchmarks derived from informationally imperfect data need to account for their inherent imprecision in a manner that attests to their ability to reliably estimate the unknown true value, while also explicitly accounting for the inherent imprecision of the estimation process. It is important to note that there are two distinct dimensions to that general idea: point-in-time resampling-related reliability, and distinct point-in-time updates of earlier estimated benchmarks. The preceding overview of the idea of expressing benchmarks as confidence intervals framed by separately estimated positive and negative variability was implicitly point-in-time focused – here, consistency and stability were considered from the perspective of deriving the initial values. The second aspect of benchmark stability and consistency arises in situations, which are quite common in applied settings, that call for updates to existing assessment standards, which are typically necessitated by the need to stay current with changing trends in states or outcomes of interest.

The general idea behind update-minded re-estimation of existing benchmarks is to keep everything as-is, except for data-derived values. In the operational sense that simply means replicating the original estimation steps using more recent data, assuming no meaningful changes in what data are captured and how those data are captured. Of course, that also requires replication of all data due diligence and data feature engineering steps that were taken to prepare the original dataset for the analysis; ideally, an operationally explicit template can be used to avoid any unintended departures from the original process. While templatizing or even automating the update process it is important to be mindful of system changes that may impact data structures. The overwhelming majority of data captured nowadays are generated by a myriad of electronic transaction processing systems, which generate data as a by-product of their functioning; as with all systems, those are also subject to ongoing technological changes, and those changes may impact data structures in ways that are not always immediately visible. For example, measure of time can be changed from the 12- to 24-h format, units of measurement of some quantities may change from pounds to kilograms, or the increase in measurement precision may result in a shift to more granular units, such as from pounds to ounces or kilograms to grams.

Turning back to the high-level typology of benchmark-setting criteria, the third and final broad category is usability, which is composed of two more narrowly framed elements of relevance and ease of administration and interpretation.

Usability

Although it may seem to be obvious that benchmarks need to be usable, the notion of what it means to be usable is in and of itself relatively vague as it may conjure up different interpretations across contexts; in view of that, the idea of benchmark usability warrants a more explicit examination. Here, of particular interest are refresh cycle, the relevance of the benchmark of interest to assessment contexts for which a particular benchmark was constructed and the ease of its administration and use.

Refresh Cycle

One of the key characteristics of sound benchmarks is their stability – to offer consistent basis for assessment standards need to remain fixed, in the sense of confidence interval expressed ranges discussed in the previous segments continuing to remain valid. Keeping in mind the general logic of range-based benchmark-setting, a question that has not been answered in the context of recomputing existing benchmarks' values using more recent data was question of benchmark refresh cadence: Given that most states or outcomes of interest (in the context of benchmarking) continue to evolve on ongoing basis, how often should a particular benchmark be updated to continue to offer timely assessment standards? The answer to this important question hinges on careful consideration of what is commonly referred to as the refresh cycle. Broadly characterized, *refresh cycle* refers to the frequency with which benchmark values are re-estimated using newer data, where 'newer' means more recent but unchanged in terms of content.

Refresh cadence determination is rooted in several distinct considerations that center on the general ideas of data availability, cross-time data consistency, and informational soundness. Setting aside any idiosyncratic, context-specific factors, data availability can be seen as a function of generalizable data source – in that sense, data can be seen as being first-party, second-party, or third-party. First-party data are captured by the organization's own systems, e.g., point-of-sales systems used by retailers; second-party data are captured by business partners, e.g., factory shipment systems used by manufacturers; third-party data comes from a variety of other sources, such as organizations that collate and sell geodemographic data. As implied by the first-, second-, third-party distinctions, data captured by the organization-own systems are generally most immediately available; second- and third-party data's availability is generally tied to specific data sharing or purchase agreements, but typically is less immediate and often less frequent. In a general sense, data availability can be seen as a factor that determines the feasible frequency of data refresh.

The second refresh cadence determining consideration is cross-time data consistency. As noted earlier, technological evolution of electronic transaction processing systems can create periodic data capture discontinuities, due largely to corresponding changes in what data are captured and how individual measurements are recorded. As can be expected, any material data discontinuity should trigger a new refresh cycle.

The third refresh cycle contributor, informational soundness, captures the applicability of historical trend-shaped standards to assessing current phenomena of interest. Of key interest here are material changes in factors that impact benchmarks as typical states or outcomes. For instance, the spread of COVID-19 global pandemic in 2020 had a profound impact on, among other things, many consumer behavior trends, rendering many pre-2020 benchmarks inapplicable. In a sense, the idea of informational soundness parallels cross-time data consistency, as both socioeconomic developments and technological innovation can be seen as extraneous forces that exert strong, but largely unpredictable impacts on states and outcomes of interest.

Relevance

At the first glance, the idea of benchmark relevance might seem superfluous, as the act of constructing a benchmark might be seen as tantamount to it being needed and thus relevant, which could likely be the case when a particular benchmark is constructed and used by the same entity. That, however, is not always the case. More and more, informational tools, such as benchmarks, are developed by specialized entities that create those tools for commercial purposes, which can create a conflict of interest: The commercial developers of benchmarking information are motivated by the desire to maximize their sales, which typically means making their offerings as universally applicable as possible; the users of that information, on the other hand, would like those benchmarks to be maximally tailored to their specific usage contexts. That conflict is loosely analogous to agency dilemma (also known as the principal-agent problem), which is characterized by a misalignment of interests between, in this case, suppliers and users of information. In short, what is good for one may not necessarily be good for the other, which means that relevance of individual benchmarks needs to be carefully considered.

Ease of Administration and Use

In the world of information, there are numerous examples of functionally excellent tools that are difficult to use, often due to nuanced complexity that carries with it a significant learning curve. Moreover, the idea of 'ease of use' is relative: What one user finds easy, another might find challenging for reasons ranging from one's professional background to involvement and willingness to learn.

Implied in the general idea of ease of administration and use is a tradeoff between informational richness and ease of use: Informationally rich applications tend to require more learning, thus are generally seen as more difficult to use (at least initially), which means that reducing barriers to use could entail making functionality related choices; as captured in the well-known expression, sometimes less is more. All considered, when it comes to usability there is no one-size-fits-all formula – each decision needs to be made in a thoughtful and considered manner, and it should reflect a realistic assessment of the needs at hand.

Chapter 5
Baseline-Setting

The introductory overview of broadly outlined benchmarking and baselining rationale offered in Chapter 1 pointed out numerous similarities between those two related
but distinct facets of comparative assessment. Those parallels carry over into more
narrowly scoped benchmark- and baseline-setting contexts, which is not surprising
since both are geared toward deriving valid and reliable state or outcome evaluation
standards; in fact, the general baseline-setting process largely parallels the benchmark-setting process. Still, mixed-in with those similarities are material differences
that emanate from fundamental differences in the type of focal phenomena: spatial
(benchmarking) vs. temporal (baselining) contrasts.

There are also notable usage-related differences between the two manifestations
of comparative assessment. Although lacking consistent framing and clear operationalization, the idea of benchmarking enjoys widespread popularity, in contrast to
which, the idea of baselining is invoked and used comparatively sparingly, and so perhaps not surprisingly, its conceptual framing and methodological foundations are
even foggier. A survey of commonly used baselining framings reveals that the most
used conception of that idea, which defines it as a process used for comparison or
control, is also its least informative characterization. Even more formal attempts fall
short of providing conceptually and operationally clear description: For instance, the
National Institute of Standards and Technology, an agency of the US Department of
Commerce, sees baselining as a 'monitoring [of] resources to determine typical utilization pattern so that significant deviations can be detected,'[1] and the American Society
for Quality, a nonprofit professional accreditation organization, sees it as a critical
part of Six Sigma, which is a set of techniques and tools for process improvement, in
the context of which the Society frames baselining as the process of establishing measurement standards.

The picture that emerges shows a need for conceptually clear and methodologically explicit framing of the general idea of baselining, along with the generally overlooked idea of baseline-setting. Moreover, it also strongly hints at the importance of
those definitional and operational descriptions reflecting baselining's status as a
mechanism of the more general process of comparative assessment, and thus a complement to benchmarking. Keeping that in mind, the goal of this chapter is to build on
the statistical foundations of baselining outlined in Chapter 3 by delving into definitional and operational specifics of baseline-setting.

---

1 https://csrc.nist.gov/glossary/term/baselining; accessed 1/14/2024.

https://doi.org/10.1515/9783111001296-005

Baselining and Baseline-Setting

The idea of baselining lacks robust ontological foundations, as evidenced by inconsistent definitional scoping and virtually nonexistent methodological foundations. In fact, the prevailing way the notion of baselining is used also makes it practically indistinguishable from benchmarking. Moreover, though somewhat less obvious, there is also a persistent lack of attention to baseline-setting, or how evaluative standards used in temporal aspects of comparative assessment are derived and validated.

To start, *baseline-setting* is defined here as the process of deriving and parameterizing temporal (i.e., across time) evaluation standards, while *baselining* is defined as a process of using those standards to carry out unbiased comparative assessment of outcomes or states of interest. It follows that baseline-setting efforts can be seen as a precondition of the baselining process, in the sense that sound comparative assessment (here, baselining) requires the existence of valid and reliable assessment standards in the form of baselines.

The distinction between baselining and baseline-setting processes is important because while ultimately interrelated, the two processes have distinct functional roles that translate into distinct sets of methodological considerations. To that end, the earlier discussed technical concepts surrounding the general ideas of estimation and parameterization play an important role in deriving valid and reliable assessment standards, i.e., baseline-setting, while the mechanisms for assessing the materiality of difference between an outcome of interest and the appropriate assessment standard, in the form of statistical significance tests and effect size evaluations, play a critical role in baselining.

Baseline-Setting Criteria

To apply to a wide range of potential usage situations, baseline-setting criteria need to be framed in sufficiently broad terms, which in turn leads to a clear overlap with benchmark-setting criteria. In fact, when looked at the perspective of general categories, the two sets of criteria are the same – differences emerge within the confines of more specific definitional and methodological details that comprise those general categories. With that in mind, the following are the core baseline-setting criteria:
1. Definitional clarity:
   a. Explicit conceptual definition of the standard
   b. Appropriateness of the standard
2. Data and methodological soundness:
   a. Data due diligence
   b. Explicit estimation and parameterization
   c. Temporal reliability

3. Usability:
   a. Refresh cycle
   b. Relevance
   c. Ease of administration and interpretation.

Definitional Clarity

One of the many dangers of an idea having a ring of familiarity is that its deeper mean-ing is often taken for granted. The very general conception of baseline as a measurement standard is the case in point here – not only does such broad framing render baselining indistinguishable from benchmarking but also opens it to numerous and varied opera-tionalizations. Consequently, even in overtly similar contexts, different interpretations of the idea of baselining may lead to differently conceived measurement standards, which can ultimately impede the generalizability of baselining-based conclusions. Hence, the importance of definitional clarity as the point of departure in framing that aspect of comparative assessment. Paralleling the earlier discussed benchmark-setting process, the derivation of clear conceptual framing of baseline-setting manifests itself in two dis-tinct facets: providing clear definition of the standard of interest, and equally clearly spelling out the uniqueness of that standard.

Conceptual Definition

The focal point of conceptual definition is to capture the essence of the phenomenon of interest in a clear yet concise manner. Within the confines of baseline-setting, that can be accomplished by focusing on two core objectives: First, to sharply articulate what the phenomenon of interest – here, a contemplated standard – is, and secondly, what it is not. In that context, it is important to be mindful of the difference between a definition and a description. A good definition is as concise as possible, which means it foregoes any descriptive nonessentials; in the way of contrast, a description can be expected to be lengthier, more narrative, and can also be expected to include implications, interpretations, and other supporting rationale. In a more technical sense, a formal definition generally consists of three parts: (1) the term (i.e., a word or a phrase) that is being defined; (2) the class of ideas or concepts to which the term belongs; and (3) the specific characteristics that distinguish it from others in its class.

Here is a simple example of setting a baseline that captures the multiyear cost trend of securities litigation settlement values. The term that is of interest here is 'set-tlement cost trend of securities litigation,' which belongs to a class of concepts that fall under the umbrella of 'executive risk,' a broad domain that encapsulates a diverse set of accountabilities of directors and offices (jointly referred to as 'executives' in this context) of public, i.e., traded on US.stock exchanges, companies. The specific characteristics that set that particular class of concepts apart from other notions that also fall under the umbrella of 'executive risk' is that the former is specific to shareholders, who allege violations of securities laws protecting their interests; as such, that class of concepts is separate and distinct from those that encapsulate allegations made by other organizational stakeholders, such as employees or creditors (and who would allege violations of different, but still executive accountability enumerating laws). In addition, to be unambiguous, the definition of 'settlement cost trend of securities litigation' also needs to address the ideas of 'cost' and 'trend,' especially given that the latter of the two can be operationalized in more than one way,[2] and it also needs to address time interval aspects, given that cross-time trends can be computed with varying degrees of granularity (e.g., monthly, quarterly, and annually). Pulling it all together, the following definition emerges: 'The trend of settlement cost of securities litigation, a subset of the broader domain of executive risk, captures the annually computed average of values of settled and/or adjudicated shareholder lawsuits alleging violations of the Securities Act of 1933 or the Securities Exchange Act of 1934.' More on that in the baselining case study in Chapter 9.

Although a sound definition needs to be as succinct as possible, it is usually beneficial to also include it more in-depth description, though care should be taken to make sure that the two are structured and seen as complementary. The overriding objective here is for the definition (and any associated descriptions) to create uniformity of understanding of the concept of interest.

Appropriateness of Standard

Why this conceptualization, why not a different one? While that may not always be the case, in situations in which there is a plurality of potential framings of a standard of interest, it is important to expressly address appropriateness of the chosen conceptualization. That is particularly important in defining evaluation standards as it is common for standards to be selected based on reasons such as tradition or availability, which can lead to chancy results: maybe the chosen framing will work well in contemplated usage contexts, or maybe it will not. With that in mind, it is important to recognize the instinctive appeal of relying on familiar or established solutions, while being cognizant of benefits of looking beyond the tried and (not always) true approaches. After all, the inevitable march of change can eventually render all approaches obsolete, or it can at least materially degrade their comparative efficacy, something that is particularly true in the data-rich and data-centric info-technological settings. Hence, the idea of standard appropriateness needs to be assessed at the time

---

2 Among the most used methods are moving average, time series analysis, and regression analysis.

at which the standard is being considered, and it needs to be set in the context of the state of knowledge at the decision point.

Data and Methodological Soundness

Assuring robustness of data and methods used to derive estimates of interest is always a challenging undertaking, primarily because it is inescapably nuanced. Even manifestly similar datasets, such as those drawn from the same population can differ in terms of the earlier discussed structural and statistical characteristics, ultimately requiring highly individualized review and problem remediation; that need for individualized attention is further amplified by the choice of different analytic approaches, and still further amplified by differences in focal informational goals. However, those context-dependent data due diligence and analysis-related actions can nonetheless be seen as situationally shaped applications of universally applicable general processes that guide review, preparation, and analysis of data. Within the confines of baseline-setting, those processes coalesce around three broad end goals: data due diligence, estimation and parameterization, and reliability assessment.

Data Due Diligence

As can be expected, prior to being used data should be carefully inspected. In principle, the review of data centers on comparing structural and statistical characteristics in the context of observed vs. expected characteristics, with an eye toward assuring *validity* and *reliability* of data-derived estimates. Or stated differently, the goal of data due diligence is to determine what, if any, corrective actions need to be taken to assure that analyses using data of interest yield truthful, i.e., valid, in the sense of factual accuracy and logical correctness, and dependable, i.e., reliable, informational outcomes. Careful and considerate review of fundamental properties of data of interest is critical in any data usage context, and it is particularly so in the context of baseline-setting, given the importance of assuring truthless and dependability of data used to derive comparative assessment standards.

In a more operational sense, given that technical steps of data review and problem remediation reflect basic data characteristics, due diligence specifics of temporal data-oriented baseline-setting can be expected to differ from the analogous spatial data-oriented benchmark-setting specifics (those differences apply to structural as well as statistical validity and reliability considerations). More on point, within the confines of time series data rooted baseline-setting, assessment of time-related aspects is of central importance; more specifically, time interval spacing, and serial dependence,[3] commonly referred to as 'autocorrelation' or 'serial correlation,' are the two focal characteristics.[4] Recalling that time series (i.e., temporal data) represent ordered sequences of values of an outcome or a state of interest measured at equally spaced time intervals, it is critically important to assure that the individual values are indeed expressed in constant time intervals. It is also important to be mindful of the fact that since time is a continuous phenomenon, time-expressed measurements can, in principle, be continuous; in fact, there are numerous time series data that are continuous, perhaps best exemplified by the various aggregate stock market indices, such as the Dow Jones Industrial Average or the S&P 500 Index. Those data, however, are ultimately composites of distinct successive measurements taken in very short time intervals, just as a moving picture is composed of many still images captured at very short, rapid, and equal intervals; and just as in a moving picture, to produce smooth and coherent image, the timing of successive intervals has to be exactly the same. The same logic applies to more coarsely measured and thus more explicitly interval-based discrete time series data.

Implied in the preceding overview of the key baseline-setting-related data due diligence considerations is a two-step process of review and subsequent problem remediation. It might seem presumptive that a review of data shall yield problems that need to be fixed, but within the context of data due diligence, the idea of 'problem' encompasses any difference between the current and the ideal states of data, where the latter reflects structural and statistical characteristics that are necessary to enable the use of data in the desired manner. So, for a particular dataset to be used as the basis for deriving a baseline of interest, that dataset needs to be appropriately structured and needs to exhibit appropriate statistical characteristics; given that the organizational structure of most datasets reflects a combination of the manner in which those data were captured and storage efficiency, and data are generally considered to be at least somewhat messy, the chances of preliminary review of data yielding no corrective actions at all are remarkably low. Dataset-specific problem remediation is commonly referred to as 'data feature engineering'; given that it encompasses structural as well as statistical 'fixes,' it requires strong technical skills, and as noted earlier, it is highly situationally nuanced. And while a more in-depth overview of that process falls outside the scope of this book,[5] the key, baseline-setting related data feature engineering considerations are outlined below.

---

3 It is worth noting that the concept of 'serial dependence' is also used in cognitive sciences, or more specifically in the study of visual perception, where it is framed as a type of sequential effect in which what was seen previously influences, and possibly biases the interpretation of what is seen next.
4 While it may not be immediately obvious, assessment of serial dependence (i.e., autocorrelation/serial correlation) incorporates the earlier (benchmark-setting) discussed data element-focused assessment of implied unit of measurement, the degree of completeness, and reasonableness of values.
5 For a more in-depth overview, see Banasiewicz, A. (2023). *Data Analytic Literacy*, De Gruyter: Berlin, Germany.

Data Feature Engineering: Temporal Focus

To start, the terms 'data feature,' 'attribute,' and 'variable' are simply different ways of saying the same thing, as they all describe individual measurable properties or characteristics of phenomena that exist as individual data points or pieces of information (referred to throughout this book as states or outcomes of interest). Hence broadly defined, *data feature engineering* is the process of manipulating and transforming raw attributes or pieces of data into analytically usable ones. That typically entails one or more of the following: Restructuring, which entails changing the physical layout of data, recoding, or changing of measurement or informational properties of data (e.g., collapsing continuous measure into a set of categories or combining categories or standalone attributes), or correcting, which entails fixing of data deficiencies, as exemplified by imputing of missing values. Of course, what constitutes 'usable data' is highly context-dependent, as it is a function of the specifics of data on hand and expected data analytic outcomes. Moreover, keeping in mind the distinctiveness of cross-time trends (baselining) and cross-group differences (benchmarking), as a subset of broader domain of data due diligence, temporal data-focused data feature engineering is markedly different from the earlier discussed spatial data feature engineering. More specifically, because in data management sense temporal datasets are collections of records that represent distinct-in-time measurements of outcomes or states of interest, the focal point of temporal data feature engineering is assuring *serial consistency*, or conformity of each individual element in the data series to a singular periodic cadence and unit of measurement. In other words, making sure that time spacing and unit of measurement are consistent across all data points in the series.

In practice, temporal, i.e., time series datasets usually contain fewer data features than spatial datasets, in part because the former tend to have narrower informational scopes in the sense of being focused on specific states or outcomes; consequently, the task of temporal data restructuring, recoding, or correcting can be expected to be comparatively less involved.[6] That is especially true in the confines of baseline-setting, where it is reasonable to expect a dataset of interest to be limited to a single or a small handful of measures. The context of baseline-setting also heightens the importance of expressly examining data feature's *periodicity*, which expands upon the idea of periodic cadence.

In simple terms, *periodicity* of data series is a measure of the frequency with which something is measured and recorded.[7] Any continuum, including time, is ulti-

---

6 There are notable exceptions to that general assertion – some widely used informational sources make data available as more complex structures that combine spatial and temporal data into single datasets. For instance, the S&P Compustat database, published by Standard & Poor's, covers hundreds of metrics describing thousands of companies tracked over multiple years; as such, S&P Compustat can be considered both spatial and temporal, and when looked at from the perspective of the latter, it contains as many (i.e., hundreds) data features as when looked at from the spatial perspective.

7 It is important to recognize the distinctiveness of those two actions; in many, perhaps even most contexts, the frequency with which a phenomenon is measured is also the frequency with which

mately a string of infinitesimally small units, an idea that is clearly evidenced by something like a visibly continuous metal rod, which upon a closer examination can be shown to be a collection of individual atoms held together electrostatic attraction. In that sense, periodicity of a particular dataset can range from very granular that, in the context of time series, is frequently characterized as 'continuous,' to comparatively coarse and thus visibly discrete. At issue here are two distinct considerations: First, is the periodicity consistent across the entire dataset to be used as input into baseline-setting, and secondly, is the level of granularity appropriate in view of the expected utility of the baseline under consideration? As it regards the first part of that question, given that the majority of data captured nowadays are generated as by-products of transaction processing, tracking, and communication systems' operations, and those technologies are subject to ongoing change and recalibration, periodicity of data captured by those systems can change unexpectedly as a result. Those changes may not always be clearly noted in accompanying documentation, assuming that there is data-describing documentation in the first place.

The second part of the periodicity clarifying question posed above – appropriateness of the level of granularity of data to be used in benchmark-setting – is highly situation dependent. At issue here is the alignment of data periodicity with anticipated baseline usage contexts. For example, given the current state of technology, stock prices can be recorded every second a given security is trading; currently, regular trading hours for the US stock market (both the New York Stock Exchange and NASDAQ) are 9:30 a.m. to 4 p.m., EST, which translates into 23,400 s, or 23,400 individual data records for a single trading day, or 5,896,800 records for a single trading year (there are 252 trading days in a year). Not surprisingly, stock price datasets tend to be offered in more compressed formats, typically ranging from a day to a month, but compressing data brings with it inescapable loss of information – for instance, the daily price of a particular stock, be it expressed as 'opening,' 'closing,' 'high,' or 'low,' is the average of smaller time intervals expressed prices, which means that expressing that price as a single daily value effectively gives up the within-day price fluctuation information. Turning back to the issue of data periodicity with anticipated baseline usage contexts, it is important to make sure that the periodicity of data used to compute the baseline is smaller than the periodicity of outcomes evaluated using the baseline in question. For example, if the baseline is to be used to compare daily stock performance to an appropriate standard, that standard should be computed using hourly or even more granular data; doing so will offer a more accurate representation of, particularly, positive and negative variability, ultimately yielding more robust baseline values.

While of paramount importance in the context of baseline-setting, serial consistency is not the only data feature engineering consideration that should be addressed.

---

those measurements are recorded, but at times the frequency with which measurements are recorded can be lower to reduce the resultant data volumes.

Also in need of attention are potential data corrections and enhancements; here, *missing value imputation* and *outlier* identification and resolution are the most commonly encountered concerns. Somewhat less common, in the context of temporal data, are data enhancements, as exemplified by deriving indicators out of existing values (e.g., using the 'date' field to create 'year' and 'month' indicators), or combining two or more separate data files, known as 'file amalgamation.' As could be expected, each of those data feature engineering activities entails numerous, situationally framed steps that typically require the ability to manipulate data and the ability to correctly interpret coding and meaning of individual elements of data, discussion of which falls outside the scope of this text.

Estimation and Parameterization

Building on time series specific data due diligence considerations, this section focuses on core methodological aspects of baseline-setting, framed in the context estimation, defined earlier as the process of finding approximate values using imperfect information, and parameterization, which is the process of selecting measurable quantities that best describe factors of interest. As can be expected, estimation and parameterization-related methodological choices are shaped by the interplay between data and expected informational outcomes; within the confines of baseline-setting, that interplay manifests itself as a conjoint of magnitude of effect and the rate and direction of change, framed here as *trended magnitude.*

The idea of trended magnitude, as used here, is derived from commonly used characterization of time series (i.e., temporal) data, which are characterized as composites of three elements: (1) the trend, or the long-term direction; (2) the cyclical or seasonal patterns; and (3) irregular, short-term fluctuations. In most informational contexts, long-term trends are considered informative, while cyclical patterns and short-term fluctuations tend to be seen as noninformative noise, elimination of which is often seen as a prerequisite to identifying long-term trends. The reason for this is that time series data are most commonly used for forecasting, which typically takes the form of projecting (long-term) trends into the future, implied in which is the focus on the general direction. Baseline-setting, however, represents a distinctly different application of time series data – in that particular context, it is not just the general direction – i.e., the long-term trend – that is important – trend-describing magnitudes also need to be taken into account, hence the notion of trended magnitudes.

Trended Magnitude Estimation

In a general sense, analyses of temporal and spatial data are built upon the same general assumption that data are a combination of informative patterns and noninformative noise, and identification of the former calls for filtering out of the latter. However, that communality manifests itself in distinctly different methodological steps when applied to analyses of temporal and spatial data, and those differences are further amplified in baseline- vs. benchmark-setting contexts. Within the confines of baseline-setting, estimation and parameterization steps are geared toward deriving directionally and magnitudinally explicit and robust trended comparative assessment standards.

As noted earlier, the temporal or time series data can be seen as a composite of three distinct elements: long-term trends, which are enduring patterns in the rate and direction of change, seasonality, which are more localized cyclical or seasonal patterns, and any unsystematic, short-term fluctuations, commonly characterized as noise.[8] With those three distinct elements of time series as a backdrop, the goal of trended magnitude estimation is to combine identification of long-term trends with explicit estimation of magnitudes of trended values. The supporting rationale for that idea is rooted in the longstanding logic of two-dimensional representation of cross-time phenomena using Cartesian coordinates: A long-term trend, expressed as a pattern of change along the x-axis (in Cartesian coordinates), is defined by a series of conjoints of time (x-axis) and magnitude (y-axis) – in that general context, trended magnitude estimation aims to capture the information contained in those two distinct dimensions in a way that accommodates the uniqueness of baseline-setting, framed here as a mechanism of deriving valid and reliable comparative assessment standards. Implicit in this line of reasoning is that netting out of seasonality, if present, and dismissing, as noise, of short-term fluctuations could potentially lead to understating of magnitudes of interest, ultimately undercutting the efficacy of baselines; that assertion is explored in more detail in the ensuring in-depth exploration of the idea of trended magnitude estimation.

Delving deeper into the idea of trended magnitude estimation brings into scope an important distinction that emanates from differences in types of comparative temporal assessments, as exemplified by the difference between assessing the relative performance of a particular stock vs. assessing the relative performance of promotional campaigns. When considered in the context of benchmark-setting, the difference between those two scenarios is illustrative of the more generalized distinction between direct and indirect baseline. Broadly characterized, *direct* baselines offer means of assessing trended magnitudinal and directional values of states or outcomes of interest under the assumption that the observed trends of interest do not need to be decomposed, while *indirect* baselines also offer means of assessing trended magnitudinal and directional values of states or outcomes of interest but require decomposing of observed trends. *Trend decomposition* is a process (discussed in more detail

---

8 It should be noted that not all time series data contain seasonal (i.e., tied to the time of year) or cyclical (not tied to specific times of year, e.g., business cycles) elements; some time series are composites of just long-term trends and noise.

later) geared toward separating the observed trend into the three distinct elements of long-term trend, seasonality, and short-term, random fluctuations. The goal of that process is to net out the impact of the latter two elements – i.e., seasonality, if present, and random, short-term fluctuations – and by doing so, to distill the observed trend to just the underlying long-term pattern.

Consider the difference between a baseline meant to be used to assess long-term performance pattern of a particular equity, and another one meant to be used to assess the longitudinal (i.e., across time) impact of a promotional campaign of interest. A common way of assessing performance of individual equities is by comparing their performance to a composite of peer equities expressed as peer group average. It is a conceptually obvious and methodologically straightforward method that calls for a side-by-side comparison of the equity of interest and its peer group across a period – this is the essence of direct baselining. In a way of contrast, assessment of the cross-time impacts of promotional campaigns typically calls for netting out effects of extraneous or spurious effects, such as seasonality and other, random effects to arrive at what is often referred to as 'unpromoted sales,' which in the confines of time series is the long-term trend – that is the essence of indirect baselining. In simple terms, direct baselines utilize observed time series as-is, which means that the trended magnitude is the observed trend; indirect baselines, on the other hand, require extracting hidden, long-term trends from observed data, and in that case, the trended magnitude is the long-term trend derived from observed data.

The idea of netting out the effects of extraneous factors, which is at the core of indirect baseline-setting, requires some additional explanation. To start with, long-term trends are themselves composite manifestations of multiple interacting causal factors; the often-overlooked implicit assumption that underpins the idea of long-term trends is that there is a reasonable degree of uniformity in those trend-shaping causal factors, but that is not always the case. For instance, in the above example of a promotional campaign, the underlying factors that together combine to form long-term trends can be expected to be highly variable across time: competitors start and stop different promotional initiatives, market dynamics change over time, consumer needs and preferences are shifty, to name just a few. As a result, the mix of causal influences that together shape the resultant long-term trends at one point in time could be quite different from those shaping that same trend at another point in time. Admittedly, it is difficult to capture, and even more difficult to quantify those types of changes, but it is nonetheless important to be cognizant of those effects.

Still, that is not all. The preceding overview might suggest that the existence of discernible long-term trend is a given, but that is not the case. Making that determination is, in the language of statistical analysis, known as assessing *stationarity* of series. A stationary time series is one whose properties do not depend on the time at which the individual values that comprise the series are captured, while nonstationary time series' values vary as a function of time. In that sense, nonstationary series can be expected to contain long-term trends, while stationary series are generally not expected to contain discernible long-term trends.

Central to the idea of stationarity is the concept of *serial correlation* (also known as *autocorrelation*), defined as the relationship of signal, framed here as a discrete value of a phenomenon of interest captured at a point in time, with a delayed copy of itself and expressed as a function of measurement delay. In that sense, the idea of serial correlation is at the heart of sequential measurements of a phenomenon of interest being expressed as a continuous trend that can be used not only to better understand past patterns but also to project, i.e., forecast those patterns into the future. However, forecasting and baseline-setting usages of time series data are markedly different. Geared toward projecting past patterns – i.e., long-term trends – into the future, forecasting is inextricably tied to full and correct description of the structure and mechanics of time series by means of series decomposition (more on that below); baseline-setting, on the other hand, is merely concerned with reducing random variability of individual elements of time series, as a means of arriving at 'typical,' trended values. In that sense, baseline-setting takes a comparatively simplistic view of temporal data: It implicitly sets aside the question of stationarity of series and instead focuses on dampening random series fluctuations as a means of identifying generalizable trends that can be used as basis of comparative assessment. Appreciating that nuanced distinction is rooted in closer examination of the structure of temporal data.

Understanding Time Series

Temporal or time series data are measurements of states or outcomes of interest recorded at distinct, typically equally spaced, points in time. In keeping with the general idea that, by and large, data available to businesses and other organizations are imperfect in the sense of not being 100% complete or accurate, each of those individual point-in-time values can be seen as a combination of informative signal and noninformative noise. With that in mind, long-term trends and seasonality (regular comparatively short-term patterns that occur with time) or cyclicality (longer-term recurring patterns, such as business cycles) are typically seen as informative signals, while short-term random fluctuations are treated as noise – the goal of time series decomposition is to identify each of those parts of the overall series. It is not an easy or foolproof process, which becomes evident when looking at temporal data in their rudimentary defining context of 'time' and 'value,' as shown in Figure 5.1.

When looked at in that rudimentary state, the pattern of values of the sample phenomenon shown in Figure 5.1 captured at successive, equally spaced time intervals is somewhat suggestive of a general long-term trend, but seasonality, cyclicality, or near-term fluctuations are not clearly discernible. Those effects, however, become more discernible when the individual values – shown as points in the two-dimensional Cartesian

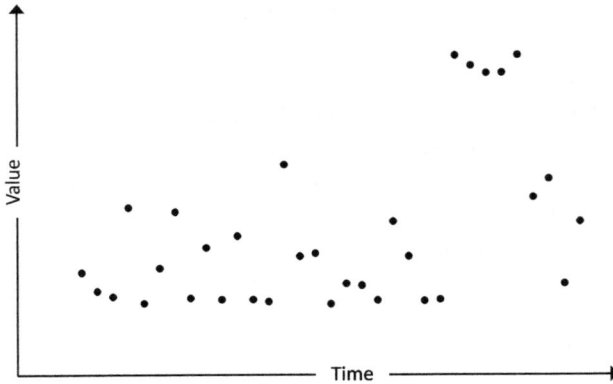

Figure 5.1: Time series as a sequence of discrete values captured at distinct points in time.

space in Figure 5.1 – are linked together with the help of straight lines, which gives rise to a noticeably different looking depiction of the same time series, shown in Figure 5.2.

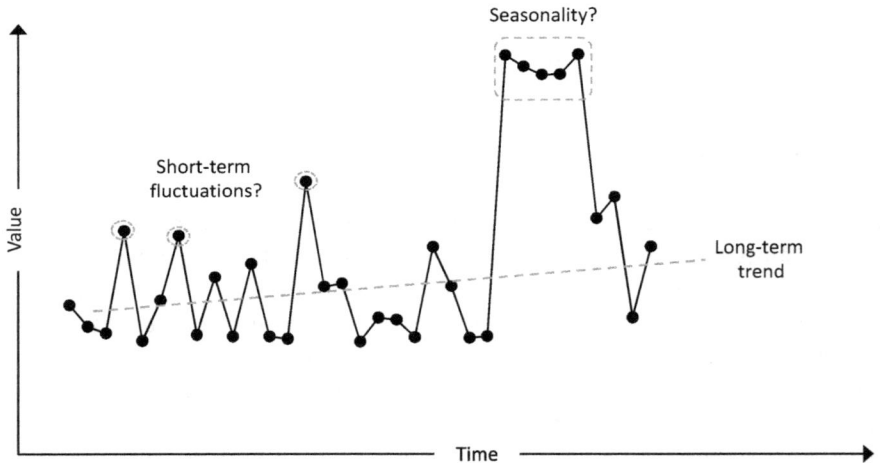

Figure 5.2: Time series as a visually linked sequence.

As graphically illustrated in Figure 5.2, simply stringing together individual data points paints an immediately clearer picture: The progression of values-implied long-term trend, representing the general time-dependent tendency of values to either increase (positive trend) or decrease (negative trend) with time, becomes more noticeable, as do the potential seasonality (or cyclicality) and near-term fluctuations. The latter two types of effects are characterized here as 'potential' because identification of those effects is considerably more speculative, not unlike the task of outlier identification discussed earlier in the context of benchmark-setting. In most situations, the ideas of seasonality and cyclicality are ascribed to observed series – meaning, their presence is ascertained outside of the specifics of data at hand, typically with the help of broader knowledge of applicable patterns, such as knowing that sales of certain types of products – ice cream or bathing suits – are higher during summer months. As can be expected, there are numerous other phenomena that do not lend themselves to such obvious conclusions, especially considering the complex web of macro- and micro-factors that jointly influence many organizational outcomes. Given those challenges, it is instructive to carefully consider the utility of series decomposition in the context of desired informational outcomes. If the goal is forecasting, series decomposition is critical because apportioning cross-time variability between long-term tendencies, seasonal or cyclical patterns, and random, near-term fluctuations is at the core of assuring maximum possible degree of forecast reliability. If, on the other hand, the goal is to arrive at a typical, as in baseline, level of states or outcomes of interest, series disambiguation is not nearly as critical – in fact, the scope of that effort can be reduced to just removing or at least dampening of the impact of noise in the form of near-term, random fluctuations. The general process of reducing the 'jumpy' pattern shown in Figure 5.2 into a more generalizable trend is commonly known as 'smoothing.'

When used in the context of time series, the idea of *smoothing* takes the form of a simple computational process of removing noise in the form of random short-term fluctuations with the goal of exposing the underlying signal, which can manifest itself as a long-term trend and possible seasonal or cyclical effects.

The general idea of smoothing out of unsystematic up and down time series oscillations is most commonly operationalized with the help of moving averaging, a process known as *moving average smoothing*. Paralleling the simple logic of arithmetic averaging discussed in the context of spatial data (benchmark-setting), the general idea of *moving averaging* can be characterized as an extension of that logic onto temporal data. In contrast to spatial data averaging, however, which is single value focused, the goal of moving averaging is to derive successively recomputed and longitudinally linked estimates of the average value of a phenomenon. In other words, it is to derive the averaged value of cross-time trends rather than single, point-in-time estimates.

One of the key benefits of moving averaging is making long-term trends and shorter-term seasonality or cyclicality patterns significantly easier to discern, as graphically illustrated in Figure 5.3. The pre- and post-smoothing sample series (the same as used in Figures 5.1 and 5.2) clearly highlights the key benefit of smoothing: By removing unsystematic, short-term fluctuations, the underlying long-term trend and what appears to be seasonality are both more clearly visible. It is also important to note that, recalling the rationale embedded in the idea of trended magnitude estimation, moving averaging preserves the magnitudinal and time-related aspects of temporal data, both of which are of critical importance to baseline-setting.

Raw Time Series Trend   Smoothed Time Series Trend

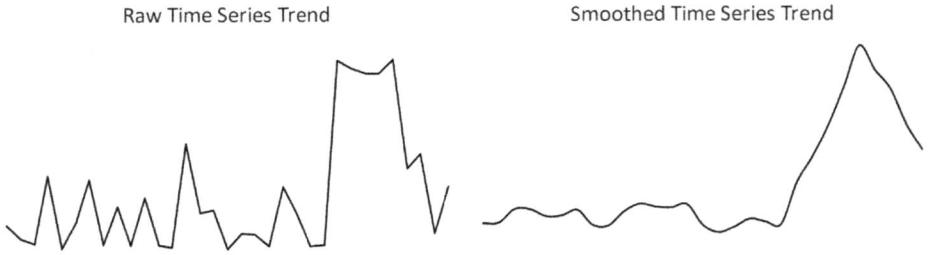

Figure 5.3: The impact of smoothing.

The most elementary implementation of the above-outlined logic is known as *simple moving average,* which simply (hence the name) averages[9] a selected range of values. The element of time, however, adds (i.e., beyond what needs to be considered in the context of arithmetic averaging) consideration in the form of the range of values to be used to compute simple moving average values. In other words, how many individual data points – i.e., successive values in the series of interest – should be used to compute the average? After all, moving average is a series itself, where individual averages are computed using some number of input values. As could be expected, that choice is usually a reflection of the specifics of a particular situation; in general, selecting a relatively narrow range, such as just three consecutive values, will yield lesser degree of smoothing than selecting a larger number of inputs, such as 30 consecutive values.

Figure 5.4 illustrates the basic logic and mechanics of moving averaging, using an example of daily stock price data that were used to compute three-day moving average.

The numerically and graphically summarized logic of simple moving averaging shown in Figure 5.4 highlights the simplicity of that basic time series smoothing approach, and it also underscores the importance of carefully considering the span of values to be used in estimating successive average values. The latter is particularly important in the context of baseline-setting, as picking a narrow span, such as three consecutive values used in Figure 5.4, will have less of a variability dampening effect than picking a wider span; on the other hand, wider span-based moving averages become less sensitive to micro but nontrivial effects, which may adversely impact the ability of a baseline to detect magnitudinally less pronounced baseline vs. outcome of interest differences. As can be expected, the choice of what is the most appropriate span of values to be used in moving averaging is highly situational; in addition, it should also be reflective of the amount of variability in data – in most situations, highly variable data tend to lend themselves to narrower input spans. Also worth mentioning is that as depicted in Figure 5.4, at its onset, *n*-day moving average becomes available starting with the last period in the input span (period #3 in Figure 5.4); in general, the

---

9 Using the basic arithmetic mean formulation, where average = sum of values/number of values.

Date	Closing Price	3-Day Moving Average
01/08/2024	$15.25	
01/09/2024	$16.01	
01/10/2024	$15.83	$15.70
01/11/2024	$16.29	$16.04
01/12/2024	$16.99	$16.37
01/13/2024	$17.01	$16.76
01/14/2024	$17.43	$17.14
01/15/2024	$17.22	$17.22

Moving Avg for 01/10/2024
Moving Avg for 01/11/2024
Moving Avg for 01/12/2024
Moving Avg for 01/13/2024
Moving Avg for 01/14/2024
Moving Avg for 01/15/2024

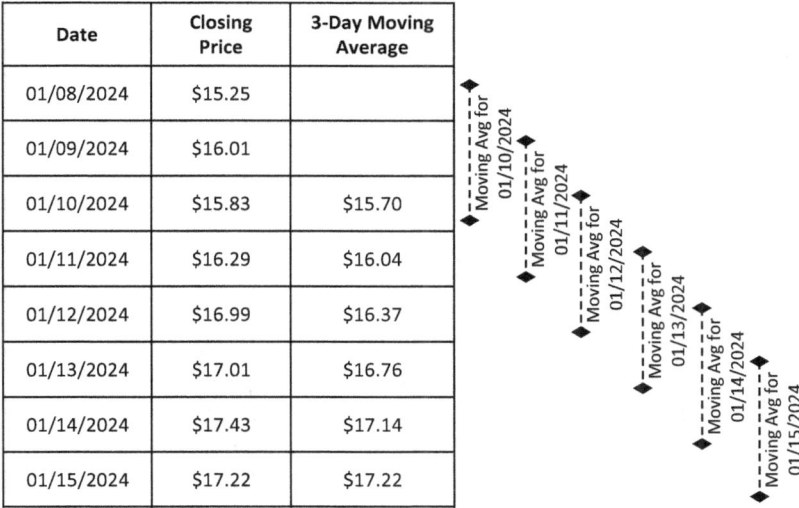

Figure 5.4: Computing moving average.

availability of the first moving average value in a series parallels the number of time periods used in averaging.

A Note on Seasonality and Cyclicality

Turning back to the earlier made distinction between long-term trends and more local-ized seasonality or cyclicality, in practice, that distinction can be hard to make. Setting aside the interpretationally obvious textbook examples of sales patterns of highly sea-sonal products such as ice cream, many other patterns may show varying degrees of variability that may not lend themselves to obvious seasonality conclusions, especially if the phenomena of interest are not widely seen as being seasonal or cyclical. Thus, in contrast to long-term tendencies that can be ascertained by simply computing averaged rate of change,[10] seasonality and cyclicality may not always be so easily discernible and may even 'blend-in' with random fluctuations. Although within the narrow context of baseline-setting, identification of seasonal and/or cyclical patterns is not as critical as it is in the context of trend forecasting; those effects can nonetheless exert potentially moderating influence of magnitudes of baseline values, which means their potential presence should not be disregarded. However, the process of identifying seasonal or cyclical patterns is not simple. To start with, there are multiple statistical expressions of those effects; at the most general level, seasonal or cyclical patterns can be either deter-ministic or stochastic, and the latter can be further broken down into stationary and

---

10 $(y_1 - y_2)/(x_1 - x_2)$, where y is value and x is time, as shown in Figures 5.1 and 5.2.

nonstationary (not to be confused with the earlier discussed idea of stationarity of the entire series). *Deterministic* seasonality, as suggested by the name, is highly predictable; it manifests itself in magnitudinally very similar (i.e., peaks and troughs are about the same) patterns recurring around the same time each year. *Stochastic* seasonality is considerably less predictable, and it is also more nuanced. More specifically, *stationary stochastic* seasonality is characterized by peaks and troughs that occur at about the same time each year (that's the 'stationary' part), but exhibit varying magnitudes from year to year (that's the 'stochastic' or random part); *nonstationary stochastic* seasonality, on the other hand, is characterized by random timing of occurrence as well as varying magnitudes of peaks and troughs, which makes that particular pattern particularly susceptible to being dismissed as random fluctuation.

One way of thinking about the different types of seasonal patterns is on a continuum ranging from most to least discernible, with deterministic representing most discernible and nonstationary stochastic the least discernible type. As can be expected, most situations will fall somewhere in-between, which means that those effects, while difficult, can be identified, especially when the 'what' of series of interest is carefully considered. What is the nature of the phenomenon that is represented by the data of interest? Or more specifically, is the phenomenon of interest expected to vary seasonally? For example, time series of aggregate milk sales and time series of aggregate ice cream sales would yield different answers to that basic question given that milk is a year-round staple product while ice cream's appeal (and thus sales) is far greater during the warm season than it is during the cold season. Consequently, ice cream sales are expected to exhibit seasonal variations, while milk sales are not; that information can be used in a manner that is loosely analogous to hypothesis testing, where presumed seasonality is empirically investigated. To that end, it is commonly recommended to begin with visual examination of plotted data; in practice, that approach might be appropriate for detecting relatively easy to spot deterministic seasonality, but it is far less reliable for detection of stochastic seasonality. Here, standardized statistical tests can be utilized; more specifically, the Friedman or the Kruskal-Wallis tests can be used to detect stationary stochastic seasonality, and Canova and Hansen test can be used to detect nonstationary stochastic seasonality.

Once singled out, seasonality needs to be addressed. While in the context of forecasting that usually means netting out its effects, within the confines of baseline-setting that is usually not the case. The reason for that goes back to the general conception of baseline-setting and baselining, where the former is framed as the process of deriving and parameterizing temporal evaluation standards, and the latter as the process of using those standards to carry out unbiased comparative assessment of outcomes or states of interest. If seasonality or cyclicality is a part of typical behavior of the phenomenon of interest, which in statistical sense is tantamount to it being nonstationary, those patterns should be embedded in baselines to be used to assess the behavior of that phenomenon as netting out those effects would likely adversely impact the validity of the assessment process. If, however, it is believed that the phenomenon of interest is stationary (i.e., the individual values do not depend on the time at which the series is measured or recorded), it is then appropriate to net out seasonal or cyclical patterns. A mechanism that is most commonly used to remove those effects is known as *differencing*, a computationally straightforward method built around estimating the difference between the current value and the corresponding value in the previous season. Differencing transforms a nonstationary series into a stationary one by subtracting the current value of the series from the previous one; that simple step removes changes in the level of a series, which has the effect of muting any nonstationary elements (i.e., long-term trend, seasonality, cyclicality) that might be present in the series of interest.

A Note on Outliers

Largely echoing the overview of benchmark-setting considerations, the problem of potentially abnormal or aberrant values also needs to be addressed in the context of baseline-setting. Within the confines of time series data, *outlier* is a value that falls outside of what can be considered an acceptable range. Keeping in mind that time series are essentially repeated – across time – measurements of outcomes or states of interest, determining what constitutes 'outlying' values can be challenging. For example, the stock price of a pharmaceutical company may suddenly sharply increase in value upon news of the approval of unique, blockbuster treatment, spiking high above its traditional range. But what if another company's stock shows a similar surge, but there is no clearly evident reason for that sudden surge? There is always, of course, a possibility of data errors that could emanate from a wide range of underlying causes, ranging from system malfunction to human error; at the same time, however, the observed spike in data could be an accurate reflection of what happened. All in all, it may not always be possible to validate the efficacy of data, but the good news is that it may not be *outlyingness* but rather the relative *influence* of abnormally large or small values that is of primary concern to baseline-setting.

The important distinction between outlyingness and influence warrants closer examination. In many organizational management contexts, abnormally large or small magnitudes of states or outcomes of interest can in fact be considered normal, as in a somewhat paradoxical sense, those outlying magnitudes might represent particularly pronounced maximum or minimum values of a phenomena of interest. For example, company stock prices may dramatically increase or decrease in response to positive or negative developments, which can recur with some degree of regularity; similarly, sales volumes may also show sudden up or down spikes driven by similar reasons. At the same time, abnormally large magnitudes may stem from truly unexpected and generally nonrecurring developments, as illustrated in Figure 5.5.

The histogram shown in Figure 5.5 depicts the annual number of securities class actions filed in the US federal courts (it starts in 1996 because that was the year that the provisions, which reset the key legal standards governing securities litigation, of a

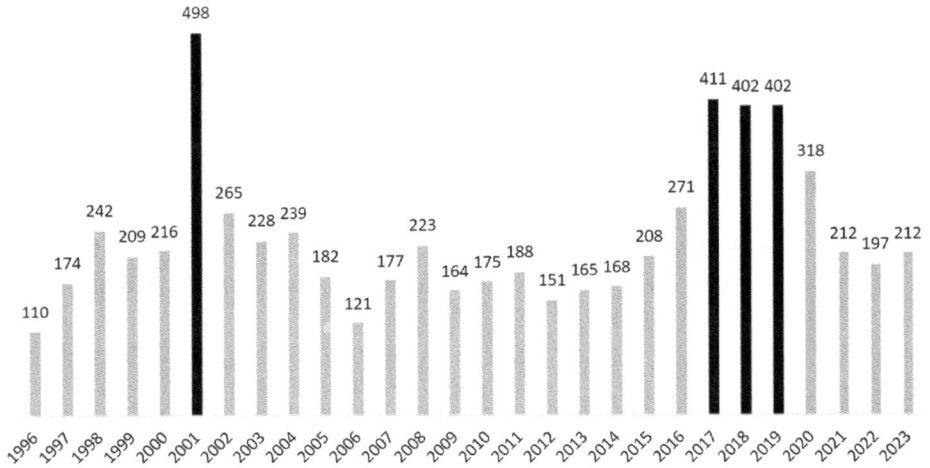

Figure 5.5: Annual frequency of securities class actions.

congressional act known as Private Securities Litigation Reform Act of 1995 went into effect). The highlighted year 2001 frequency of 498 cases is clearly the highest, followed by three consecutive years of 2017, 2018, and 2019. The large 2001 spike was caused by what is now known as the IPO[11] laddering scandal, which was precipitated by a combination of two distinct factors: The first of those was the so-called dot-com bubble, which was a rapid rise in equity (i.e., stock) valuations of internet-based companies during the bull market of the late 1990s; the second contributor was the so-called laddering practice, where the allocating underwriter required its customers to buy additional shares of the stock in the aftermarket as a condition for receiving initial shares at the offer price. The combination of such extortionary stock purchase agreement practices and irrationally exuberant valuations makes the 2001 rush of securities lawsuits a unique event, one that is not expected to recur, at least not in that form. It is quite a different story with years 2017, 2018, and 2019, which also have the appearance of outliers, but lack the unique characteristics of the year 2001 escalation. Ultimately, only year 2001 meets the full definition of outlyingness, but making that determination requires comparatively deep knowledge of the precipitating factors, which cannot be assumed.

The example depicted in Figure 5.5 is also meant to illustrate the difference between aberrant and influential values, as seen from the perspective of baseline-setting. The abnormal circumstances that precipitated the sudden and sharp year 2001 increase warrant seeing the resultant 498 cases as a true anomaly, the inclusion

---

11 Initial public offering (IPO) is the process of offering shares of a private corporation to the public in a new stock issuance for the first time.

of which has the potential to artificially inflate the magnitude of estimates of typical frequency of securities litigation filings. On the other hand, the values associated with years 2017 through 2019 do not warrant being seen as anomalous, because of the underlying precipitating factors. All in all, if included in moving average calculations, the year 2001 values would upwardly bias the resultant estimates, whereas inclusion of 2017 through 2019 values would not be expected to have the same type of biasing impact.

In a more general sense, to yield robust, meaning unbiased and stable estimates, baseline-setting cannot be unduly influenced by atypical values, but as illustrated by the example summarized in Figure 5.5, the notions of 'undue influence' and 'atypical values' need to be carefully considered within the confines of individual datasets. The very essence of baseline-setting is to derive evaluation standards that are, among other things, not only magnitudinally robust but also reflective of typical circumstances. It thus follows that achieving that goal is contingent on estimates not being skewed by aberrant values, and also on being responsive to what might be infrequent but nonetheless not aberrant changes in the underlying patterns. After all, the core function of baselines is to serve as bases for assessing magnitudinal impacts of outcomes or states of interest in a way that reflects the prevailing conditions within which those phenomena exist. All considered, baseline-setting demands explicit assessment of the degree of outlyingness, with an eye toward identifying values that could bias or exert analytically undesirable degrees of influence on estimates of interest. In an operational sense, it calls for a two-step process of, first, identify outlying values, and secondly, remediating any undue influence of those values.

Admittedly, identification of truly anomalous values can be a vexing undertaking that can yield imperfect outcomes; thus approaching that task with care is of paramount importance. Of particular interest here is what could be characterized as a chicken-and-egg problem that is at the core of the outlier identification mechanics: The commonly used detection approaches are built around assessing deviations of individual values from the mean, which requires computing the mean prior to outlier detection. The problem with that scenario is that, absent other means of detecting and eliminating outlying values,[12] all available values, including the potentially outlying ones, are used in computing the mean, which results in upwardly or downwardly (depending on the dominant skew of outlying values) biased mean. In other words, the process that relies on the use of the mean to detect outlying values is self-discrediting because its identification logic is rooted in using the very information it aims to create.

In view of the self-discrediting nature of the standard outlier detection mechanism, the type of background knowledge discussed in the context of Figure 5.5 exam-

---

12 Which seems unlikely, given that availability of other outlier detection mechanisms would render any further outlier detection needs unnecessary.

ple offers the best chances of singling out truly aberrant values, but such depth of data familiarity cannot be expected as the norm. In situations in which that is not the case, it is generally advisable to make use of a somewhat more generic approach, one built around the idea of simply truncating a predetermined % of values, under the general assumption that whatever the underlying root causes of those fringe values, simply eliminating them will reduce the chances of upwardly or downwardly biasing the resultant estimates. In those situations, the most common approach is to truncate the total of 5% of all values, which usually means 2.5% of the smallest and 2.5% of the largest values.

Trended Magnitude Estimation and Direct Baselines

Building on the preceding overview of the general idea of trended magnitude estimation and the examination of key aspects of temporal data, let us now turn back to the two general types of baselines: direct and indirect. Direct baselines, which offer means of assessing trended magnitudinal and directional values of states or outcomes of interest under the assumption that the observed trends do not need to be decomposed, are more straightforward to conceptualize and explain and are also easier to construct. The reason behind that broad characterization is they are derived directly from values of data used in analyses, i.e., the observed trends, of course subject to the earlier outlined data analytic considerations.

However, that general characterization obscures one of the key challenges of direct baseline-setting: derivation of magnitudinally valid and reliable standards from imperfect data. As graphically illustrated in Figure 5.1, at their core, time series are sequences of singular values; thus, baselines derived (with the help of moving averaging and smoothing) from those data can also be expected to be expressed as sequences of singular values or to use a more technical characterization, as point estimates. Recalling the earlier discussion of the need to factor-in the nearly inescapable data imperfections, those point estimates should be recast as standard error-framed ranges. The logic of doing so parallels the logic of framing benchmark ranges discussed in Chapter 4 – in both contexts, the goal is to express evaluative standards, in the form of baselines and benchmarks, as probable spans of values. However, the mechanics by means of which that goal of accomplished differs between structurally and informationally distinct temporal and spatial data: Confidence intervals are implicitly temporally fixed in the sense of encapsulating the relative instability of estimates at a point-in-time, which means they are ideally suited for use with spatial data, but not necessarily with temporal data. The reason for that is that doing so would require computing confidence intervals for each individual point in time, which is not possible given the informational structure of temporal data.[13] In view of that mix of notional similarity and methodological distinctiveness, it is advisable to use somewhat different labels when referring to computing probable ranges of values, simply to avoid confusion. To that end, baseline-setting analog to benchmark-setting confidence intervals is hereon referred to as *confidence bands*.

Formally defined here as a method for capturing the degree of imprecision in estimated trend lines, confidence bands frame moving average (point) estimates using upper and lower confidence bounds, which are expressions of estimates' variability and the desired level of confidence. Figure 5.6 shows the general rationale of the idea of confidence bands and also highlights the notional similarity of those two methodologically distinct expressions of probable value ranges.

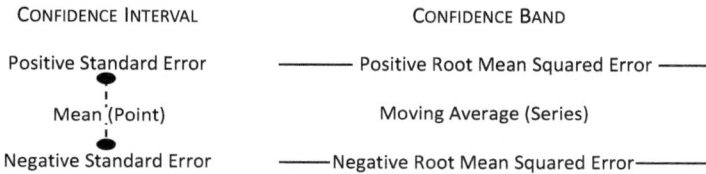

CONFIDENCE INTERVAL   CONFIDENCE BAND

Positive Standard Error   ──────── Positive Root Mean Squared Error ──────

Mean (Point)   Moving Average (Series)

Negative Standard Error   ──────Negative Root Mean Squared Error──────

Figure 5.6: Confidence intervals vs. confidence bands.

The computational logic of the upper and lower confidence bounds graphically depicted in Figure 5.6 is notionally analogous to the logic of upper and lower confidence intervals, framed in the *variance* → *standard deviation* → *standard error* progression detailed in Chapter 4. Taking into account differences in informational contexts and keeping in mind the importance of separately estimating positive and negative variability, the temporal analog of that computation progression is as follows: *sum of squared errors (SSE)* → *mean squared errors (MSE)* → *root mean squared errors (RMSE)*. In other words, SSE can be seen as temporal data's equivalent of variance, MSE as the equivalent of standard deviation, and lastly, RMSE as analogous to standard error.

An aspect of upper and lower probability estimation limits that is unique to time series data is the *recency* of data, which encapsulates freshness or timeliness of data. When used to make forward-looking predictions, more recent data are generally more indicative of the future, because the more recent states and outcomes can be expected to have stronger influence of what happens next, as opposed to older states or outcomes. The same general logic can be applied to baseline-setting, in the sense that, at least in some contexts, more recent data points might need to be weighted

---

13 More specifically, in time series variability is expressed longitudinally, or along the time dimension, and since each point in a series is represented by only a single value, it is not possible to compute point-in-time variability for individual elements in a series.

more heavily. However, the basic logic of moving averaging weighs all values equally, which means that the oldest value in a particular time series has the same impact on the moving averaging estimates as the most recent value. That limitation can be circumvented by replacing simple moving averaging with *weighted moving averaging*, but doing so comes with additional considerations.

There are numerous approaches that could be used to weigh the impact of individual components of time series (specifics of those approaches are discussed in numerous time series analysis texts); perhaps the most widely used is *exponential smoothing*, which is built around the idea that as individual values get older (i.e., are further back in time), they are assigned exponentially decreasing weights. While the more technical treatment of the computational specifics of exponential smoothing falls outside the scope of this overview, it is worth pointing out that the reason this weighting schema is called 'exponential' is because it is rooted in the mechanics of geometric series. According to its logic, the decrease in relative impact itself shrinks with each consecutive time period, and the amount of that shrinkage is determined by a quantity known as the exponential factor.[14]

The idea of trended magnitude estimation discussed here in the context of direct baselines implicitly assumes that time series of interest are composites of long-term trends, seasonal or cyclical influences, and near-term, random fluctuations, and the necessary (to baseline-setting) decomposition can be effectively accomplished with the help of moving averaging rooted approaches. But what if the series of interest also includes material but nonsystematic patterns? That question is addressed next.

Trended Magnitude Estimation and Indirect Baselines

The idea of baseline, as a tool of comparative assessment, is tied to the ability to reduce available and applicable time series data down to the underlying, persistent patterns, even if those patterns are expressed in probabilistic terms (i.e., framed as confidence intervals). In that sense, data used in baseline-setting are typically seen as a combination of systematic patterns (i.e., long-term trends and seasonal or cyclical patterns) and random noise, but there are situations in which that view might not be in keeping with true informational composition of data. More specifically, time series of interest may also include nonsystematic patterns, which are discernible influences that do not occur in a predictably repeating manner; in those situations, the 'standard' moving averaging-based baseline-setting approaches might yield methodologically and thus informationally unsound outcomes. Phrased in the language of comparative

---

14 Operationally, the simplest approach to computing the exponential factor, also known as the smoothing factor, is: 2/(number of time periods +1). Using that simple formula, a 7-day exponential factor would be 0.25 (2/(7 + 1)), and a 30-day exponential factor would be 0.0645 (2/(30 + 1)).

assessment, informational composition of data may render *direct assessment*, i.e., direct baselines, inappropriate, triggering a need for an alternative, *indirect assessment* minded baseline-setting approach. Framed here as indirect baselining, it offers a way of deriving magnitudinal estimates in situations in which those effects are confounded with other effects.

In less abstract terms, *indirect baselines* offer solutions to problems that arise when states or outcomes of interest are measured in a manner that confounds multiple effects. A good example of informational challenges that arise in those situations is offered by sales data, which track volumes of products sold across time. Upon careful consideration, it becomes clear that the individual values that comprise those series can be impacted by periodic events, such as temporary price reductions. If left unaccounted for, the presence of those factors would raise the specter of systematic error, because impact of such influential but random (as seen from the perspective of their occurrence in data series) events can be expected to be as consequential as impact of seasonality or cyclicality. But simply averaging, or more specifically, attempting to address the informational complexity of data series with the help of moving averaging would merely dampen the overall variability without differentially addressing localized aspects of it. In view of that, a different approach is needed to derive valid and reliable baselines from such compositionally complex data – that approach is indirect baselining.

Implied in that characterization is a greater degree of baseline-setting complexity: Having to be derived from more informationally complex data pushes indirect baseline into the realm of *statistical inference*, broadly defined as a structured process of drawing conclusions about an underlying population based on a subset of the data. The general notion of statistical inference is operationalized with the help of numerous statistical techniques designed to adapt that idea to a wide range of data analytic contexts; in the context of baseline-setting, of particular interest is a method known as *linear regression*. Broadly characterized, linear regression is a statistical technique used to estimate the linear relationship[15] between a target variable (i.e., a state or outcome of interest) and one or more explanatory (also known as predictor or independent) variables;[16] within the confines of indirect baseline-setting, a specific application of linear regression – temporal linear regression – is of particular interest.

In very general terms, *temporal linear regression* (TLR) is mathematical expression of generalized relationship between a target variable and time. Using the same data as the earlier discussed moving averaging approaches, TLR offers a more effective way of netting out the effect of material but nonsystematic – i.e., not recurring with a predictable degree of consistency – effects. In a more operational sense, rather

---

15 Represented by a straight line in the context of the two-dimensional Cartesian coordinates shown in Figure 5.1.
16 A more in-depth overview is offered in Chapter 8.

than merely attenuating random fluctuations (as is the case with moving averaging), TLR singles out that part of the overall cross-time variability in the phenomenon of interest that is due to persistent, long-term patterns; by doing so, it effectively nets out the effect of random influences, such as the earlier mentioned temporary price reductions. The mechanics of that process are explained in more detail in Chapter 8; for now, let it suffice to say that the part worth attribution process of temporal linear regression uses probabilistically estimated coefficients, known as 'regression weights,' which capture the generalizable relationship between the phenomenon of interest (i.e., the target variable) and time as the sole predictor.

Temporal Reliability

No data analytic undertaking is free of assumptions of judgment calls. From data due diligence to discerning the informational structure of data to making methodological choices – transforming raw, and typically messy data into valid and reliable information requires choosing among competing courses of action and acting on incomplete or imperfect knowledge. Hence ironically, while manifestly geared toward reducing the impact of cognitive biases, data analytic processes are themselves prone to biased decision-making, which underscores the importance of careful and thorough validity and reliability assessment. Within the confines of the baseline-setting process, temporal reliability is of particular concern. Framed here is the cross-time dependability of a comparative assessment mechanism, the idea of temporal reliability encapsulates the extent to which individual baselines can retain their evaluative consistency with passing time. Embedded in that characterization is the question of the length of time, as given a long enough stretch of time, any assessment standard can be expected to become outdated.

The timing question that is at the core of the idea of temporal reliability can be brought to life with the help of a simple scenario: A retailer is considering developing objective comparative assessment standards, in the form of sales baselines, to help them estimate the impact of various promotional activities over time. Having identified outcomes of interest, the company analysts are now beginning to compile daily sales data, and in doing so need to answer a key question: How far back should the selected sales data go? 12 months? 18 months? 24 months? Still further back?

It is a difficult question to which there is no singular answer because it depends on an array of factors that uniquely define individual situations. Primary among those are product/service characteristics, most notably product or service type (e.g., perishable vs. nonperishable, staple vs. luxury, etc.), sales volatility, and average product repurchase cycle; also consequential is the expected refresh cycle, framed earlier as re-estimation cadence, or the frequency with which individual baselines are updated with more recent data[17] (discussed at length in the next section), as well as the anticipated baseline usage frequency, and accessibility of data. And lastly, the type of baseline – direct vs. indirect – also needs to be factored into those considerations.

Turning back to the question of data recency, a good starting point in making those determinations is to think in terms of the number of repurchase cycles. Using that criterion, fast-moving, i.e., high repurchase frequency products and services are suggestive of reliance on more recent data, e.g., 12 months rather than 18 or 24 months; the opposite is true for slow-moving products or services. However, that conclusion might need to be adjusted based on the expected refresh cycle, with lower refresh cadence being suggestive of longer data time horizons (i.e., choosing 24 months over 12 or 18 month); additionally, the availability of 'fresh' might also need to be considered, especially if focal data come from outside parties (e.g., business partners or others). The picture that emerges is one of a careful balancing act, where the above outlined decision influencing factors are jointly taken into account to arrive at an answer that is in closest alignment with the goal of assuring temporal reliability.

Stability vs. Responsiveness

Softly implied in the preceding section is an interplay between two somewhat contradictory characteristics of baselines: stability and responsiveness. On the one hand, comparative assessment standards are expected to exhibit reasonable degrees of cross-time consistency to support credible assessments of phenomena that are relatively close in time, but, on the other hand, the same evaluation standards are also expected to be reasonably responsive to factors that materially impact the level or the direction of the trend of interest. It is not easy for a single solution, in the form of either direct or indirect baseline, to simultaneously satisfy both of those requirements.

Of major concern in addressing the interplay between stability and responsiveness is dealing with short-term random fluctuations in data series. Be it choices related to the specifics of how time series smoothing was approached when deriving direct baselines (the type of smoothing approach used and the rationale for selecting smoothing factors), or steps taken to fit the final regression model used to derive indirect baselines, that important tradeoff should be explicitly and carefully considered. It is important to keep in mind, however, that sometime either stability or responsiveness might need to be given more weight to accommodate the need at hand – in those situations, whichever of the two effectively becomes the secondary consideration

---

17 The importance of that consideration is more pronounced for baselines derived using the method of least squares than for those derived using moving averages because the mechanics of the former are rooted in concerted re-estimation efforts (in a sense of committing to periodic re-estimation of otherwise stationary estimates); the computational logic of moving averages is rooted in ongoing periodic re-estimation.

should be subsumed, not overlooked. In other words, temporal reliability cannot be assured by only focusing on stability or responsiveness.

Usability

The utility of evaluation standards, here in the form of baselines, is largely self-evident in the general sense, but that does not mean that individual operationalizations of that idea can be presumptively assumed to hit the proverbial mark. As can be expected, some applications can meet or even exceed expectations, and others can fall short. What are the difference makers? In the majority of applied organizational settings, they can be grouped into three general categories refresh cycle, relevance, and ease of administration and interpretation.

Refresh Cycle

Briefly mentioned in the context of temporal reliability, the notion of *refresh cycle* encapsulates the frequency with which baseline values are re-estimated using more recent data, keeping in mind the continuous character of many modern data sources. For instance, during trading hours, stock prices are tracked on practically a continuous basis, in a manner that is notionally reminiscent of a flowing stream; in the sense, baseline values can be assumed to be continuously changing. In practice, however, that implicitly continuous process is in fact periodic due to two distinct factors: estimation mechanics and data access.

Estimation mechanics refers to specific techniques used to compute baseline values; those are the earlier discussed moving averaging and temporal linear regression. Although different in terms of their methodological foundations and computational processes, both require a foundation of distinct *periodicity*, or clearly specified time intervals used to encode values of interest. For example, the price of a particular stock traded on a public stock exchange is fluid, meaning that it continuously fluctuates during the trading hours; however, to be able to capture and record those continuously changing data requires choosing specific time intervals – those time intervals can be granular, such as hours, minutes, even seconds, or comparatively coarse, such as days or even months. Moreover, the estimation process is itself static, meaning that it requires that a subset of data be extracted, prepared (see the earlier discussed data due diligence) and then analyzed. All in all, estimation of baseline values derived from principally continuous time series data is, in practice, periodic, and thus in need of periodic refreshments.

Implied in that line of reasoning is a yet another manifestation of periodicity of baseline estimation mechanics. Estimates of interest are computed at a point-in-time (not to be confused with point-in-time or spatial data used in benchmarking), meaning that input data need to be 'frozen' in time, to allow for computing of deterministic values. Consequently, the inescapable passage of time coupled with time series estimation mechanics creates the need for an ongoing refresh cycle.[18]

That need is further compounded by the second of the two reasons behind the periodic character of baselines, data access, which stems from, typically, multistep data capture and utilization processes. Setting aside edge analytic[19] applications, the bulk of operational and related data are first captured, then transferred into storage environments, typically in the form of data warehouses, from which data are extracted for analyses. The separation of data capture and data utilization renders analyses of, principally, continuous data flows periodic, because new data need to be extracted and made usable (e.g., restructured, amalgamated, recoded, etc.) before it can be analyzed.

The overall baseline refresh cycle rationale is graphically illustrated in Figure 5.7.

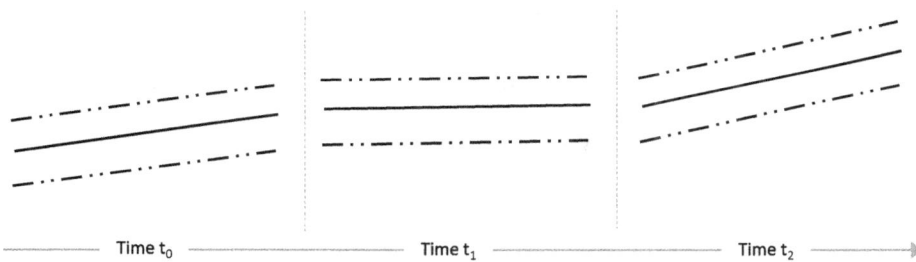

Figure 5.7: Static refresh cycles.

As depicted in Figure 5.7, periodic refresh cycles introduce distinct discontinuities in the ongoing process of baselining; those repeat re-estimation related discontinuities can become amplified in the presence of any data capture or structure related changes. While it is difficult to discuss any specific data discontinuity remedies, care must be taken to minimize any period-to-period differences.

Relevance

At its core, the question of relevance is the question of connectivity – how connected, in the sense of meaning and/or content, is one idea to another idea? In a more specific

---

18 As described here, the idea of refresh cycle implies scheduled, often in fixed time intervals such as 6 or 12 months, updates, framed here as static updates; an alternative, more ad hoc update method is dynamic update, discussed in more detail in the next chapter.
19 A subset of data analytics where automated algorithms built into data capture systems process data captured by those systems at the point of collection, typically on ongoing basis.

context of informational tools, such as baselines, it is an expression of the degree of applicability of a tool to the problem at hand. As can be expected, relevance is highly situational, as the same tool may be in good alignment with informational needs in one context, but not so in another. Hence, the question that arises is how, exactly, is relevance of a baseline to be determined?

The most obvious way is to compare data used to build the baseline with data representing phenomenon to be assessed, focusing primarily on origin and informational content; it is intuitively obvious that a high degree of similarity is suggestive of the benchmark's relevance. That is not all, however; also important is timing of data. A benchmark can be rendered inapplicable by simple passage of time, especially if the focal phenomenon is impacted by changing trends. For example, trends of filings and settlements of shareholder litigation class actions, which are at the center of baselining case study discussed in Chapter 9, are strongly impacted by changes in laws and regulations that govern shareholder rights; those changes can have trend-discontinuing impact, so much so that baselines based on prematerial change have greatly reduced applicability to assessing postchange outcomes.

There is still more. Continuing with the example of cross-time stock price assessment used throughout this chapter, performance of a stock of interest can be evaluated in various contexts, ranging from the overall market to just a small number of handpicked peers – which of those many potential frames of reference is most relevant?

There are some potentially conflicting considerations. Continuing with the stock price performance assessment example, on the one hand, it is intuitively obvious that a carefully picked set of most alike stocks would yield a maximally similar comparison set, but, on the other hand, the resultant peer group would likely be quite small, which could ultimately give rise to undesirable estimation related consequences. Recalling the computational mechanics of variability, or more specifically the standard error, there is an inverse relationship between estimated variability and the number of records (here, peer companies) used in computing those estimates – in other words, the smaller the number of companies, the larger the estimated variability of outcomes of interest, in this case stock performance. When put in the context of confidence bands discussed earlier, larger variability in the form of larger standard error will inescapably give rise to wider confidence bands, which may ultimately impede *evaluative sensitivity* of the evaluation standard. More specifically, a narrowly defined evaluation standard is likely to be downwardly biased, which means only capable of detecting large deviations from the norm, dismissing smaller differences as random fluctuations.

Swinging to the other end of the peer group continuum and opting for a comparatively much broader set of companies, e.g., all firms comprising an industry, raises a different set of issues. First, even though the term 'industry' may sound unambiguous, that is not the case. To start with, there are multiple, in fact about a dozen different industry classificatory taxonomies, with each producing materially different compositional structures. A company that wants to identify all industry peers is likely to end up with different sets of industry peers, depending on which industry classification schema it chooses to use (more on that in Chapter 9). But the ambiguity does not end there. For example, using the popular GICS (Global Industry Classification Standard) taxonomy,[20] a healthcare organization may see itself as being a part of a large healthcare sector or just a more narrowly framed healthcare equipment and services industry group, or a still more narrowly framed the healthcare providers and services industry, or an even more narrowly framed healthcare services subindustry.[21] Each choice comes with a tradeoff: Casting a wide net by selecting all companies grouped into the healthcare sector will yield many entities that will ultimately translate into heightened evaluative sensitivity, but the potentially highly heterogeneous mix of companies will adversely impact the degree of similarity of the so-derived standard. Choosing a more narrowly defined set, in the form of industry or even subindustry, can be expected to heighten the degree of similarity but at the expense of reduction of evaluative sensitivity.

All in all, the idea of baseline relevance is highly nuanced and cannot be fully operationally resolved outside of the specifics of individual situations. Such a nonspecific conclusion should not be seen as being dismissive of the idea of baseline relevance but rather as a recognition of the importance of purposeful and careful examination of usability-impacting choices.

Ease of Administration and Interpretation

As noted in the context of benchmark-setting, in the very broad realm of information, there are numerous examples of functionally excellent tools that are difficult to use, often due to nuanced complexity that often manifest itself in steep learning curves. Of course, complexity is, at least to some degree, subjective, with differences in background knowledge, experience, and aptitude (and, at times, attitude) playing a strong role in whether a particular informational tool is seen as complex or not. It thus follows that developing a robust understanding of who will be using the baseline under consideration, and what kind of informational utility is expected by those users is a critical part of baseline development.

The related but distinct ease of administration implicitly assumes a three-party baseline usage context of developers, administrators, and users, although it should be

---

20 Developed in 1999 by MSCI and Standard & Poor's, it groups companies into MECE (mutually exclusive and collectively exhaustive) segments using a four-tier system of sectors (11), industry groups (25), industries (74), and subindustries (163).
21 GICS taxonomy uses a four-tier, hierarchical structures starting with sectors (the most aggregate), which are then subdivided into industry groups, which in turn are subdivided into industries, which are made up of subindustries (the most disaggregate).

noted that in some cases, developers could also serve as administrators. Assuming a three-party baseline ecosystem, ease of administration is another important aspect of baseline-setting, and it warrants a closer look.

Broadly framed, baseline administration is the process of managing the use and usability of baselines. The former entails access and making use of those tools, while the latter involves making sure that the tools in question are still relevant given the expected needs at hand. Recalling the earlier discussed temporal reliability and refresh cycle considerations, the latter is particularly critical to baselines remaining in good working condition, as it is aimed at assuring ongoing usefulness of those tools as mechanisms of comparative assessment. In that context, ease of administration is tantamount to updatability. Implied in that broad requirement is a clear understanding of what exactly needs to be done, and when those specific tasks need to be accomplished to assure uninterrupted availability of structurally, methodologically, and otherwise consistent baselines.

It goes without saying that the baseline-setting rationale outlined in this chapter is comparatively simple and transparent, and that is precisely one of the goals. Transparent, easy to retrace computational logic coupled with structurally simple and validated data have a strong, positive impact on believability of results. Simple systems are far less likely to lead to *cognitive dissonance*, or perception of contradictory information, because informational outcomes of those systems lend themselves to comparatively easy validation and rationalization. When it comes to baselines, the ultimate success, as measured by user acceptance, of those informational tools hinges on how easy they are to use and interpret.

Chapter 6
Static vs. Dynamic Standards

The general benchmark- and baseline-setting processes discussed in Chapters 4 and 5 are rooted in the idea of initially setting up and subsequently periodically re-estimating comparative assessment standards. In that context, benchmarks and baselines are derived using data that are, in effect, frozen in time, thus both of those standard-setting processes can be characterized as *periodic* standard-setting, which are rooted in the general logic of derive – deploy – refresh – redeploy. In a more general sense, that approach can be seen as a part of the traditional data analytic paradigm, which is built around the process of extracting data out of their native environments, putting extracted data through a thorough due diligence and feature engineering process, and lastly, analyzing data. That process has its advantages, in the form of carefully planned and executed analyses, and its disadvantages, in the form of time delays and static (between refreshes) nature of the resultant estimates. However, rapid advances in computational processing capabilities coupled with easier data access are now making it possible to circumvent the main shortcomings of that approach which, in the context of comparative assessment discussed here, is the static nature of benchmarking and baselining values. In more and more organizational settings, it is now feasible to institute an alternative benchmark- and baseline-setting mechanism, where those assessment standards are derived on-the-fly, an approach framed here as *dynamic* standard-setting.

It is important to note, however, that the choice between static and dynamic standard-setting approaches should not be reduced to technological capabilities. Behavioral characteristics of states or outcomes of interest are just as critical to that choice, simply because not all phenomena warrant investing in, typically, more resource-intensive dynamic standard-setting capabilities. Of particular interest here is volatility of the phenomena of interest, as well as stability of the system within which those phenomena exist. As can be expected, some phenomena fluctuate a lot more than other ones, and some systems are comparatively less stable than other ones. For example, within the realm of insurance, the annual aggregate accident rate trends, both frequency and severity, remained remarkably stable over the course of the last decade even though the number of drivers, and thus the vehicles, has been steadily increasing; along similar lines, driving-related rules and regulations also remained relative unchanged. At the same time, frequency and severity of natural disasters varied noticeably within the same time frame, and there have also been numerous shifts in the way those risks are mitigated. With that in mind, choosing between static and dynamic standard-setting capabilities needs to balance data and technological possibilities and behavioral characteristics of broadly framed phenomena of interest.

https://doi.org/10.1515/9783111001296-006

Static vs. Dynamic: The Distinction

The definition of what constitutes 'static' and 'dynamic' varies quite a bit across contexts, with somewhat different meanings associated with, for instance, static and dynamic systems, websites, lists, and even characters in a story. Within the context of interest here – the development of assessment-related standards – *static*[1] standard is framed as a value or a set of values that remain unchanged within a specific time; in contrast to that, *dynamic* standard represents a value or a set of values that are updated on an ongoing basis. Implicit in this distinction are three key factors of timing, intentionality, and feasibility.

When considered as a factor contributing to the distinction between static and dynamic assessment standards, the general idea of *timing* has a nuanced and complex meaning (and the root notion of *time* has, upon deeper reflection, mind-bending meaning, though those considerations fall outside the scope of this overview). To start with, in the context of organizational management, as well as broader behavioral settings, it is difficult to think of phenomena that are not subject to change, given a long enough time horizon (as noted earlier, that is not the case with the so-called universal constants used in natural sciences). Hence, in principle no behavioral state or outcome is truly static, but the frequency and the magnitude of change can vary considerably across different measurable states and outcomes. Moreover, the notion of timing can be used as a part of larger description of the phenomenon of interest (e.g., timing of purchase), and it can also be used in framing of the process of assessing of that phenomenon (e.g., timing of data refresh); and lastly, it can also be expressed in terms of 'degree of' continuum as well as 'yes vs. no' discrete choices.

In the context of interest here, which is development of probabilistic, i.e., derived from analyses of applicable data, assessment standards, the notion of *timing* is used in a narrower context of informational updates. Given the inherent change that underpins behavioral outcomes, all behavioral assessment standards will eventually become outdated, which means that the design of robust benchmarks and baselines needs to incorporate refresh considerations. In a very general sense, updates can be either periodic or dynamic – the former entail re-estimation of values of standards of interest at distinct, often fixed points in time, whereas the latter entails situational derivation of those values on extemporaneous basis. With that in mind, periodically re-estimated standards are referred to here as static because their values remain unchanged until re-computed, in contrast to dynamically updated standards the value of which is derived anew each time a particular standard is accessed.

---

1 It is important to note that the notion of 'static' is used here in the sense of being unchanged within some period of time; it should not be confused with universal standards, such as the speed of light or the value of π, or pi, which are expected to remain unchanged in perpetuity.

An equally important distinction between static and dynamic standards is *intentionality*, a general state of mind that manifests itself as deliberate, purposive focus on some phenomenon or state. In contrast to time, that somewhat difficult to clearly frame the mental state of being directed toward some state of affairs, intentionality captures the reasoned action aspect of standard-setting. More specifically, setting up a benchmark or a baseline as static is a result of willful choice that, ideally, reflects a thoughtful and well-founded evaluation of the behavioral characteristics of the phenomenon of interest, the key usability-related considerations, data access, and technological (i.e., data processing) capabilities. In that sense, intentionality encapsulates what should and what could be done. A quantity that is comparatively stable within a relatively short period of time, such as a year, can be reasonably well approximated by a point-in-time-based estimation process, with the resultant estimate used as a fixed or static quantity for a year or so thereafter. On the other hand, a phenomenon that exhibits comparatively high degree of short-term variability may be deemed to need dynamic estimation, provided it is technologically feasible.

And in fact, *feasibility*, commonly defined as the possibility that something can be done, is the third key point of distinction between static and dynamic estimation. Dynamic estimation implies ad hoc, or as needed, re-estimation cadence which in turn necessitates ready access to the required data, and data processing infrastructure that can support such on-demand analytic processing. Not surprisingly, that may simply not always be the case, even if being able to do that is highly desirable. The reasons can be wide ranging, including transactional for data that are purchased, in which case data purchase agreements may call for periodic, such as monthly or quarterly data deliveries, or they may be operational, as is the case when cumbersome data capture and processing mechanisms lead to long time delays in user access. Specific reasons notwithstanding, dynamic standard-setting may be desirable, but may turn out to be ultimately infeasible.

But what if dynamically updated comparative assessment standards are both desirable and feasible? The remainder of this chapter looks at that question from the perspective of, first, benchmarking, and then baselining.

Benchmarks

Broadly characterized, data analysis-derived *benchmarks* are spatially oriented assessment standards that are either static within a defined time frame or are dynamically updated. Benchmarks can also be thought of as either externally or internally sourced – the former originate outside, while the latter are created inside a particular organizational ecosystem. Externally sourced benchmarks, especially the so-called rule of thumb, are predominantly static, whereas internally developed benchmark can be either fixed or dynamic, depending on the combination of time-, intentionality-, and feasibility-encapsulated characteristics. As noted earlier, however, it is important to keep in mind that the distinction between 'static' and 'dynamic' reflects a difference of degree and not of kind. In organizational and other behavioral settings, static benchmarks' values are not permanently fixed (in the sense of universal constants, such as the speed of light); similarly, while dynamic standards are recomputed on ad hoc basis, the amount of change in their values, if any, is tied to the amount of change in the source data. Given that somewhat fuzzy distinction, a closer look at the difference between static and dynamic benchmarks is warranted.

Static Benchmarks

In a very general sense, fixed points of reference represent arguably the most familiar type of evaluative standards, though the idea of being 'fixed' has a somewhat nuanced meaning in the context of benchmarks. As noted earlier, within the very broad realm of behavioral phenomena, which encompasses organizational functioning and management, all states and outcomes are ultimately subject to change; consequently, notionally static benchmarks are not fixed in the absolute sense. More on point, the 'static' designation is borne out of the interplay between time, intentionality, and feasibility, rather than being an expression of just the time dimension. In that sense, *static benchmarks* can be characterized as evaluative assessment standards that are intentionally fixed for some amount of time; further embedded in that broad framing is that static benchmarks can be fixed due to systemic or nonsystemic reasons. Systemic reasons are typically tied to data constraints (e.g., new data are made available in quarterly intervals); nonsystemic reasons are typically tied to need and/or preference.

A good example of static benchmarking is offered by the task of tracking organizational performance outcomes, typically focused on widely used metrics such as return on investment (ROI). While business companies often track ROI and other key financial performance outcome measures monthly, that information is usually made available to the investing public quarterly and annually (the latter includes a more comprehensive set of financial outcome measures), which effectively determines the cadence of organizational performance benchmarking updates. That process, however, is somewhat more complicated than what might meet the eye. To start with, a common approach to framing performance benchmarks is to compile peer group averages, but the required data may not all be available at the same, or even near the same time. There are several reasons for that: First, while most companies use the calendar year for accounting purposes, not all do; for example, Apple Inc.'s fiscal year runs from October through September. Second, companies generally have several weeks to submit their reports to the Securities and Exchange Commission, which means that the full complement of required data might take several weeks to become available. And lastly, companies can request reporting extensions, which can cause further benchmark data delays. In that general context, availability of all required data effectively dictates the cadence of performance benchmarks' updates; given that availability of the full complement of required data can vary depending on the above outlined factors, scheduling of performance benchmarks' updates is typically based on worst-case – data availability-wise – scenario.

There are, of course, numerous other contexts where the requisite data are readily available in a highly predicable manner, and where there is a compelling need to use as recent as possible information. For example, investors evaluating companies' performance from the standpoint of equity valuation (i.e., stock price) are keenly interested in benchmarking the behavior, i.e., upside and downside volatility, of a stock of interest in reference to the most up-to-date benchmarking information, which might call for weekly or even daily update cycle (ideally, those investors might be interested in dynamic benchmarks, discussed next, but that functionality may not always be technologically and otherwise feasible). And lastly, there are also numerous other benchmark examples that do not include predetermined updates and are updated on a more or less ad hoc basis, meaning whenever newer version of the requisite data becomes available. For example, one recent email marketing-related set of general benchmarks stipulates average open rate of 21.3%, average click (on a link included in the email) rate of 2.6%, and average unsubscribe rate of 0.3%.[2] As noted on the site that communicates those benchmarks, their values were last updated in October 2019 and remained in place till the early part of 2024; moreover, it is unclear if those benchmarks will be updated, and if so, when. In some instances, such general benchmarks can evolve into general rule of thumb that are taken as true on their face value, at times long past their informational reliability.

When to Consider
Implied in the preceding general static benchmark characterization are contexts that are particularly well suited to the use of that type of assessment standard. However, it is not so much 'when' or 'where' but 'what' that determines the appropriateness of using static benchmarks. Slow changing, low-frequency outcomes are ideally suited to static benchmarking because the potential loss of information is minimized by their slow-moving characteristics. In principle, static encapsulation of information that is, in terms of the underlying data, subject to ongoing change entails some degree of loss of informational precision, but that degradation is a function of the degree of variability in those states or outcomes, and the frequency with which those phenomena are measured; together, those two considerations are framed here as the *opportunity to vary*. Overall, the lower the opportunity to vary, the lower the potential loss of informational precision. But what is the line of demarcation between the low and high opportunity to vary states and outcomes?

It is a difficult question to answer because such determinations are almost inescapably perspective laden. For instance, within the broad realm of risk management, those

---

2 https://mailchimp.com/resources/email-marketing-benchmarks/

focusing on severe weather-related threats are accustomed to dealing with relatively small numbers of qualifying events occurring on annual basis – for instance, according to NOAA's National Hurricane Center, there are, on average, 12 major hurricanes in the Atlantic basin (and thus of interest to the US forecasters) annually. Within the same broad domain of risk management, other types of risks, such as those relating to management liability, which typically manifest themselves in filings of securities litigation, exhibit somewhat higher annual frequency of, on average, a little over 200 qualifying events per year (in the United States). Still other areas of risk management, such as automotive liability, have comparatively voluminous data, given the high frequency of auto accidents (according to recent statistics, over 6 million per year in the United States alone). Within that general context, the first case (severe weather) could scarcely be seen as anything other than infrequent, while the last case (auto accidents) could scarcely be seen as anything other than frequent – using those two contrasting cases as the opposite ends of the frequency continuum suggests that the 200 or so annual securities litigation filings ought to be viewed as relatively infrequent.

To restate the earlier point, while the frequency of occurrence of the phenomenon of interest is important, so is the comparatively more nuanced behavioral profile of that phenomenon. A single, particularly destructive storm, such as hurricane Katrina (2005) or the more recent (2022) hurricane Ian, both of which caused well above $100 billion in damages, can have an outsized impact on benchmark values, which warrants close and careful consideration. The nearly reflexive inclination to eliminate or at least trim, magnitude-wise, those outlying events need to be balanced with other considerations, such as the trend of climate change-precipitated worsening of the impact of severe weather.

Dynamic Benchmarks

In a very general sense, the distinction between static and dynamic benchmarks can be characterized as the difference of degree and not of kind, with degree once again being a function of time, intentionality, and feasibility. Dynamic benchmarks are updated each time they are accessed; hence, to be deemed 'dynamic,' values of so-derived standards need to include the most recent data available. Implied in that characterization are clearly manifest informational needs – i.e., it is important for benchmark values to be highly responsive to any new developments – and operational feasibility, which centers on the availability of the necessary data capture and processing infrastructure. Thus, in contrast to static benchmarks, which remain fixed between periodic updates, dynamic benchmarks are, in principle, ever changing.

Such timely comparative assessment standards are appealing, but it is important to be mindful of potential challenges. By and large, data used in organizational analyses (benchmarking, baselining, and others) are imperfect, which means that data require careful due diligence and preparation, which can be a tedious, time-consuming, and largely manual (i.e., carried out by human analysts) process, but immediacy-oriented dynamic benchmarking only allows for templated data preparation steps. In other words, it restricts data review and corrections to just those actions that have been identified during the initial setup and were subsequently built into the data processing logic. As a result, the possibility arises that previously unencountered new data abnormalities may not be treated in the most appropriate manner, which can ultimately adversely impact the efficacy of recomputed standards, especially those generated with the help of increasingly popular edge applications.

Edge computing is an umbrella term for a wide range of technologies for bringing data storage and computation closer to the sources of data, which, from data processing and analysis perspective represents a more advanced data utilization mechanism, geared toward making data analytic outcomes available in near-real time. Edge applications offer an alternative to the traditional, multistage-based data capture and utilization paradigm where data capture is distinct from data storage and aggregation, and data storage in turn is separate from data processing and analyses; typically, each of those distinct stages has its own processes and applications, resulting in the overall data capture-to-insight process being time-consuming and resource-intensive. Edge computing eliminates many of the 'hand-offs' and points of separation by incorporating data processing and analysis functionality into the same general systems that capture data, which greatly compresses the capture-to-insight processes. Currently, many automated and autonomous systems, such as those used in smart grid applications, predictive maintenance, or patient monitoring use edge analytics as a part of their architecture, but those systems also rely on externally validated performance benchmarks, which underscores the importance of carefully considering the advantages and shortcomings of dynamic benchmarking.

A good in-between (the traditional stepwise data analytic processing and edge computing) option to consider are purpose-designed database reporting environments known as *datamarts*. Those data systems are typically subsets of large data repositories (known as data warehouses) and are designed expressly to retrieve and process specific data and to generate predetermined data analytic outcomes, typically used to support a specific undertaking, such as customer relationship management. When used to support ongoing benchmarking efforts, datamarts can greatly expedite to update the process, while still allowing for more involved ongoing data review.

When to Consider

Building on the rationale outlined in the context of static benchmarking, assuming it is feasible, dynamic benchmarking is, in principle, well suited to outcomes characterized as both more volatile and higher frequency. The combination of high frequency and high volatility is necessary to assure that dynamically updated assessment standards can be reflective of potentially material near-term changes in underlying trends, while at the same time also encompass large enough number of data records to smooth out the impact of potentially nonsystematic near-term random oscillations.

Once again, however, just because something can be done does not mean that it should be done, dynamic benchmarks may simply not be what is called for in a particular usage context. Some decisions such as those surrounding risk transfer in the form of insurance coverage are very infrequent, typically annual; other types of decisions, such as investment portfolio management, are very frequent and need the support of most up-to-date information. Deploying dynamic benchmarking capabilities to support the latter scenario would be highly desirable; it would not, however, be an optimal choice to support the former scenario because those capabilities would far exceed informational needs at hand.

Baselines

Comparatively less frequently invoked in applied and theoretical work alike, but nonetheless highly complementary in terms of their informational value, baselines are temporally oriented assessment standards, meaning, they are focused on cross-time trends rather than implicitly point-in-time cross-entity comparisons. It thus follows that baselines are complementary to benchmarks because while the latter offer 'us' vs. 'others' (i.e., spatial) comparisons, the former contribute 'now' vs. 'before' (i.e., temporal) comparative dimension, which broadens the evaluative perspective. Paralleling benchmarks, baselines can also be either static or dynamic, a distinction that once again is rooted in three key factors of timing, intentionality, and feasibility. In a general sense, differences that separate static and dynamic baselines largely mirror those that separate static and dynamic benchmarks, though, as can be expected, there are also several unique considerations.

Static Baselines

A point-in-time snapshot of a trend provides perhaps the most accurate summarization of the idea behind static baselines. Notionally paralleling static benchmarks, fixed-in-time baselines offer means of assessing cross-time change, as seen from the perspective of a particular point in time. The general estimation logic that underpins static baselines is implicitly rooted in the traditional data analytic paradigm, which is built around distinct data capture and storage → data retrieval and preparation → data analysis stages. As such, static baselines tend to be easier to develop, test, and implement; the ease of implementation aside, static baselines tend to be preferred in situations where the state or outcome of interest is relatively stable, at least in the short term.[3]

Paralleling the earlier discussion of benchmarks, the idea of a derived evaluative standard being 'static' needs to be framed in the qualifying context of time: To be deemed 'static,' a baseline needs to remain unchanged across usages within some reasonable period of time (as noted earlier, given the ever-changing nature of behavioral phenomena, to remain informative, eventually all baselines need to be brought up to date). Of central importance to that framing is the idea of 'across situations,' which implies repeated usages. More specifically, static baseline content (i.e., individual values and long-term trends) has to remain fixed between periodic updates.

One of the major advantages of static baselines (and static assessment standards in general) is that it allows careful and deliberate examination of input data, primarily geared toward identification and remediation of aberrant values, both from the standpoint of their validity and outlyingness. It is important to note, however, that being able to carefully examine data characteristics is not synonymous with readily available solutions to observed data anomalies, as illustrated by the commonly encountered problem of dealing with large, outlying values. The earlier mentioned examples of outlyingly large economic damages caused by hurricanes Katrina and Ian can exert highly influential impact on baseline trends, which suggests the appropriateness of either eliminating those values altogether or at least trimming their impact (the standard statistical treatment of outlying values); at the same time, however, artificially dampening the impact of what is, after all, valid data can have the undesirable consequence of understating the 'typical,' as in average, impact of extreme weather events (and by extension, of climate change). Still, periodic re-estimation cycles naturally lend themselves to methodical and careful examination of data, as well as ongoing methodological review.

There are, however, some distinct downsides to static baselines. Perhaps their most obvious limitation is the inability to account for near-term changes in trends of interest, which can lead to unexpected 'jumps,' either up or down, in successively updated patterns. Even if near-term trend volatility turns out to be relatively modest, repeat re-estimation discontinuities, first mentioned in Chapter 5, are unavoidable. Keeping in mind that baselines are means of carrying out longitudinal comparisons, static baselining is tantamount to taking repeated snapshots of continuous flows at different points in time, as graphically depicted in Figure 6.1.

The hypothetical example shown in Figure 6.1 depicts a relatively close alignment of periodic static baselines with the underlying long-term trend, which could be expected in situations in which the baseline is re-estimated in fixed and relatively close intervals. That, however, is not always the case; baselines can be re-estimated on as-

---

3 In most applied organizational settings, the line of demarcation separating the short and long term is 1 year: Time frames of up to 1 year are generally seen as short term, and those greater than 1 year as long term.

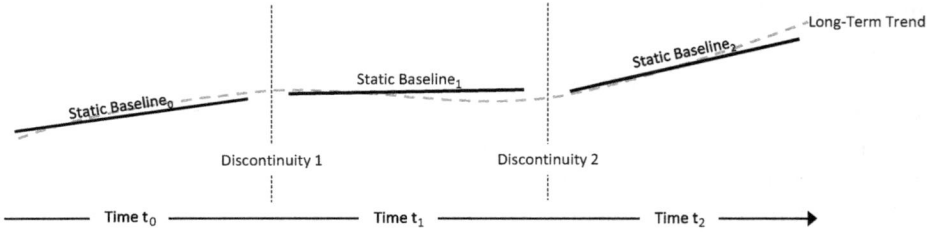

Figure 6.1: Repeat re-estimation discontinuities.

needed basis, which could be expected to yield unevenly spaced intervals, a situation that would likely amplify long-term trend vs. period-specific baseline differences.

When to Consider

The spatial vs. temporal distinction notwithstanding, there are close parallels between optimal usage situations for static baselines and benchmarks. With that in mind, tracking of long-term patterns of slow-changing, low-frequency outcomes encapsulate the ideal usage situation, primarily because capturing snapshots of the underlying long-term trends of such phenomena at distinct, and possibly infrequent, points in time can be assumed to yield the lowest potential loss of information. In more operational terms, it minimizes any repeat re-estimation discontinuities, as graphically illustrated by the two contrasting scenarios depicted in Figure 6.2.

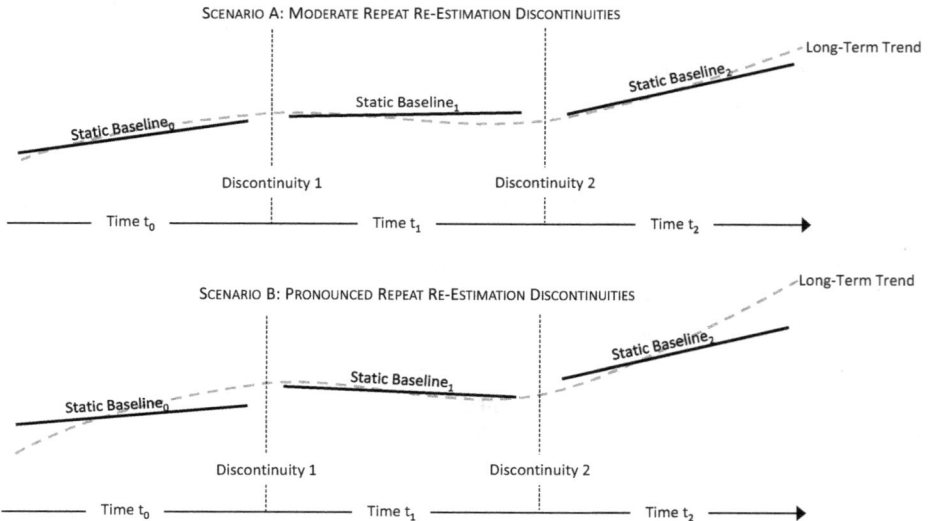

Figure 6.2: Moderate vs. large repeat re-estimation discontinuities.

Labeled as 'moderate' in Figure 6.2, the loss of informational precision associated with scenario A is indeed relatively small, so much so that in many common organizational usage contexts the point-in-time static baseline snapshots would likely be deemed to be sufficiently close approximations of the underlying long-term trend. On the other hand, scenario B illustrates more pronounced deviations of static baselines from the long-term trend, which would likely render static baselines a comparatively poor approximation of the true characteristics of the underlying pattern of change.

Dynamic Baselines

Continuously updated reference trendlines, perhaps best exemplified by financial indices, such as the Dow Jones Industrial Average, are some of the most widely recognized examples of dynamic baselines. (It is instructive to note that those indices are frequently mischaracterized as benchmarks, despite their obvious longitudinal qualities.) Paralleling the distinction between static and dynamic benchmarks, the difference between static and dynamic baselines boils down to data source connectivity: Static baselines are derived using data extracts, which are then subjected to stepwise data processing flows, characterized earlier as the traditional data analytic paradigm, built around distinct data capture and storage, retrieval and preparation, and analysis steps. Dynamic baselines, on the other hand, are derived by querying live source data, as graphically illustrated in Figure 6.3.

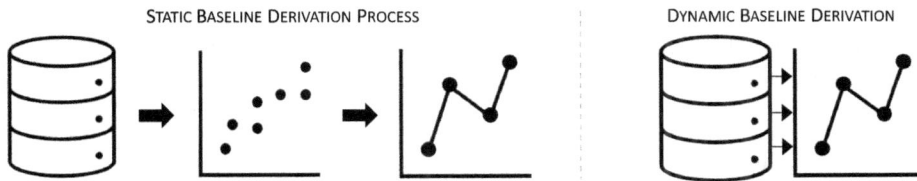

STATIC BASELINE DERIVATION PROCESS   DYNAMIC BASELINE DERIVATION

Figure 6.3: Static vs. dynamic estimation.

The obvious appeal of dynamic baselining is its responsiveness to changes in the underlying data, while its equally obvious shortcoming is exposure to potentially unchecked hitches. Dynamic baselining data query and subsequent estimation processes can, of course, include data validation and correction routines, but dealing with potential data shortcomings is rarely a 'set and forget' type of a problem. Newly captured data may exhibit previously not encountered and thus unaccounted for in the built-in data validation routine abnormalities, which may potentially distort data analytic outcomes. Still, as data validity routines are improved over time, the chances of encountering more unexpected – and material – data problems tend to diminish.

In a more general sense, and again paralleling the distinction between static and dynamic benchmarking, timing, intentionality, and feasibility play a key role in opting for dynamic rather than static baselines. The idea of timing encapsulates *data capture cadence,* or the frequency with which new measurements of the same entity are taken, which can range from nearly continuous to very sporadic. Stock market data is a perfect example of the latter as equity trading volumes and prices are continuously updated; on the other hand, financial disclosure data, which are typically made quarterly and annually, offer a good example of the latter. As can be expected, dynamically updated baselining is a far better fit for stock market data than for financial performance data.

The idea of intentionality combines elements of functionality, purpose, and utility associated with a baseline; in a somewhat more abstract sense, it also tackles the idea of 'just because it can be done, should it be done?' Baselines serve a particular purpose, and thus their design needs to be considered within the confines of that purpose. For example, if a particular baseline is used only sporadically, is dynamic functionality worthwhile, especially if it entails higher levels of resource commitments? At their core, baselines (as well as benchmarks) are informational tools, and as such they have a certain degree of implied value, thus should be assessed from the perspective of cost-benefit trade-offs.

The third and perhaps the most obvious consideration is that of feasibility. As graphically illustrated in Figure 6.3, dynamic baselining requires a high degree of integration between data capture, storage, and analysis, which is generally not the norm as data capture and storage environments tend to be separate from data analytic environments. The two alternatives discussed in the context of benchmarking – edge computing and datamarts – are also the go-to solutions here; as can be expected, dealing with potential data anomalies is also the key concern that arises in the context of, primarily, edge-computed baselines.

When to Consider

When trying to capture the nuanced nature of high-velocity outcomes, as illustrated by aggregate equity market tracking indices, such as the Dow Jones Industrial Average, dynamic baselines are the natural choice, given those tools' high degree of responsiveness to change in the underlying patterns. Given that, can dynamic baselining be assumed to be equally appropriate to use as an evaluative assessment tool on a more micro scale, here, to evaluate the performance of individual stocks?

Assuming that it is feasible in terms of the requisite ongoing data access and computational resources, the answer to this question centers on desired functionality. When, for instance, the intended use is to actively manage individual investments (i.e., stocks), dynamic baseline would offer the desired level of informational precision, but when the intended use is associated with a passive investment strategy, often referred to as 'buy and hold,' dynamic baselining would likely yield excessive level of utility, ultimately resulting in poor ROIs that are necessary to build and maintain such a system.

Chapter 7
Machine Learning and Standard-Setting

Artificial intelligence (AI), broadly characterized as computing systems capable of replicating human problem-solving abilities, is emerging as a topic of conversations in an
ever-wider range of organizational management contexts; hence, it is important to ex-
plore the impact on those rapidly evolving technologies on derivation and use of benchmarking and baselining. Once largely a domain of computer scientists, AI is now a part
of a common vernacular, though the manner in which that broad designation is used
often obscures some important distinctions between related but distinct areas of *AI* and
machine learning, which is of particular interest in the context of derivation of evaluative assessment standards. Further adding to that, fuzziness is the notion of *algorithm*,
commonly understood to be a defined set of computational procedures geared toward
arriving at specific types of outcomes. Even though the idea of algorithm is not limited
to computer processing, nor is the notion of machine learning synonymous with AI, the
use of those terms can signal that standards of interest were derived using autonomous,
i.e., lacking direct human intervention, data processing means. In view of that, it is important to draw a clear distinction between when and how assessment standards in the
form of benchmarks and baselines are derived using the traditional, human analyst-
centric methods, and when those standards are derived using modern automated and
even autonomous information technologies.

Starting with a high-level overview of AI and machine learning, the goal of this
chapter is to sketch out an outline of how machine learning applications can be used
in benchmark- and baseline-setting. More specifically, it is to take a closer look at one
of the nagging questions that emanate from ceaseless and, in fact, accelerating march
of info-technological progress: Can the traditional 'does it make (human)sense' standard be replaced with synthetic algorithmic logic? And, is the emerging reality in
which AI systems are ingesting massive amounts of multisource data and deriving
evaluation standards in a nonexplainable manner spelling doom for the traditional,
human analyst-led approach to standard-setting?

Artificial Intelligence

The idea of *AI* cannot be fully appreciated without a clear understanding of *human*
intelligence, and the efforts to develop the former are best illustrated in the context of
the game of chess. This centuries-old game (it is believed to have originated in India
around sixth century AD) is held by many as a true test of cerebral fitness because to
prevail, a player needs to consider a wide range of available strategies and tactical
moves, all while recognizing and adapting to the opponent's moves. Given its highly
analytical, zero-sum (one player's gain is the other player's loss), perfect information

https://doi.org/10.1515/9783111001296-007

(all positions are perfectly visible to both players), and combinatorial (each successive move generates a typically large set of possible responses) nature, the game of chess was recognized early as a perfect setting for the design of artificial learning systems, commonly referred to as AI.

AI research and development centers on one basic question: Can a machine be made to think like a person? Almost from the start, that question was tied to the question of whether a machine could be made to play chess, as the strategic nature of that game embodies, in many regards, what we tend to view as a uniquely human combination of reason and creativity. Building on the work of Alan Turing,[1] John Von Neumann, Claude Shannon, and other early twentieth-century information theory pioneers, computerized chess-playing system designers forecasted that machines would come to dominate humans as early as the 1960s,[2] but it took three more decades of algorithmic design and computing power advances for that forecast to come true (now computerized chess systems routinely beat the best human players, so much so that those systems play other such systems for the 'best of the best' bragging rights). That tipping point was reached in the famous 1997 match in which the reigning chess world champion Garry Kasparov was defeated by a supercomputer known as IBM Deep Blue.[3] The news of Deep Blue's victory stirred worldwide sensation, but looking back it is hard not to ask why it took that long for a computer to better the best human player, especially in view of combinatorial character of chess.

To that end, the truly fascinating aspect of Kasparov's duel with Deep Blue was the astounding informational asymmetry: Capable of processing more than 200 million instructions per second, in a timed match where a player has on average 3 min to make a move Deep Blue was able to evaluate millions of possible move sequences; in contrast, human *cognitive* information processing is incomparably slower,[4] so much so that Kasparov was only able to carefully consider maybe 10 or so move sequences. Further adding to that disparity was the fact that while the designers of Deep Blue had access to hundreds of Kasparov's games, Kasparov himself was denied access to recent Deep Blue's games. All considered, the contest pitted a human chess player relying primarily on intuitive *ends-and-means heuristic* against a computer programmed with the best strategies human chess players – as a group – devised, lightning-fast access to dizzying number of alternatives, and an equally lightning-fast decision engine powered by the

---

1 The famed Turing's machine, originally built to break the Nazi's Enigma code and designed around the concept of 'mechanized thought,' now forms one of the core theoretical constructs in computer science.

2 For instance, following their 1957 discovery of 'refutation screening,' which is a method for optimizing move evaluation, a team at Carnegie Mellon University predicted that a computer would defeat the world human champion by 1967.

3 It is worth noting that the 1997 event was a rematch between Kasparov and Deep Blue; Kasparov won the initial match held a year earlier 4–2.

4 The human brain can process about 11 million bits of information per second, but conscious thinking can handle only 40–50 bits of information per second.

most advanced algorithms devised and programmed by leading scientists. And, like all machines, Deep Blue was not hindered by factors such as fatigue, distraction, or recall decay. In view of the enormous informational and computational disparity, it is nothing short of amazing that the human champion convincingly won the initial 1996 about 4–2 and was only narrowly edged out in the 1997 rematch, where in six games there were three draws, two games were won by Deep Blue and one by Kasparov.

Understanding the underlying root causes of why such overwhelming computational advantage on the part of the computer did not immediately translate into a crushing defeat of the human chess champion is at the core of appreciating the essence of AI. There is a lot more to it than merely being about to rapidly carry out a vast number of calculations.

The Computational Mind

It is well known that even the slowest electronic computers are many orders of magnitude faster than human 'mental computing'; the fallacy of that thinking, however, is confounding of the idea of conscious cognitive reasoning with largely subconscious information processing carried out by the human brain on an ongoing basis. When considered from the perspective of raw, meaning largely subconscious, processing power, even the fastest supercomputers lag the human brain.

In a physical sense, the human brain can be described as approximately £3 of very soft and highly fatty (at least 60% – the most of any human organ) tissue, made up of some 80–100 billion nerve cells known as neurons, the totality of which comprises what scientists refer to as 'gray matter.' Individual neurons are networked together via exons, which are wire-like connectors numbering in trillions (it is believed that each neuron can form several thousand connections, which in aggregate translates into a staggering 160+ trillion synaptic connections) and jointly referred to as 'white matter.' Function-wise, gray matter performs the brain's computational work, while white matter enables communication among different regions of the brain which are responsible for different functions and where different types of information is stored; together, this exons-connected network of neurons forms a single appliance-like storage, analysis, and command center, which can be thought of as a biological computer.

The nexus of the processing power of that biological computer goes beyond the number of cells and connections that comprise that network – if each of those 100 billion or so neurons was only capable of storing a single memory, the entire human brain network would only be capable of a few gigabytes of storage space – about the size of a small capacity flash drive. According to the recent research, however, those individual cells 'collaborate' with one another in a way that each individual neuron helps with many memories at a time, which exponentially increases the brain's storage capacity, bringing it to about a million gigabytes – a staggering difference. How, exactly, that 'collaboration' happens is not yet fully understood; one of the leading explanations suggests that it appears to be rooted in neurons' geometrically complex structure endowed with multiple receptors (dendrites) and a highly branched outflow (an axon) capable of extending over relatively long distances. Moreover, emerging research also suggests that while the brain's storage capacity can grow, it does not decrease (what drops off, at times precipitously, is the retrieval strength). And so even though the amount of storage in the human brain certainly cannot compete with what is, in principle, a nearly infinitely expandable amount of electronic storage, it is far greater than commonly believed.[5]

But the amount of storage is, of course, only a part of what makes the human brain so amazing – in fact, its true power lies in its computational processes. In contrast to machine-executed computational steps, which can be broadly characterized as one-dimensional and explicit, meaning they tend to follow a specific step-by-step logic built around sequential input-output processes, brain's computation is dominantly nonexplicit and multidimensional, meaning that we are not consciously aware of the bulk of computations running in our mental background. And that is the essence of the fallacy of comparing the speed with which a human can consciously execute a specific computational task to the speed with which the same task can be accomplished by a machine – it contrasts only the speed of human rational reasoning with the full computational capacity of a machine. Commonly referred to as 'thinking' or 'cognitive reasoning,' those processes are slow and deliberate, and perhaps even more importantly, not at all indicative of computational prowess of the human brain.[6] Framed in the context of the ends-and-means heuristics relied on by Kasparov when playing Deep Blue (or any other opponent), that small handful of move sequences that Kasparov was able to consciously consider was supported by a tremendous amount of subconscious information processing leveraging brain's nonexplicit and multidimensional processing infrastructure. And given that every player has a particular bias in their choices, was Kasparov was able to study Deep Blue's games the way the computer was able to study Kasparov's past matches, the outcome of the 1997 match might have been different.

---

5 For instance, the raw storage power of the human brain is sufficient to record about 300 years' worth of nonstop television programming.

6 In contrast to electronic devices that can be either digital or analog, the human brain is effectively both, which creates exponentially greater depth of computing capabilities, all rooted in the use of probabilistically interacting biomolecules for computation, which in turn encompasses higher-order information processing and more sophisticated ways of storing, consolidating, and retrieving information than in electronic computers. While the ever-advancing designs of ANNs aim to emulate the intricacies of the biochemical structures and processes of the human brain, those biological intricacies simply cannot be understood as elements of electronic systems, thus as acknowledgement by the leading research in the area of computer design, the brain entails many more computing options than any supercomputer in existence; today, it is hard to imagine an artificial system capable of performing abstract and complex tasks such as intuition or anticipation.

Although the stir caused by Big Blue's triumph has long faded away, the quarter of century that passed since that memorable event witnessed steady growth and proliferation of increasingly more capable applications of AI, most recently exemplified by the rise of *generative AI*. When looked at as a multipronged domain encompassing a broad mix of tried-and-true and still under development technologies, there are currently four general types of AI systems, which are in different stages of evolutionary development: (1) reactive, which is the simplest of all, containing no memory and only able to respond to specific stimuli; (2) limited memory systems, somewhat more advanced applications that rely on ongoing learning to improve their responses; (3) theory of mind systems, which are more advanced designs aiming to understand the needs of other intelligent entities (both human and nonhuman); and (4) self-aware artificial systems, the pinnacle of AI where artificial systems exhibit human-like intelligence and self-awareness. As of the time of this book (2024), the first two are commonplace, the third is rapidly emerging, but the fourth type of AI is still in the development stages (at least as far as can be discerned based on public sources).

Nowadays, the state-of-the-art AI systems, such as ChatGPT, Microsoft Bing, or Google Bart are all powered by complex *deep learning* algorithms (more on those later). As a class, however, machine learning algorithms span a wide range of sophistication, from highly complex deep learning to comparatively simple regression applications. In that sense, it is important to differentiate between appliance-like – i.e., combining computational hardware and software into a single processing unit – AI systems and individual, standalone machine learning algorithms. In a general sense, no machine learning algorithm can be expected to exhibit the degree of computational transparency that is associated with the use of simple statistical reasoning outlined in earlier chapters; however, the line of demarcation between statistical analysis and machine learning is blurry, with some of the most widely used statistical techniques – most notably, linear and logistic regression models – are also seen as supervised machine learning algorithms. Clearly, that overlap is confusing and counterproductive – if classical statistics and machine learning are to represent two distinct data analytic modalities, a particular data analytic technique can be a part of one, but not both modalities. That assertion is further strengthened by the well-known fact that while the general idea of learning is at the core of classical statistics and machine learning algorithms, the two domains have distinctly different conceptions of who is the learner, which is at the core of understanding how manifestly the same type of data analytic outcomes can be generated using very different approaches to extracting insights out of data.

The Heart of AI: Machine Learning

A subset of the broader category of AI, machine learning is how an artificial system develops its intelligence. The actual 'learning' part is encapsulated in algorithms, which are structured procedures for performing specific computations by following an exact and unambiguous sequences of instructions, geared toward specific end goals. Machine learning algorithms that are at the core of AI systems are capable of optimizing their operations to improve their performance by learning from data, which is at the core of the idea of developing 'intelligence' over time.

There are four distinct types of machine learning algorithms: supervised, unsupervised, semisupervised, and reinforcement. In *supervised learning*, the system is taught using explicit examples, which means that those algorithms require datasets that include not only inputs of interest but also clearly labeled outputs (commonly referred to as labeled data); implied here is some degree of causal, or at least correlative relationship between available inputs and outcomes of interest. Given the requisite data, supervised learning algorithms are then to find methods to determine how to arrive at those sample outputs using available inputs;[7] the resultant model can then be used to explain or predict outcomes of interest. In contrast to that, in *unsupervised learning*, the system (i.e., a specific algorithm) studies available data to identify patterns without the benefit of examples, in that sense, it uses unlabeled data. Here, the machine learning algorithm is left to interpret informational contents of datasets using only a combination of its built-in logic and patterns it identifies in data. As can be expected, unsupervised learning algorithms are used primarily for exploratory analysis, or search for previously unknown patterns and relationships.

Wedged between those two pure-type machine learning algorithms are the two hybrid approaches: semisupervised and reinforcement learning. The former can be seen as a crossover between supervised and unsupervised machine learning in that it uses both labeled and unlabeled data; the primary advantage of this mode of machine learning is that it allows the algorithm that is being trained to learn how to label unlabeled data. Reinforcement learning, which is the second of the two hybrid machine learning mechanisms, is somewhat different in its character as it is focused on maximization of the cumulative reward. In other words, it is geared toward artificial systems learning to take suitable actions to achieve the most optimal results.

Implied in the very high-level summarization of the four distinct variants of machine learning algorithms is the limited degree of human control over what machines learn and – to a large extent – how they learn (and thus improve over time). That is noteworthy because while the logic imbedded in individual algorithms is the logic of human programmers, suggesting that machine learning processes should be understandable to humans. Those learning processes, however, are stochastic, because of the interplay between built-in algorithmic logic and particulars of individual datasets. In short, learning by machine can take varied and unexpected pathways. Moreover, some of the more complex machine learning algorithms, most notably artificial neu-

---

7 It is important to not interpret the term 'supervised' learning to mean that which is guided and directed by a human analyst (it is not); as used in this context, supervised simply means learning from examples.

ral networks (ANNs), which are inspired by the desire to imitate a simplified version of biological brains' neural structures, process data in a manner that is simply too complex for cognitive human processing (an ironic contradiction). In the end, data analytic outcomes generated by machine learning algorithms are not human sense-verifiable, meaning they generally cannot be understood in terms of the underlying processes; in that sense, it is analogous to subconscious human sensemaking. After all, what is commonly thought of as intuition or gut feeling is in fact a product of subconscious information processing, and the manner in which many if not most of those gut feelings are generated is not any more explainable than the outcomes of complex machine learning systems.

As noted earlier, however, human influence goes beyond the design of machine learning algorithms themselves – data used by those algorithms are selected, and oftentimes curated[8] by human analysts. Here, perhaps the most visible illustration is offered by supervised and unsupervised learning algorithms. In the context of supervised learning, human analysts influence the learning process by choosing what data and what specific examples to include; that influence is less pronounced in unsupervised learning due to its reliance on unlabeled data, but those data are still chosen and possibly curated by human analysts. It is worth noting that those choices can lead to *algorithmic bias*, which is typically unintended systematic and repeatable departure from the intended function of the algorithm.

It is hard to resist the temptation to ruminate, if only just a little, when thinking about the idea of algorithmic bias. To start, that notion is somewhat reminiscent of the idea of reality, in the sense that it touches on the elusive distinction between subjectivity and objectivity. A particular object may exist independently of anyone perceiving that object, but that does not mean that the object is perceived the same way by all onlookers. Similarly, as a matter of practicality if nothing else, all algorithms need to be designed by someone or by some ones, and data used by those algorithms also need to be selected by someone or some ones, and it is simply not possible for those 'ones' to be everyone, which suggests that bias is an inescapable consequence of how we, as human society, do what we do. In short, when considering the idea of algorithmic bias, it is important to be explicit and purposeful in what, exactly, are the undesirable influences that should be identified and remedied. This is where machine learning and classical statistics intersect: In both settings, the ideas of representativeness and generalizability play an important role in assuring validity and reliability of outcomes.

---

8 As used here, it encompasses a wide array of data due diligence and data feature engineering steps, typically geared toward identifying and rectifying data abnormalities and irregularities.

Machine Learning and Standard-Setting

While AI-powered systems have been widely commercially available for quite some time (e.g., Apple's Siri, the first popular virtual assistant, was released in 2011), the 2020 release of OpenAI's GPT-3, a deep learning[9]-based system capable of writing computer code, poetry, creating reports, etc., sparked a wildfire of interest in AI technologies. Can AI-powered systems be used for the purpose of standards-based assessments? And more specifically, can they be used to derive valid and reliable benchmarks and baselines?

The difficulty that arises when trying to answer these questions can be encapsulated in a long-standing philosophical quip: How does one know that one knows? According to some philosophical perspectives, there is no definitive way to affirm knowledge of anything at all; Friedrich Nietzsche, a noted nineteenth-century philosopher, famously asserted that 'there are no facts, only interpretations.' Of course, much of contemporary science is rooted in verified objective knowledge, in which sense Nietzsche's claim appears to be clearly false. But the questions raised above are of an altogether different nature – rather than asking about objectively verifiable facts, they ask about the soundness of a particular *belief*, in this case, belief that AI systems are capable of generating true and dependable assessment standards. And in that context, Nietzsche's supposition rings true, as here it boils down to subjective beliefs rather than objectively verifiable facts. Some may indeed believe that AI-powered systems can be trusted to generate valid and reliable assessment standards because they have faith in those technologies; others, on the other hand, may be skeptical, usually not because of the technology per se but because of the inability to validate the efficacy of outcomes. For some, there simply is no trust without validation.

Recalling the logic of statistical inference-rooted approach to extracting insights out of data, results produced with the help of that general method are deemed believable because of the relative transparency of the underlying mathematical reasoning. Consequently, statistical inference-derived assessment standards, in the form of benchmarks and baselines discussed in the preceding chapters, exhibit high degrees of *face validity*, or the degree to which a particular approach appears effective in terms of its stated goals. It is important to emphasize the 'appears' part of that characterization – face validity is simply the appearance of truthfulness, as seen from the perspective of individual onlookers. To that end, some AI-generated outcomes may appear to be valid in instances where those outcomes – such as generative AI-written computer code or narrative summaries – lend themselves to the 'does it make sense' type of human validation. In those situations, even though the manner in which those outcomes were

---

9 Deep learning is a more advanced variant of machine learning built around the use of multiple layers (hence the term 'deep') of data processing and analytic sensemaking; it represents an evolutionary step forward when compared to single layer-based machine learning networks.

generated is unintelligible, if the outcomes themselves pass the human correctness or reasonableness test, face validity will likely attach. Other types of AI-generated outcomes, however, such as numerically expressed comparative assessment standards simply do not lend themselves to that type of validation, and thus may lack face validity. More on point, unintelligible processes generating uncertain outcomes can lead to cognitive dissonance, or a state of mental discomfort brought about by inconsistent or contradictory information. Cognitive dissonance can be especially pronounced in instances where AI-generated outcomes conflict with long-held beliefs; in those situations, even recognizing that those systems are capable of impressive feats, there is still awareness of their fallibilities, which amplifies the onset of cognitive dissonance.

The problem of believability of AI-generated assessment standards can be summarized with the help of a somewhat philosophical question: How does one assess the validity of an assessment standard itself? After all, standards are norms that are to be used in comparative evaluations, which suggest that standards do not lend themselves to being assessed. With that in mind, when a standard is derived using the transparent logic of statistical inference-based approaches (see benchmark-setting and baseline-setting discussions in Chapters 4 and 5, respectively) and the validity of that standard needs to be ascertained, that standard can be expected to derive its validity from the broadly framed logical and transparent – i.e., verifiable by human reason – derivation method, which encompasses data validation and preparation as well as subsequent analyses. Similar types of standards derived using machine learning-based computational approaches cannot be validated in that manner, which can raise acceptance barriers.

Machine Learning and Benchmarks

Implicit in the idea of comparative assessment, and thus in benchmarking, is that evaluation is retrospective with regard to outcomes of interest. For example, a recently concluded marketing campaign produced $X\%$ increase in repurchase rate of the product of interest; how does that result compared with industry average? Needless to say, that type of evaluation is critical to the practice of evidence-based management, and in more general sense, to the ongoing organizational learning – however, it only addresses one aspect of how modern organizations use data to support better decision-making. Just as important to organizational management is *predictive decision-making*, which is built around using forward-looking, probabilistic estimates of states or outcomes of interest as the basis for making decisions. When used in that context, benchmarking is commonly seen as a way of assessing the efficacy of predictive algorithms,[10] many of which are created using machine learning. And while on the surface that general usage context may seem quite like benchmarking past outcomes, there are in fact notable differences, which are tied to two distinct manifestations of timing misalignment.

The first of those is misalignment of the timing of data used to compute assessment benchmarks and data representing measurements of states or outcomes of interest. When benchmarking is used to assess past outcomes or developments, the benchmark and the phenomenon of interest are generally contemporaneous, which allows to control for the impact of random differences that may emerge simply due to the passage of time. In a very general sense, that type of benchmarking alignment is analogous to controlling for extraneous variation in the context of an experiment, where the goal is to prevent spurious influences from tainting experimental effects. However, when benchmarking is used to assess the impact of future events, there is a clear misalignment, as benchmarks need to be computed using currently available data with the intent of being used to assess the impact of not-yet-materialized outcomes. And in that particular context, random, passage of time-precipitated differences between past-rooted benchmarks and future-oriented outcomes of interest can be expected to arise, and such easy to overlook disparities may end up having a disproportionate impact on the efficacy of the resultant assessments, in a manner that is reminiscent of the butterfly effect.[11]

The second timing misalignment manifestation takes the form of compositional appropriateness of benchmarks as assessment standards. It is a comparatively more straightforward source of potential disparities, as it reflects the fact that in broadly framed behavioral contexts, everything is subject to change with the passage of time, including the definitional framing of benchmarks. For example, the composition of a peer group used to frame a particular set of benchmarks may be materially altered by developments such as mergers or rise of new companies,[12] to name just a couple of many potential sources of compositional peer group instability. It is intuitively obvious that those types of shifts may render past frames of reference less applicable as comparative assessment standards. Though of the two manifestations of timing-

---

10 The use of the term 'algorithm' can be confusing; as used here, it refers to specific machine learning techniques, such as neural networks or random forest, as well as to models generated by those techniques, where models are mathematically expressed generalized relationships that can be used to explain or to predict a phenomenon of interest. Thus, for instance, a random forest algorithm can generate an algorithm that can be used as a mechanism of making forward-looking predictions in regard to a particular outcome.

11 In chaos theory, it describes sensitive dependence on initial conditions, where a small change can result in disproportionately large consequences (the idea originates in the study of weather, where a butterfly flapping its wings has the potential to create tiny changes, which could alter the trajectory of much larger phenomena, such as hurricanes).

12 The 'rise' that is contemplated here is primarily focused on initial public offerings, which is selling of shares of (privately held at that point) companies to institutional and retail investors.

related misalignment it is an easier one to discern, it nonetheless creates a problem in terms of applying standards that are rooted in what is true today to assessing yet-to-materialize future outcomes.

Still, while the use of machine learning–derived benchmarks lends itself particularly well to predictive decision-making, that approach to baseline-setting can also be used in contemporaneous contexts, which is to say that it can be used to assess the efficacy of past outcomes of interest, where no timing-related misalignments are present. With that in mind, a closer look at the potential use of machine learning in benchmark-setting is warranted.

Machine Learning and Benchmark-Setting

It is to start with a brief methodological note: The distinction between machine learning and methods characterized earlier as classical statistics (so labeled here because their origins predate the computer age) is not always clear – in fact, some of the more commonly used predictive techniques, such as linear or logistic regression, are, in the eyes of many, considered to be both: classical statistical techniques and machine learning algorithms. The reason for that, however, has more to do with how those methods are 'packaged' as software products than with their mathematical foundations. More specifically, many commercially available machine learning software packages include methods like linear and logistic regression simply because those are widely used techniques, and not including them would likely adversely impact the appeal of those products. Such unfortunate blurring of the line of demarcation does more to confuse than it does to inform; the position taken here is that analytic techniques that impose specific assumptions on data (e.g., linearity, independence, and homoscedasticity) should be seen as classical statistical techniques, and those that do not impose such assumptions and are also built around the general principals of mathematical optimization[13] should be seen as machine learning algorithms.

In fact, not being rooted in specific assumptions regarding input data but instead utilizing *heuristics* of mathematical optimization[14] is a key advantage of machine learning algorithms, especially when dealing with voluminous datasets, which are

---

13 In simple terms, it is the selection of best elements, with regard to some criteria, from a set of available alternatives.

14 In a general sense, the term 'heuristics' is used to describe any approach to problem solving that is built around some type of a practical method; it could be as simple as a rule-of-thumb or a mathematical procedure that determines near-optimal solution to an optimization problem (the term is also used to describe mental shortcuts used to avoid cognitive overload). As used here, heuristic is a general approach to finding an approximate solution to a problem solving, especially in situations when classic techniques (i.e., those rooted in specific assumptions) or either too slow or altogether unable to find an exact solution.

commonplace nowadays. In a more practical sense, there are decision contexts, as illustrated by corporate mergers and acquisitions, that call for reasonable assessments (i.e., best informed guesses) of future states and quick estimation turnaround times – in those situations, machine learning algorithms often offer the most viable estimation options. The high-level general process of that approach is graphically summarized in Figure 7.1 using the general supervised learning process (it is worth noting that when considered in terms of such high-level process flow, the difference between supervised and unsupervised learning is reduced to the absence of 'Labeled Examples' shown in Figure 7.1).

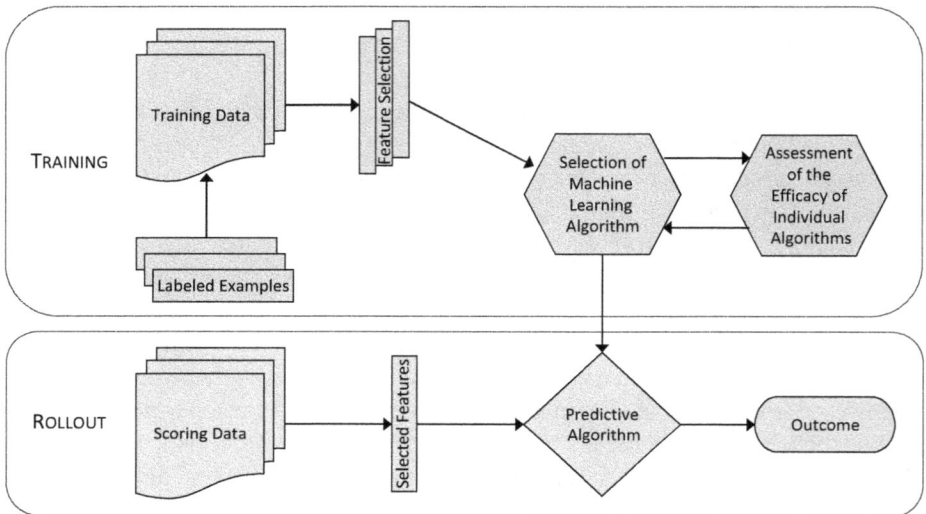

Figure 7.1: Supervised machine learning process.

Deriving forward-looking estimates with the help of supervised machine learning entails two multistep sets of activities: training and rollout. As illustrated in Figure 7.1, there are four key components that comprise the algorithm training process: (1) specifying data to be used in training; (2) creation and adding of clearly labeled examples of outcomes of interest; (3) selecting data features or variables to be used in the analysis; and (4) selecting a machine learning algorithm to be used.[15] The first three of those are data steps entailing the earlier discussed data selection and curation, and those steps are particularly critical in the context of machine learning. That is because those steps offer an opportunity but also present a threat, in that they open an avenue

---

15 For completeness, it should be noted that the selected algorithm could itself be a combination of several algorithms; the so-called ensemble methods generate the same type of results (i.e., models) using competing algorithms and then combine them to produce overall improved results.

for infusion of human interpretation of data of interest. Whichever machine learning algorithm is selected in the next step, its largely self-guided processing of data will be influenced – either positively, through sound data selection and preparation, or negatively, through biased data-related choices – in a way that will be very difficult to discern by looking at the outcomes.

Algorithm selection, which follows data selection and preparation, quite often entails choosing among competing techniques, as there are typically multiple methodological solutions to a given data analytic problem at hand. Selecting from a set of several available and applicable alternatives can be difficult, given the typically nuanced differences that separate competing methodologies; in view of that, in practice, selection of the 'best' approach often comes down to trying multiple algorithms and selecting the one that delivers the best predictive accuracy.[16] Given the speculative (i.e., probabilistic) nature of predictive accuracy assessment, meaning that there is a possibility that the cross-model assessment is inaccurate, rather than selecting a single algorithm, it might be deemed more appropriate to use the average of all individual models (that is essentially the logic of ensemble methods mentioned earlier).

It is important to keep in mind that within the confines of benchmarking, the analytic end goal is to derive an estimate of a measurable (i.e., continuous) quantity, thus the outcome of interest, and therefore the labeled examples, should be continuously measured quantities, such as revenue. Consequently, only those machine learning algorithms that can accommodate continuous response (i.e., dependent) variables should be considered; those techniques are usually grouped under the general umbrella of regression algorithms[17] (those focused on categorical response variable are known as classification algorithms), which can be confusing, given that there are also regression analysis (briefly mentioned earlier and discussed in more detail in the next chapter). To appreciate the distinction between a class of machine learning algorithms that are focused on regression, and a family of statistical techniques also built around the idea of regression, a quick regression sidebar might be helpful here.

In a general statistical sense, *regression* is a measure of the relationship between the value of the response variable and corresponding values of predictor variables. While the term 'regression' in everyday language means to return to a previous and less advanced or worse state, in the context of statistical analysis it refers to structured mathematical processes geared toward relating the variability of a state or outcome of

---

16 Although discussion of the specifics of that process falls outside the scope of this book as that topic is covered in detail in numerous other sources, the general approach to assessing and comparing predictive efficacy of supervised learning algorithms entail splitting (at random) of the training dataset into 'analysis' and 'validation' subsets, followed by training each algorithm on the analysis subset and comparing model's predictions to known, by virtue of labeled data, outcomes using the validation subset.

17 Some of the more popular supervised learning algorithms that can accommodate continuous response variable include ANNs, decision trees (most notably, random forest), and SVMs.

interest, i.e., the response variable, to the variability of one or more explanatory or predictor variables, which are believed to have causal impact on the value of the response
variable. Being able to do that is informationally attractive because it helps to explain
the behavior (variability) of the phenomena of interest and being able to explain the
causes of those oscillations then makes it possible to predict the future value of that
phenomenon. Depending on the measurement characteristics of the response variable,
which can be either continuous or categorical (and the latter can be either dichotomous
or multichotomous), and the nature of the target-predictor(s) relationship, which can be
either linear or nonlinear, there are numerous mathematical solutions to the problem
of estimating response-predictor(s) relationship, which manifest themselves in the form
of distinct variants of regression analyses, which are among the best known and most
widely used classical statistical techniques. Some of those techniques, such as linear
and logistic regression, are oftentimes also included in popularly disseminated lists of
supervised learning algorithms, alongside the likes of ANNs or support vector machines
(SVMs), even though, as noted earlier, linear regression is fundamentally different from
ANN and SVM in terms of its underlying assumptions and computational logic. In view
of that, when used in the context of (supervised) machine learning, the notion of regression is used here in reference to assessing the relationship between – in the case of
benchmarking – a continuous response variable and one or more (continuous or categorical) predictor variables using distribution-free (i.e., no underlying distributional
assumptions) and mathematical optimization-powered algorithms. That framing of machine learning regression expressly excludes the method of simple linear regression,
which in the confines of this overview is considered to be a part of classical statistical
techniques, a distinct and separate family of data analytic approaches rooted in specific
distributional assumptions and numerous other assumptions imposed on data.

Turning back to the high-level summary of the supervised machine learning process
depicted in Figure 7.1, the second of the two broad sets of activities entails 'rollout' of
the generalizable model built in the 'training' phase of the process. In more application-
clear terms, the explicit separation of rollout and training underscores the distinctives
of derivation of predictive algorithms, and the use of those algorithms as benchmark-
setting mechanism. When contrasted with the 'one-and-done' process of setting benchmarks using classical statistical techniques (see Chapter 4), the use of machine learning
algorithms expands it into a two-step – derive and, separately, apply – process. And
somewhat hidden from view here is that machine learning, as softly implied by the
name itself, is geared toward deriving data processing mechanisms, commonly referred
to as models or algorithms (as noted earlier, care should be taken to be mindful of the
different contexts in which the term 'algorithm' is used), rather than merely estimating
narrowly defined sets of parameters. Stated differently, while it is possible to use machine learning algorithms to derive benchmark values, doing so may come at a cost of
amplifying the shortcomings of that broad data analytic approach, most notably limited
data preparation, while at the same time taking limited advantage of its strengths, in the
form of ongoing and adaptive data processing. This line of reasoning also suggests that

investing in the process of training and validating a machine learning model to use it only once (since benchmark re-estimation, as discussed earlier, would call for a fundamental model re-development) may be quite inefficient. Models developed using the general process outlined in Figure 7.1 are fine-tuned solution engines that tailor their outputs to the specifics of individual datasets, a value proposition that is markedly different from a fixed formula of classical inferential statistical techniques discussed in earlier chapters; moreover, it may also run counter to the general idea of fixed standard-oriented comparative assessment. More specifically, in contrast to intentional and periodic benchmark re-estimation discussed in Chapter 4, where a particular set of benchmark values remains fixed across multiple usage situations (i.e., different datasets), the use of the same machine learning algorithm with different datasets would have the effect of recasting benchmark-setting into a process of fitting new sets of benchmarks to each individual dataset, and thus allowing benchmark values to be highly responsive to idiosyncrasies of datasets, effectively eliminating the fixed assessment standard.

Machine Learning and Baselines

Recalling the general goal of baselining, which is to derive temporally oriented assessment standards, machine learning is of interest in this context and is capable of forecasting values of magnitudes of interest across time. In terms of data, baselines are derived from temporal or time series data, which represent the measurement of states or outcomes of interest at different, and typically equally spaced points in time. In a more practical sense, baselining is geared toward identification of longitudinal trends that can support 'now vs. before' comparative assessments – given such limited focus, can machine learning be used to delineate long-term trends of interest? The short answer is a qualified 'yes,' but as discussed below, doing so may not be practically appealing.

In terms of methods, if the difference between classical statistics and purely machine learning algorithms is not always clear in the context of benchmarking, it is even less so in the context of baselining. The most widely used forecasting techniques are *autoregressive (AR) models*, of which there are several variants, offering progressively greater degrees of controlling for extraneous, trend-impacting influences. The basic AR model simply aims to extrapolate past into the future without explicitly accounting for any factors that may impact the direction of long-term trends; in other words, it aims to predict future values using past values, assuming some correlation in value series. Built atop of the basic AR model are two methodologically more advanced members of the AR model family: AR-integrated moving average (ARIMA) and seasonal ARIMA. The former aims to predict future values by 'explaining' current values using lagged versions of selves, while the latter also factors-in seasonal patterns. AR models, however, are not assumption-free – the underlying data are assumed to stationary, lagged values are assumed to be linear, and error terms (described in earlier chapters of near-term fluctuations) are assumed to be random or nonsystematic; in view of that, it is difficult to see AR models as pure machine learning approaches.

Narrowing the scope to distributional assumption-free techniques points to a general category of *recurrent neural networks (RNNs)*,[18] and particularly to a specific machine learning algorithm known as the long-short-term memory (LSTM) network algorithm. In simple terms, by retaining information about prior values, LSTM is capable of learning order dependence in sequential or time series data, in a manner that is generally analogous to AR models. The somewhat puzzling 'long short-term memory' characterization of the LSTM algorithm reflects the fact that RNNs have long-term memory in the form of long-term trend influencing weights that change slowly during the training process, but those long-term weights are also impacted by short-term changes. All considered, LSTM algorithms, and RNNs in general, are examples of a more complex, multilayered subcategory of machine learning known as *deep learning* networks. Those more evolved data processing mechanisms are more computationally involved and more self-guided than the traditional (supervised, unsupervised, etc.) machine learning algorithms; a high-level difference between 'standard' machine learning algorithms and deep learning is graphically illustrated in Figure 7.2.

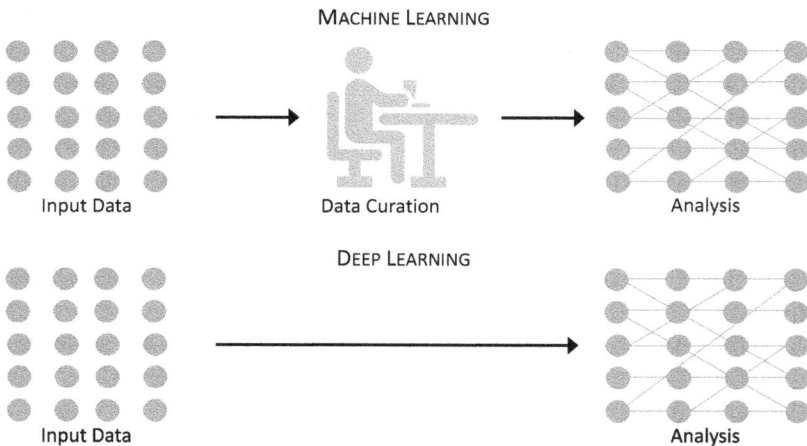

Figure 7.2: Machine leaning vs. deep learning.

---

18 In a very general sense, there are two types of ANNs: convolutional and recurrent. Convolutional neural networks (CNNs), or feed-forward networks, are well suited for spatial, textual, and image data, while RNNs, or networks that feed the results back into the network, are ideally suited for working sequential or time series data. The distinction between CNN and RNN is also reflected in a somewhat more general distinction between *recurrent* and *recursive* neural networks: The former, which entails repetition, is ideal for capturing sequential, as in time series, dependencies, whereas the latter, which entails a procedure that invokes itself, excels at tasks' hierarchical structures.

As shown by that very abstract comparison, the key difference between 'standard' machine learning and deep learning algorithms is that the latter obfuscates the need for data preparation. While in some situations that may be appropriate, even desirable, it is not in the narrow context of baseline-setting. Recalling the baseline-setting-specific estimation and parameterization considerations discussed in Chapters 3 and 5, it is easy to see that fully entrusting data-related choices to self-contained algorithmic logic of deep learning systems opens the possibility of data aberrations influencing baseline estimates in ways that are not easily discernible. And of course, given the unintelligible way RNNs generate their estimates, the so-generated outcomes are difficult to validate in a convincing manner. Interestingly, because deep learning algorithms aim to mimic the functioning of the human brain, their outcomes can be as hard to rationalize as human intuition.

There are also a number of more pragmatic considerations that speak against using deep learning algorithm for baseline-setting: Unlike the less sophisticated machine learning algorithms that can perform well with relatively small datasets (by today's standards that means thousands of records), to support their far more complex learning needs, deep learning algorithms require much larger datasets (i.e., millions of records); moreover, machine learning algorithms can be trained relatively quickly, typically as quickly as just a few seconds to maybe a few hours, while deep learning networks require much more time to be trained, ranging from a few hours to multiple weeks.

The picture that emerges here is that while broadly defined machine learning can indeed be used to generate assessment baselines, it may only be practical to do so in atypical situations. Setting the relative complexity of deep learning algorithms aside, the large volumes of data required to train those systems coupled with potentially long training time frames may render the use of those complex computational technologies to solve a fundamentally simple task of extracting analytically robust long-term trends out of time series data impractical, if not outright infeasible.

Chapter 8
Predictive Standard-Setting

The previous chapter's high-level overview of applicability of machine learning to benchmark- and baseline-setting broadened the methodological framing of how comparative assessment standards are derived by injecting the notion of forward-looking estimation. Building on that, this chapter delves deeper into that idea, by taking a closer look at the idea of predictive standard-setting.

Within the realm of statistical analyses, one of the most fundamental ways of grouping statistical techniques is along the descriptive vs. predictive dimension, with the former being focused on what is, and the latter peering into what is most likely to materialize in the future. The overview of various facets of benchmarking and baselining presented in Chapters 1–6 is implicitly descriptive, because it is rooted in using currently available data to derive estimates that are valid at the present time. That framing of benchmarking and baseline is well aligned with the goal of assessing past outcomes, as exemplified by a recently completed marketing campaign, but it is not well aligned with the goal of assessing expected future impact of contemplated courses of action. To that end, there are numerous decision-making contexts that require a more anticipatory or forward-looking assessment, which calls for future-minded evaluation standards.

Inferential vs. Predictive Standards

The conventional portrayal of comparative assessment is retrospective, and it is also rooted in the general notion of statistical inference. It is retrospective because assessment standards, here in the form of benchmarks and baselines, are derived from past events or outcomes; it is rooted in statistical inference because the process of measuring past events and outcomes is imperfect and thus yields imperfect data, and transforming those data into valid and reliable standards requires the application of sound mathematical reasoning. In that sense, probabilistic benchmark-setting and baseline-setting outlined in Chapters 4 and 5, respectively, can be framed as *inferential standard-setting*, and derivation of inferential assessment standards is well served by classical statistical reasoning and techniques. The reason for that is that retrospectively minded comparative assessment standards can be seen as expressions of distilling applicable and properly prepared data into averages (benchmarking) and long-term trends (baselining).

The inferential standard-setting approach is well suited to situations such as choosing among competing promotional alternatives, where the informational need at hand is to assess a set of competing outcomes in relation to applicable standards. But there are other decision contexts, which fall under the broad umbrella of specula-

https://doi.org/10.1515/9783111001296-008

tive actions, where competing alternatives need to be evaluated in the context of expected future outcomes. In that context, benchmarks and baselines need to be framed as *predictive assessment standards*. The general difference between inferential and predictive standard-setting is graphically illustrated in Figure 8.1.

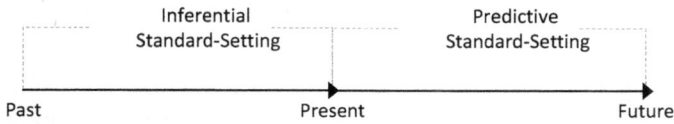

Figure 8.1: Inferential vs. predictive standard-setting.

It is important to note that, due to various types of data imperfections discussed in earlier chapters, both the inferential and predictive standard-setting are probabilistic processes because their values need to account for data imperfections. That said, predictive standard-setting is also impacted by forecasting error, which reflects general uncertainty surrounding the future.

In some respects, the idea of predictive standards might be seen as antithetical to the notion of standards, as an accepted norm. It is difficult to dispute the apparent contradiction; however, the idea of standards is looked at (in this book) from the perspective of that which can be used as the basis of comparative assessment, and in that context, the idea of standard is framed as average or typical value of something. In other words, it is not expected to be a universally acknowledged norm, just a point (in a generic sense) of reference that can be used in a particular evaluative context. That framing effectively recasts the idea of standards as localized, situational norms that reflect the specificity of information needs at hand, which is in keeping with the nuanced nature of organizational decision-making, and more broadly defined behavioral contexts.

Prediction and Forecasting

In a general sense, analysis of data entails peering into past trends and associations to unearth insights that can inform forward-looking decisions. Within that general context, there is a distinct subset of data analytic approaches and techniques that are geared toward estimating the likelihood or the magnitude of future outcomes of interest – that subset of data analytics is commonly known as *predictive analytics*. A closely related but somewhat distinct idea is that of *forecasting*, which involves projecting historical trends into the future. Although differences between those two areas can be easily blurred – for instance, forecasting is often characterized as predicting future values – there is an important distinction: When considered from the perspective of value estimation, *prediction* is typically framed in the context of the degree of certainty, e.g., a particular estimate is statistically significant at $\alpha = 0.05$, while forecasts are most commonly framed in terms of the level of uncertainty, usually expressed with the help of the root mean square error (RMSE) statistic. Moreover, softly implied in the prediction vs. forecasting distinction is the difference in the type of outcome and, by extension, in input data: Prediction entails estimation of the expected future value of a specific parameter of interest, which can take the form of probability of group membership, as exemplified by predicting which of several vehicle types (e.g., an electric, a hybrid, or a gas-powered) is a buyer most likely to purchase, or the magnitude of a continuous outcome, as exemplified by expected future spending level. Forecasting, on the other hand, is typically concerned with projecting historical trends into the future, as exemplified by forecasting the level of the stock market. All in all, prediction is ideally suited for spatial data and thus for benchmarking, while forecasting is well suited for temporal or time series data, and thus for baselining.

Whether it is characterized as prediction or forecasting, estimation of expected future values is inescapably speculative, which, as noted earlier, can be difficult to reconcile with the idea of assessment standards. However, it is important to keep in mind that, in principle, all data analytic outcomes are at least somewhat speculative, given that data tend to be incomplete and messy; after all, that was the key reason for expressing benchmarks and baselines as confidence intervals and confidence bands, respectively. Hence, the somewhat paradoxical value of data: While the vast and diverse varieties of data generated by the modern electronic infrastructure are informationally rich, those data nonetheless contain varying degrees of noise, which renders resultant informational outcomes approximately true, i.e., probabilistic. With that in mind, peering into the future adds an additional element of error stemming with projecting future values of states or outcomes of interest using information about the past. All considered, the reasoning that is at the heart of ideas outlined in this book is that of relative benefit: Systematic analyses of imperfect data that use methodologically sound approaches can be expected to outperform the alternative, which manifests itself as different forms of guessing; the basis for that assertion is graphically illustrated in Figure 8.2.

The abstract rationale depicted in Figure 8.2 captures the advantage of using predictive statistical models, such as logistic regression, commonly used to predict the probability of specific types of outcomes, with the goal of identifying entities (individuals, companies, etc.) that exhibit heightened likelihood of making choices of interest. The basic rationale for the use of those decision-aiding tools is that, even though the resultant predictions are imperfect, meaning that many, perhaps even most turn out to be inaccurate, the models nonetheless materially outperform the alternative in the form of random selection, which is effectively guessing. The context used in this illustration is prediction of the likelihood of individual companies incurring shareholder class action litigation (that example will be explored in more depth in the next chapter).

The two Cartesian coordinates graphs connected with the straight solid line labeled random selection show that, on average, a certain proportion of companies,

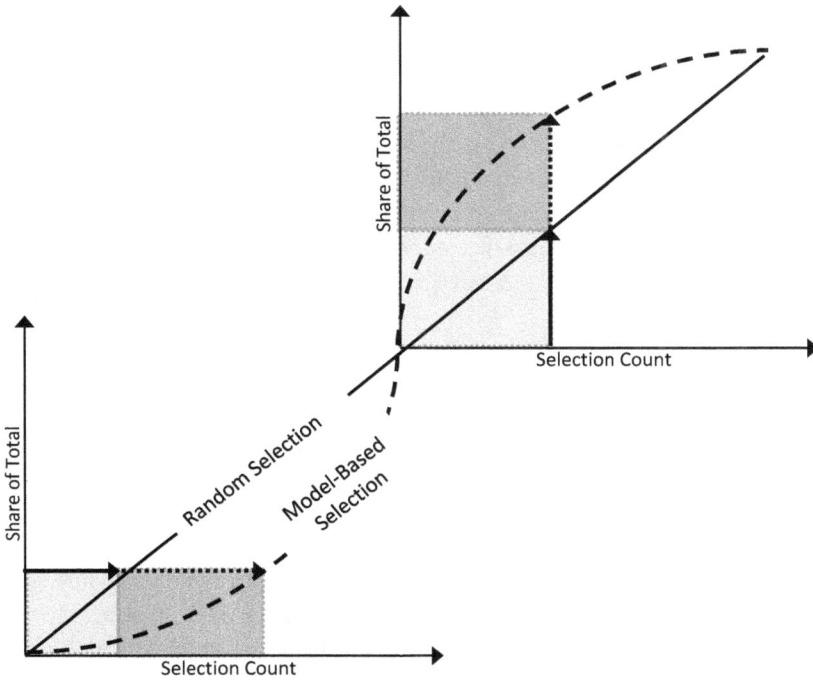

Figure 8.2: The relative benefit of data-derived estimates.

let's say 10%, can be expected to account for a proportional share (i.e., 10%) of shareholder class action litigation filings, as portrayed by the light-shaded regions in both the upper and lower graphs. The goal of predictive models, such as logistic regression, is to skew those proportions, in the manner shown by the dotted line labeled model-based selection, with the expected gains shown by the dark-shaded regions in both graphs. Here, the intersection of dotted curve and the dotted arrow (extending from the shaded area) shows the amount of lift generated by the model, where *lift* represents the increase in predicted classification accuracy over the 'no model' or random selection. In terms of subsequent performance measurement, a well-performing model is one that can attain the greatest degree of lift, which is where a relatively small proportion of the total number of companies, such as the 10% noted earlier, accounts for a disproportionately large share of the total number of securities class action filings (i.e., significantly more than its 'fair share' of 10%). In practice, it is common for such models to generate a lift of 3× to 5×, meaning that the top 10% of model-scored companies would contain 3–5 times as many lawsuit-prone companies as the randomly selected 10%. In other words, focusing on the model-identified 'most likely to be sued' 10% of companies will lead to 3- to 5-fold increase in predictive accuracy.

The key takeaway here is simple: While imperfect (most of the companies falling into the aforementioned top 10% of the 'most likely to be sued' companies), methodologically sound predictions and forecasting can be expected to yield material gains in the accuracy of future estimates of magnitudes of interest, when compared to the alternative in the form of random selection. Applying that rationale to the idea of standard-setting, when a situation arises that calls for assessment of the expected future impact of speculative actions, structured predictive modeling techniques can offer material improvement in estimating expected values of future states or outcomes of interest.

Regression as a Tool of Prediction

The example of comparative advantage of data-derived estimates captured in Figure 8.2 uses the context of logistic regression, a popular statistical technique used to estimate the likelihood of a binary outcome. Logistic regression is a part of a broad family of statistical techniques built around the idea of estimating the relationship between an outcome of interest, referred to as the response or dependent variable, and one or more predictor or independent variables that are believed to measurably impact the value of the response variable. Depending on the measurement properties of the response variable, which can be either continuous or categorical,[1] and the nature of the response–predictor(s) relationship, which can be either linear or nonlinear, there are numerous types of regression techniques, including linear, logistic, polynomial, ridge, and lasso. Specifics of individual regression techniques notwithstanding, utility-wise, statistical regression offer a way of explaining the variability in the response variable, which can then be used to make forward-looking predictions; consequently, the idea of regression is at the core of predictive standard-setting.

Of particular interest within the context of benchmarking and baselining is *linear regression*, which is one of the most widely used regression techniques (and also one of the simplest in terms of the underlying mechanics). There is, however, an important distinction between how regression is used with spatial and temporal data, or benchmarking and baselining, respectively. That distinction centers on the idea of *independence*, which, in statistics, means that the value of one data record does not influence or affect the value of other data records; that core assumption is common to most spatial data statistical techniques, including linear and other types of regression analysis. However, temporal/time series data are serially correlated (or *autocorrelated*, which is another commonly used label), which clearly violates the indepen-

---

1 Categorical outcomes can be further broken down into dichotomous and multichotomous phenomena, which in the context of regression analysis has important methodological considerations, meaning that there are methodologically distinct variants of logistic regression designed for use with dichotomous and multichotomous response variables.

dence assumption. Given that, analyses of time series data make use of a distinct variant of regression known as *autoregression* – rather than using a predictor variable to forecast the value of the response of interest, autoregressive models use past values of the response variable to forecast its future value.

Predicted Benchmarks

Recall that benchmarks are points of reference that represent typical or average values, and in terms of measurement, those values are expressed as a continuous numeric magnitude. Applying those foundational idea to forward-looking estimation, *regression analysis* quickly comes to mind as an appropriate method that can be used for predictive benchmark-setting. As noted earlier, regression analysis is a family of statistical techniques that encompasses about a dozen or so of distinct methodologies, each designed with different combinations of response variables' measurement properties (continuous vs. categorical; dichotomous vs. multichotomous) and response–predictor(s) association types (i.e., linear vs. nonlinear) in mind. One variant of regression analysis, *linear regression*, which was designed to assess linear association between a continuous response and one or more (continuous or categorical) predictor variables, is commonly used to predict the future value of continuously measured outcomes of interest, and thus it is well aligned with the general goal of predictive benchmarking. There are two general variants of linear regression: simple, which relates only a single predictor to the response variable of interest, and multiple, which simultaneously estimates the impact of two or more predictors on the response variable of interest. Given that the key estimation mechanisms are the same for simple and multiple regression, the ensuing overview focuses on the easier to describe simple linear regression.

Linear Regression

The logic of linear regression is built around the *method of least squares*; in fact, the two techniques are so intertwined that one is often used to define the other. For instance, the least squares method can be defined as a form of mathematical regression used to find the line that best fits a set of data. Figure 8.3 offers a graphical summary of the logic of the method of least squares.

As shown in Figure 8.3, the least squares method is a conceptually straightforward mechanism for finding a line that best fits a set of data; within the confines of simple linear regression, the least squares line, known as the *regression line*, is representative of generalized response–predictor linear relationship. It is represented by a straight line, the slope of which is determined by the smallest sum of squared errors, which are positive and negative deviations of individual values (shown as dots in Figure 8.3) and the overall average. The computational process involves squaring of posi-

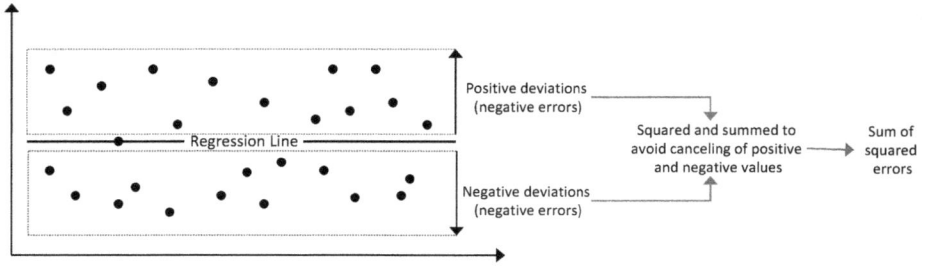

Figure 8.3: The method of least squares.

tive and negative deviations (to avoid canceling of positive and negative deviations during the summing process); thus, the immediate product of that step, known as 'sum of squared errors'[2] or SSE, is not directly interpretable. However, when divided by the number of records[3] used in the analysis, SSE yields the now-familiar measure of *variance*, computed as follows:

$$\text{Variance} = \frac{\text{SSE}}{n-1}$$

where SSE is the sum of square errors and n is the number of data points in time series.

The now-familiar computational progression of variance → standard deviation → standard error can now be employed to derive the standard error of predicted benchmark values, as summarized below:

$$\text{Std deviation} = \sqrt{\text{Variance}}$$

$$\text{Std error} = \frac{\text{Std deviation}}{\sqrt{n}}$$

where x_i is an individual measurement (e.g., location-specific employee theft-related shrinkage);is mean; n is number of cases (e.g., location-specific values).

Within the confines of predictive benchmarking, the so-estimated standard error becomes an important *unit of predictive imprecision*, which encapsulates the expected

---

2 It is worth noting that in statistical analysis, the term 'error' is not used to communicate a misstate but rather to denote deviation from the mean or other estimates.

3 The formulas used here use the number of records minus 1 or '$n-1$' rather than just the number of records because of the underlying assumption that in the vast majority of applied situations records used in analyses represent a subset of all possible like records, i.e., can be construed to be a sample, and $n-1$ (rather than just n) gives a more accurate estimate of the spread (i.e., it yield an unbiased estimate). In a more technical sense, where the number of records is framed as the so-called degrees of freedom, or the number of unconstrained data that can be used to compute a statistic, one degree of freedom is lost (before variance calculation) to estimation of the mean, which has to be done before variance can be computed.

amount of error in the predicted benchmark value. In an operational sense, it enables unbiased and robust transforming of inherently inaccurate exact value-based benchmark estimates into far more informationally robust interval-based estimates, using a simple formula of mean ± standard error × multiplier, where the multiplier is the number of standard errors, which could be 1 or higher (typically 2 or 3, depending on the desired degree of informational precision of the resultant interval). The end goal of this series of computational steps is to convert the exact value-expressed regression line as shown in Figure 8.3 into a confidence interval bound range that encapsulates the aforementioned predictive imprecision.

Simple Linear Regression

Turning back to the overview of simple linear regression and the method of least squares as the method of quantifying generalizable response–predictor relationship, it should be noted that while inseparable in some contexts, the notions of linear regression and the least squares method are phenomenologically distinct. In a general sense, linear regression is a broader concept that is focused on estimating of causal relationships between variables, whereas the method of least squares is the specific estimation technique used within linear regression (there are numerous variants of regression analysis (e.g., logistic, ordinal, ridge) and most use other than the method of least squares approaches).

Briefly described, *simple linear regression* is the simplest of all regression techniques, though the 'simple' part of the technique's name is not meant to communicate the technique's simplicity but rather that it relates only a single predictor to the response variable of interest (when more than a single predictor is used, the technique is referred to as 'multiple linear regression'). The response variable must be a continuous value, such as 'purchase amount,' but the predictor can be either continuous or categorical; also, the relationship between the response and the predictor is assumed to be linear. As used in statistical analyses, *linear* relation, which can be graphically represented by a straight line, connotes that the change in the response variable is constant across different values of the predictor variable. That is obviously a critical assumption, and its implications should be carefully considered, especially given that many observed phenomena are subject to law of diminishing returns-like effects. (There are more methodologically advanced regression models that relax the linearity assumption, i.e., consider nonlinear predictor–response relationships; application of those nonlinear regression techniques, however, is usually tied to nuances of individual datasets and thus falls outside the scope of this general overview.)

Keeping the preceding considerations in mind, the generalized form of simple linear regression can be expressed as follows:

$$Y = \beta_0 + \beta_1 X + \varepsilon$$

where Y is the response variable, β_0 is the intercept term, $\beta_1 X$ is the predictor X, and ε is the error term.

Recasting the formulaic expression shown above graphically offers a clearer illustration of the linearity of predictor-response relationships, and it also captures the earlier discussed (see Figure 8.3) logic of the method of least squares.

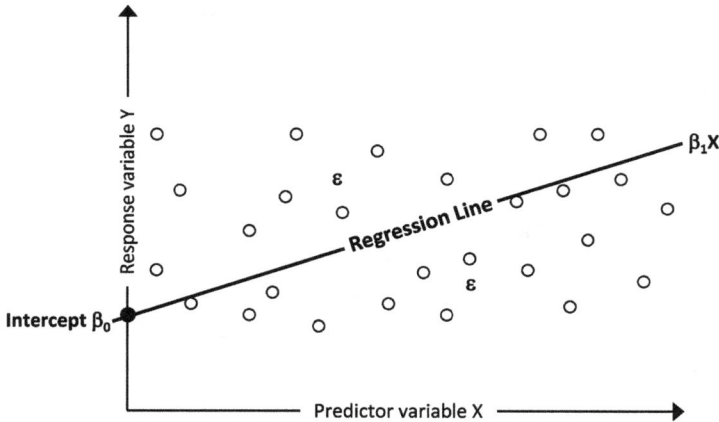

Figure 8.4: Simple linear regression.

Highlighted in the generalized graphical representation of simple linear regression shown in Figure 8.4 are the core elements of interest to benchmarking: The intercept term (β_0), which captures the expected value of the response Y variable in the absence of any impact of the predictor variable X, the regression line $\beta_1 X$, which captures the change in values of the response variable Y associated with changes in values of the predictor variable X, and short-term positive (up from the regression line) and negative (down from the regression line) fluctuations (ε). Within the confines of benchmarking, the β_0 intercept term encapsulates the expected or predicted benchmark value, and coefficients representing the impact of individual predictors (commonly referred to as 'regression weights'), e.g., $\beta_1 X$, where β_1 represents the expected incremental, i.e., over and above the value of the β_0 intercept, impact associated with predictor X, can then be interpreted as expected values of quantities being benchmarked. Lastly, the ε error term encapsulates the measure of estimation-related imprecision, which can be used as the basis for transforming chancy point estimates into more informationally dependable confidence intervals discussed in Chapter 5.

A quick point of clarification: It is important to not confuse the regression line, shown in Figures 8.3 and 8.4, with long-term trendlines and trended estimation idea that are at the core of baselines. Within the confines of benchmarking focused simple linear regression, the regression line captures the relationship between response and predictor variables as the function of values of the two variables; that relationship is assumed to be linear, hence it is represented by a straight (regression) line. In other words, within the confines of benchmark-setting, the regression line is a point-in-time estimate of the linear association of the joint variability of the response variable of interest and its predictor (only one in simple regression, and more than one in multiple regressions). A positively sloped, i.e., upward pointing (as in Figure 8.4) line communicates positive linear relationship, meaning as the magnitude of the predictor increases so does the magnitude of the response; the steepness of the slope captures the strength of that association, where the steeper the slope, the stronger the association. As can be expected, the reverse logic applies to negatively, i.e., downward sloping lines.

Forecasted Baselines

The idea of predicted standards is equally applicable to baselines, characterized earlier as level of uncertainty framed trends of reference that can be used to assess cross-time changes in states or outcomes of interest, even if the context of change over time might blur the distinction between retrospective and forward-looking estimates. The general rationale summarized in Figure 8.1 applies here as well: Retrospective longitudinal standards (i.e., baselines) offer the means of assessing change in the already materialized (i.e., past) outcome of interest, whereas prospective longitudinal standards offer ways of making anticipatory assessments. The task of forecasting baseline values can be carried out using one of several distinct applications of the general idea of statistical regression, keeping in mind the critical distinction between spatial (i.e., point-in-time, cross-entity variability) and temporal (i.e., cross-time, single entity variability).

Before delving into those methods, it is instructive to note a couple of foundational considerations, starting with the idea of *serial correlation* (also known as autocorrelation). Technically, it is the relationship of a signal (a discrete value at a point in time) with a delayed copy of itself expressed as a function of delay; in more everyday terms, it is a measure of the relationship between the current value of a variable of interest and the values of the same variable in prior time periods. The idea of serial correlation is critical to forecasting because it is indicative of the presence of discernible and thus projectable patterns in data series.

The second key consideration is the notion of *stationarity* of series. A stationary time series is one whose properties do not depend on the time at which the series is observed, while nonstationary time series' properties vary across time. Therefore, time series that contain long-term trends or seasonal or cyclical patterns, or both, are nonstationary, which means that the value of the series at different times is impacted by long-term and/or seasonal trends. Stationarity of series is an important forecasting consideration as well, because the accuracy of forecasts is inextricably tied to full and correct description of the structure and mechanics of time series.

The General Idea of Time Series Regression

In analyses of spatial data, time is effectively not considered since spatial data represent values of a phenomenon of interest at a point in time – in contrast to that, time is one of the key elements in analyses of temporal data; that difference is of core importance to how the general idea of regression is operationalized in the context of predictive baselining. In the computational sense, that difference is visible in the mathematical formulation of time series regression, which is as follows:

$$Y_t = \beta_0 + \beta_1 X_t + \varepsilon_t$$

where Y_t is the response variable at time t, $\beta_1 X_t$ is the time-lagged value of the response variable, and ε is the error term at time t.

Contrasting the above time series regression equation with its analog discussed in the context of spatial data, the absence of the intercept term is immediately apparent. The reason for that is rather simple. In the context of spatial linear regression, the intercept term has a clear and rational interpretation: it encapsulates the value of the response variable when values of all predictors are set to 0. An everyday example of that situation is offered by analysis of aggregate sales (response variable) where the value of the predictor – such as advertising spending – is set to 0; in that context, the intercept could be interpreted as the unpromoted level of sales, which is the level of sales that could be expected absent in any promotional spending (in addition to that, the intercept term also helps with the mathematical problem of finding the best fitting regression line). That type of an example, however, has no analog in the context of time series regression where the de facto predictor is time – setting the value of time to be equal to 0 is, in the context of time series data, noninformative, nor does it aid in the mathematics of regression line fitting.

Factoring those differences into the general, graphically depicted logic of simple linear regression is shown in Figure 8.4; time series specific representation of the logic of linear regression is depicted in Figure 8.5.

Another important consideration that also needs to be addressed in the context of using time series regression as a mechanism of forecasting baseline values is accounting for uncertainty of regression-estimated forward-looking estimates. Here, the earlier discussed idea of *confidence bands*, framed using the mean ± standard error × multiplier formulation (where the multiplier is the number of standard errors), can be used to reframe the implicitly point estimate-based regression line shown in Figure 8.5 into an estimate that expressly accounts for forecast's uncertainty, as shown in Figure 8.6.

The preceding overview was focused on the application of 'generic' linear regression models to time series data; as noted earlier, however, time series forecasting can also be operationalized using time series specific modeling techniques that fall under the umbrella of autoregressive models. The next section offers a high-level overview of those techniques.

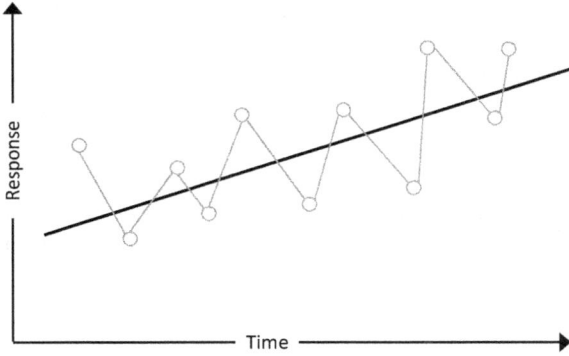

Figure 8.5: Time series regression.

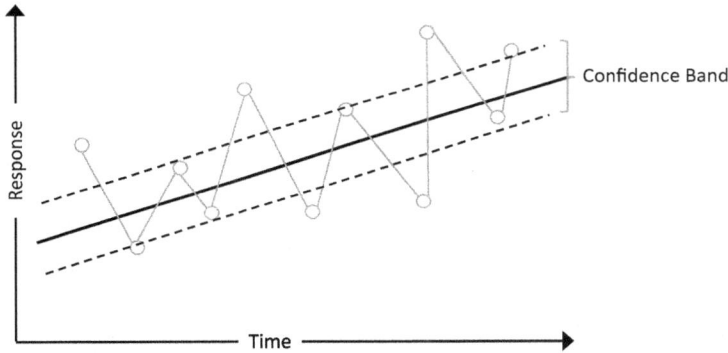

Figure 8.6: Time series regression confidence bands.

Autoregressive Forecasting Models

While similar in terms of general characteristics, linear regression and *autoregression* differ in some important ways: Most notably, linear regression aims to predict the value of the response variable using either one or multiple predictors – in contrast to that, autoregression merely extrapolates the patterns contained in time series. Stated differently, linear regression uses explanation as the forecasting mechanism while autoregression extends past patterns in phenomena of interest into the future. Implied in that contrast is that linear regression is well suited to situations characterized by rich data, or data that includes trend impacting variables, while autoregression is better suited for applications with more limited, in terms of informational scope, data.

However, limited informational scope is not tantamount to limited informational content. Recalling the three key components of time series – long-term trends, recurring seasonal and/or cyclical patterns, and random short-term fluctuations – data limited in scope might be informationally comparatively rich; in keeping with that, there are several distinct variants of the general autoregressive model that made different assumptions about data. The simplest, and typically the most widely used, of those techniques is the basic *autoregressive* or AR models. That foundational AR model assumes at least some serial correlation but no underlying seasonal or cyclical patterns, and thus views time series of interest as a combination of informative long-term trends and noninformative near-term random noise. Simply put, the basic AR model aims to extrapolate past trends into the future. In that sense, the AR model takes a literal view of time series: a sequence of time-dependent values that can be regressed on their own prior values.

In many situations, the basic AR model is simply too coarse to offer adequate predictive power – in those cases, one of several more evolved autoregressive approaches to forecasting time series can be utilized. The simplest of those is the autoregressive moving average, or ARMA, which merges the basic autoregressive (the 'AR' in ARMA) and moving average (the 'MA' in ARMA) models. Here, the autoregressive model makes predictions based on previous values; the addition of moving average adjusts the initial AR model using average prediction errors, which often results in better predictive accuracy.

A more methodologically evolved variant of the basic autoregressive model is the autoregressive integrated moving average or ARIMA for short. As clearly visible in the side-by-side name comparison, i.e., AR vs. ARIMA, the autoregressive integrated moving average builds on the basic logic of the AR model by adding two additional elements: The first of those elements is integration (the 'I' in ARIMA), or differencing of raw values to allow the time series to become stationary, which is accomplished by replacing the original values with the difference between the current (time$_0$) and the previous (time$_1$) values. The second add-on element is the moving average (the 'MA' in ARIMA), which incorporates the dependency between individual values and residual errors from a moving average model applied to lagged observations.

A still more evolved variant of the basic autoregressive model is the seasonal autoregressive integrated moving average or SARIMA. Building on the ARIMA approach, it explicitly accounts for the seasonal component of the series, which is the 'S' part of SARIMA. It can be seen as a sensitive, in terms of its trend-decomposing abilities, variant of the general autoregressive model, which, for data that are expected to include a persistent long-term trend and seasonal or cyclical patterns, should yield the highest forecasting accuracy.

Implied above is an evolutionary progression of the successive autoregressive models where the basic AR model represents the crudest, or methodologically least advanced forecasting approach, and SARIMA demarks on the opposite end of the methodological sophistication continuum. It is important to note, however, that the use of more methodologically advanced autoregressive models is only appropriate with data that can be reasonably expected to contain embedded elements, such as seasonality; in other words, in some contexts the rudimentary AR or ARMA models may yield forecasts that are as dependable (or as rough) as those generated by more methodologically involved ARIMA. All considered, the implied evolutionary methodological progression of the individual autoregressive models can be summarized as follows:

AR: Autoregressive (i.e., pattern extrapolation)

ARMA: Autoregressive + Moving Average

ARIMA: Autoregressive + Moving Average + Trend Differencing

SARIMA: Autoregressive + Moving Average + Trend Differencing + Seasonal Differencing

Figure 8.7 shows the graphical representation of the expected gains in predictive accuracy associated with the progressively more trend-nuance-sensitive AR → ARMA → ARIMA → SARIMA autoregression modeling progression.

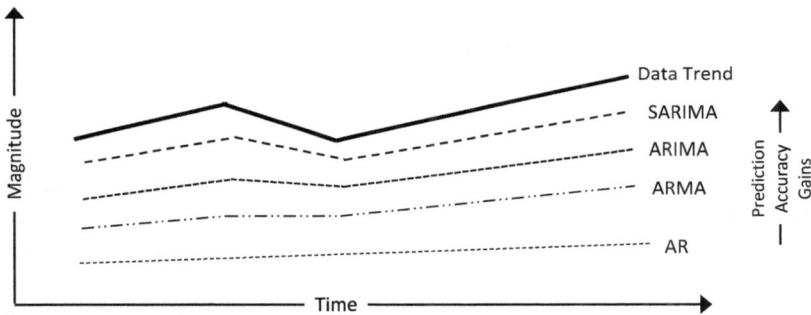

Figure 8.7: Expected predictive accuracy gains.

A consideration that should not be overlooked is that the choice of an autoregression variant should carefully weigh model specific expected predictive accuracy with characteristics of time series of interest. Although in the general sense SARIMA can be expected to yield the most accurate forecasts, it does not mean that it is always the most appropriate choice – if series of interest do not contain any discernible cyclical patterns, SARIMA will likely not outperform the comparatively 'coarser' ARIMA; in fact, it may perform worse due to the model algorithms heightened possibility of incorrectly interpreting some parts of random variability as cyclical patterns. Recalling the machine learning vs. deep learning distinction drawn in the previous chapter, all four of the autoregressive models are machine learning-like, in the sense that while their built-in data analytic routines are largely self-sufficient, they nonetheless rely on human analyst-led data selection and curation. At the same time, paralleling linear regression and other classical statistical techniques, autoregressive models impose explicit assumptions on input data: Data are assumed to be stationary, lagged values are assumed to be linear, and error terms (described in earlier chapters as near-term fluctuations) are assumed to be random or nonsystematic.

Some Usage Considerations

The idea of benchmarking and, to a lesser degree, the idea of baselining have been used in applied contexts such as organizational management for many years, but the way those notions are operationalized lacks consistent conceptual and methodological foundations. Commonly used as evaluative frames of reference, framing of those assessment standards is frequently reduced to accepted norms or so-called rules of thumb; when assessment standards are derived from available and applicable data, the underlying logic and methodological processes are not always carefully considered, and quite often vary across usage situations. At the same time, the well-known modern data riches are creating unprecedented opportunities to establish robust evidence-based decision-making culture, built around objective assessment of states and outcomes of interest, but that cannot happen without thoughtful rethinking of the very conceptions of benchmarking and baselining. That means that, first, in contexts in which objective assessment-enabling data are available, steps should be taken to move away from anecdotal norms and rules of thumb and toward objective, data-derived standards; secondly, conceptually clear, and methodologically sound benchmark- and baseline-setting foundations need to be developed and deployed. The ideas outlined in the preceding pages are aimed at those two broad objectives.

The overview of data-driven benchmarking and baseline presented in this book was inspired by the desire to offer conceptually clear and methodologically unambiguous mechanisms for deriving probabilistic – in view of imperfect data – evaluative reference standards. Central to those processes is the idea of expressing assessment standards of interest not as absolute magnitudes (statistically known as point estimates), but rather as probable ranges that explicitly account for the nearly inescapable informational imprecision of those values. That is an important point because unlike universally constant physical phenomena, such as the unquestionably precisely measured and unchanging speed of light, measurement of behavioral states and outcomes can only be deemed approximately correct, primarily because of data imperfections due to factors such as incomplete coverage or missing or incorrect values. Used here as an umbrella term, the idea of *informational incompleteness* is encapsulated in a simple assertion that not all that can be known about a particular behavioral outcome of interest is encoded and available as data; for example, sales data do not contain any direct measurements of buyers' attitudes or other emotional states. In short, while available data are highly informative, those data generally do not encapsulate all that can be known about a phenomenon of interest; at the same time, assessment standards (and other insights) derived from available data offer generally superior decision-making foundation.

Lastly, tacitly implied in the preceding overview is an important though not always clearly noted consideration of usage context. Data do not exist in a vacuum, and overtly similar data types may require nuanced analytic treatment to correctly extract and interpret informational content contained therein. In other words, to get the maximum informational value out of data-encoded outcomes or states of interest, it is essential to develop robust understanding of data generation mechanisms, as to a large degree, that understanding informs the key data utilization steps. For example, one of the staples of data due diligence and feature engineering is identification and remediation of outlying values; in some contexts – most notably, risk management – simply eliminating outlying values (a textbook remedy) may run counter to the informational needs at hand (e.g., sound potential impact assessment), which then may call for more out-of-the-box thinking on how to address that particular problem.[4] All considered, effective use of the ideas of benchmarking and baselining discussed in this book calls not only for thoughtful and carefully executed data analytic steps but also for a deeper understanding of the broader context in which those data are used – the next two chapters highlight two distinct case studies that illustrate those ideas.

---

4 In the context of risk management, where the goal is to obtain a realistic assessment of likelihood and potential severity of adverse developments of interest, simply trimming or outright eliminating outlying values would likely lead to systematic underestimation of the magnitude of outcomes of interest.

Part III: **Putting It to Work**

Chapter 9
Baselining Case Study – Macro Standards

If a picture is worth a thousand words, a good illustrative case study ought to be even more convincing. With that in mind, this chapter offers a case study that typifies the use of data-driven baselining in applied business analyses, in the context framed here as macro, as in high-level, general trends, standards. The decision-making context used here is that of risk management, a broad domain built around identification, evaluation, and mitigation of threats facing business and other organizations. More specifically, the case study is focused on what is known as executive risk, which encapsulates an array of legal accountabilities associated with duties carried out by directors and officers of (typically, public, i.e., with stocks traded on public stock exchanges) business enterprises. While incredibly important to senior organizational managers, the domain of executive risk is poorly understood by many others, at times even those charged with helping organizations assess and mitigate those risks. In view of that, the case study begins with a broad overview of the key risk exposure shaping considerations, which is then followed by a real-life example of available data can be used to help individual organizations objectively assess their exposures and identify the most appropriate risk response actions.

It should also be noted that the introductory, foundational overview of the basic concepts and considerations that jointly form the domain of executive risk is also meant to underscore the importance of developing a broader understanding of a phenomenon that is being, in this case, baselined. Data are not just numbers and other symbols – they encapsulate distinct elements of meaning, which cannot be fully discerned without the foundation of background knowledge.

The Broad Context: Security Class Action Litigation Trends

Among the most visible characteristics of large public business enterprises is the separation of ownership and management, a situation which creates an almost inescapable informational dependence of the former on disclosures by the latter. Framed variously as *agency dilemma*, principal-agent problem or agency theory, the investor-manager informational asymmetry can lead to conflict when objectives of the two parties are misaligned. More specifically, executive managers, who are typically corporate officers entrusted with day-to-day running of a company, and corporate directors, tasked with overseeing of executive managers' adherence to sound corporate governance practices, jointly referred to as corporate management, act as shareholder agents and are thus expected to make decisions that maximize shareholder wealth. That goal, however, may at times run counter to managers' desire to maximize their own wealth, which may compel them to make choices that suboptimize or even im-

https://doi.org/10.1515/9783111001296-009

pair shareholder value.[1] When shareholders have reasons to believe that management's disclosures were incomplete, inaccurate, untimely, or otherwise misleading, not just in regard to the 'what' of company performance-impacting decisions, but also of the 'why,' or reasons behind those decisions, and they also suffered economic harm (in the form of associated precipitous stock price decline) as a direct result of those decisions, they may take legal action aimed at recouping their investment losses. This general scenario is at the root of securities fraud litigation, a key manifestation of what is commonly known as *executive risk*, one of the most economically and reputationally damaging expressions of organizational risk.

Those fundamental, disclosure-related shareholder rights were established in the early 1930s (in the aftermath of the Wall Street Crash of 1929) with the passage of the US Securities Act of 1933 and the US Securities Exchange Act of 1934.[2] Jointly known as *securities laws*, those statutes require all companies traded on US public exchanges to timely, accurately, and completely disclose all pertinent and material financial details; failure to meet those obligations allows economically harmed shareholders to seek legal relief, typically in the form of financial compensation. Broadly known as securities litigation, the resultant shareholder lawsuits can be pursued individually by single shareholders or as a group known as a 'class,' the former known as securities class actions, or SCAs. Given the economic efficiency of class actions,[3] the vast majority of securities fraud lawsuits are SCAs.

When considered from an organizational perspective, *shareholder class actions* represent one of the most economically and reputationally damaging risks confronting directors and officers of public companies,[4] and the companies themselves. Though relatively infrequent – on average, about 200 of companies traded on US stock exchanges incur securities litigation annually – those suits can nonetheless result in substantial, i.e., multimillion, even multibillion-dollar, losses, not to mention negative publicity. To

---

1 A fairly common example is offered by revenue recognition: At the year's end, a company may opt to recognize a large part of revenue for a project that has been booked but not yet completed because doing so may lead to larger end-of-year management bonuses; if the project ultimately does not materialize, the company will then likely need to restate its earlier reported revenue, which then may cause a downward slide in its stock price, ultimately resulting in economic harm to shareholders.

2 The 1933 Act governs the registration of newly issued securities, while the 1934 Act controls trading of those securities; the former also created the US Securities and Exchange Commission (SEC), an independent federal agency tasked with enforcing of those and ensuring laws against market manipulation.

3 Securities fraud cases are lengthy (average duration is about 3 years from filing to disposition) and complex (require specialized legal knowledge and significant investments of time and effort) which renders the prosecution of those cases far more economically feasible for a large group rather than a single investor, unless, of course, that single investor is a large institutional holder or other, similarly resourced entity (hence it is a fairly common occurrence for such entities to opt out of class actions and pursue their claims individually).

4 Commonly referred to as Directors' and Officers', or D&O for short, liability, a subset of a larger domain of executive risk (for more in-depth discussion see Banasiewicz, 2015).

make matters worse, the traditionally financial disclosures focused scope of what triggers SCA is expanding, as what investors consider to be 'pertinent' and 'material' information is now beginning to encompass not only financial performance related disclosures, but also those addressing the increasingly more important environmental, social, and governance (ESG) considerations. In particular, organizational disclosures addressing policies and practices reflecting companies' sustainability related choices along with social fairness and equality related efforts are playing an increasingly important role. Consequently, developing well-founded expectations regarding the likely future impact of the threat of securities litigation on organizational management calls for an in-depth examination of historical trends and triggers of SCA claims, and an assessment of the changing nature of the broadly defined organizational citizenship.

Private Securities Litigation Reform Act

At the tail end of 1995, the US Congress once again delved into securities market manipulation considerations by enacting the Private Securities Litigation Reform Act (PSLRA), which was aimed at stemming frivolous or unwarranted securities fraud lawsuits alleging management misrepresentations. The key provisions of the Reform Act were centered on strengthening evidence required to successfully prosecute allegations of managerial malfeasance. More specifically, following passage of the Act, investors alleging management misrepresentations are now required to bring forth particular fraudulent statements made by organizational management, are further required to assert that those allegedly fraudulent statements were reckless or intentional, and lastly, also need to offer proof that they suffered financial losses resulting from the alleged fraud. Effectively, the enactment of PSLRA gave rise to what can be considered the 'modern era' of securities litigation.

When considered from the standpoint of benchmarking and baselining, by fundamentally re-writing some of the key legal provisions of shareholder litigation, the passage of PSLRA introduced discontinuity into long-term trends. For that reason, the year 1996 is now considered 'Year 1' in long-term shareholder litigation tracking, and pre-1996 outcomes are effectively ignored in all descriptive and predictive analyses focused on shareholder litigation.

The Modern Era of Shareholder Litigation

While the enactment of the Private Securities Litigation Reform Act (PSLRA) at the tail end of 1995 effectively redefined the key aspects of how, and under what circumstances shareholders can hold directors and officers of business companies accountable for the content and timing of pertinent and material disclosures, that was not the only material change to the fabric of executive risk. In fact, the so-called modern era of shareholder litigation has since been punctuated by numerous other legal develop-ments, each with a potential to also alter the long-term shareholder litigation trends. In that sense, while PSLRA can be seen as the point of origin of the 'modern' share-holder litigation trends, the subsequent legislative, regulatory, and judicial actions[5] can also factor prominently into continuity of long-term shareholder litigation trends. All considered, while the passage of the Reform Act of 1995 had trend-resetting im-pact, the post-PSLRA era has also been shaped by additional legal developments that further refined filing and prosecution of securities fraud cases – some of those devel-opments were in the form of US legislative acts, and others in the form of applicable US Supreme Court rulings, both graphically summarized in Figure 9.1.

U.S. LEGISLATIVE ACTS

Private Security Litigation Reform Act of 1995	Sarbanes-Oxley Act of 2002		Dodd-Frank Act of 2010	

| | Dura Pharmaceuticals 2005 Ruling | Tellabs Inc 2007 Ruling | Halliburton Inc 2014 Ruling | Cyan Inc 2017 Ruling |

U.S. SUPREME COURT RULINGS

Figure 9.1: Key securities litigation-related legal developments: 1995–2021.

Though an in-depth discussion of the federal acts and court rulings delineated in Figure 9.1 falls outside of the scope of this research, it is instructive to note some key takeaways. First, the two post-PSLRA legislative acts mandated a number of reforms aimed at en-hancing corporate responsibility and the clarity of financial disclosures as means of combatting corporate and accounting fraud (Sarbanes-Oxley Act), in addition to also re-shaping the US regulatory system in a number of areas including strengthening of inves-tor protection through more effective oversight of corporate governance and disclosure practices, and further enhancing management transparency (Dodd-Frank Act). Second, the core outcomes of the US Supreme Court rulings summarized in Figure 9.1 was fur-ther clarification of loss causation (causal connection between alleged management mis-representations and shareholder losses) and scienter (wrongful state of mind) principles, both of which are at the heart of securities fraud allegations. Building on the founda-

---

5 While congressional acts, most notably PSLRA along with the earlier mentioned US Securities Act of 1933 and the US Securities Exchange Act of 1934 form of backbone of legal obligations of corporate directors and officers, the US Securities and Exchange Commission (established as one of the provi-sions of the Securities Exchange Act of 1934) also has rulemaking powers; moreover, given that the United States is a common law country (meaning that the legal fabric of the United States is rooted in unwritten, in the sense of not being formulated as legal statutes, laws based on legal precedents estab-lished the courts), legal opinions passed down by the courts, especially the US Supreme Court, also factor into the larger schema of shareholder litigation.

tional provisions of the Securities Act of 1933 and the Securities Exchange Act of 1934, the legislative and judicial developments summarized in Figure 9.1 now shape the general outline of public disclosure related responsibilities of managers of publicly traded companies, as seen from the perspective of shareholder rights. It is important to note that the definition of 'disclosure' includes both written statements, such as the annual financial statements communicated via the SEC Form 10-K, and verbal communications, such as comments made during analyst calls. Moreover, the rights of shareholders in that regard are absolute, which means that no distinction is made between intentional and unintended errors, omissions, or misstatements – in other words, any written or verbal, formal or informal disclosure related error or omission can be seen as a violation of securities laws, even if no discernible intent to deceive is evident. All in all, understanding of those key legal considerations is critical to correctly interpreting long-term filings and subsequent dispositions of shareholder lawsuits, and ultimately, to deriving valid and reliable assessment standards.

However, that is not all. Even though any incomplete, misleading, or inaccurate managerial disclosure automatically creates potential legal liability, in order for shareholders to have grounds for initiating a securities fraud case there also has to be manifest economic loss, typically in the form of precipitous stock price drop that can be causally attributed to alleged management misrepresentations. In other words, shareholder litigation arises because of (alleged) managerial misrepresentations and a corresponding – i.e., having occurred within the same timeframe and being causally attributable to the said misrepresentations – shareholder loss; if shareholders did not suffer economic harm in the form of management information-precipitated share price drop they have no grounds for seeking compensation, even if management misstatements are clearly manifest. (The loss provision only applies to shareholder litigation; management can also be held legally accountable by regulators, most notably the Securities and Exchange Commission). The reason for that stems from the fact that ultimate goal of securities laws is to contribute to efficient functioning of capital markets by providing assurance of legal recourse to investors who, as company outsiders, have to depend on completeness, accuracy, and timeliness of investment-pertinent information provided by organizational managers.

Organizational Duality and Shareholder Actions

In the legal sense, a corporate entity is endowed with a person-like status; thus, it is separate and distinct from individuals that comprise it; at the same time, from the organizational theory point of view, a business organization is a group of individuals joined together in pursuit of commercial goals. One of the numerous aspects of that duality is that shareholder litigation can be directed either at an organization as a separate legal entity, or at individual organizational decision-makers, typically the key corporate officers and directors (or at both, as is often the case in securities fraud litigation). Moreover, as noted earlier, while shareholder lawsuits tend to be focused on compensation for incurred economic damages, they can also seek changes in policy or personnel, stemming from shareholders' belief that managers' actions are causing harm to the organization itself. The result is a multiplicity of shareholder disputes and securities litigation actions, which includes the above discussed class action securities fraud suits, as well as derivative litigation or regulatory enforcement actions, typically by the Securities and Exchange Commission. While all of those different manifestations of what is broadly known as executive risk can have significant economic and reputational impact, of interest to this research are just the economic damage-focused SCA lawsuits.

Reliance and Materiality

As noted earlier, the two key securities fraud allegation triggers are the ideas that (1) shareholders relied on the allegedly incorrect, misleading, or untimely disclosures, and (2) that those disclosures were material to their decision-making. Recognizing the difficulty – in reality, practical near-impossibility – of convincingly establishing investor-level reliance on incorrect, misleading, or incomplete management disclosures, while at the same time also discerning the degree of materiality of any such misinformation, adjudicators[6] of securities fraud allegations have been relying on a broad legal doctrine known as fraud-on-the-market. It holds that price of a security traded on an efficient market reflects all public material information, thus any material misrepresentations can be expected to translate into substantive change in investors' evaluations of the company's past performance and/or its future prospects. In short, once made public, management disclosures are assimilated by the marketplace and all market participants are then assumed to rely on that information. Implied in the idea of efficient capital markets' rapid incorporation of pertinent information is that revisions of substantive financial measures can be expected to have considerably more pronounced impact on investors' evaluation of a stock's investment-worthiness than 'cosmetic' corrections, such as those addressing nonmaterial typographical and other stylistic errors. Moreover, within the realm of substantive revisions, direction and magnitude of initial misrepresentations further moderate their impact – as can be expected, magnitudinally large negative corrections, as exemplified by steep downward revisions of earlier reported profitability measures, will have far more profound impact on investor evaluations than comparatively modest revisions of the same outcomes.

---

6 In the post-PSLRA era just federal courts, until the 2018 US Supreme Court's *Cyan v. Beaver County Employees Retirement Fund* ruling which expanded it to also include state courts (as in the pre-PSLRA era).

Outcome Scenarios

The brief schematic of securities fraud litigation would not be complete without briefly outlining the key case disposition outcomes. In principle, securities fraud cases that are not initially dismissed[7] (typically due to insufficient evidence) are either tried in court (which can lead to a jury or bench verdict) or are settled out of court. Interestingly, of the more than 6,000 individual SCAs that have been filed in the post-PSLRA era (Securities Class Action Clearinghouse, 2022), a grand total of just 21 cases went to trial – of those, only 14 have been tried to a verdict, while the remaining 7 were settled out of court prior to reaching a verdict. Hence even taking into account that roughly 40% of initial securities fraud allegations are dismissed, a conservative estimate of a securities fraud case being tried to a verdict is trivially small, roughly 1-in-250 cases, or 0.4% (14/(6,100 × 0.6)). In view of that, quantifying the threat of shareholder litigation is ultimately focused on tracking of SCA filings, which reflects the frequency and SCAs, and settlements, which captures the severity dimension of that facet of executive risk.

The brief synopsis of the key legal considerations that give rise to shareholder lawsuits is an example of what was earlier characterized as 'usage context.' When considered in the context of three distinct components of time series data – i.e., long-term trends, seasonality and/or cyclicality, and short-term, irregular variation – understanding of usage context is notionally reminiscent of discerning seasonality or cyclicality in data series, in the sense that it offers a lens through which cross-time variability can, really should, be examined. In short, derivation of valid and reliable baselines and benchmarks is contingent on that level of understanding of data-encoded outcome patterns. Quite often, overtly simple looking data call for a surprising degree of nuanced interpretation.

Key Shareholder Litigation Trends

SCAs are often characterized as low frequency, high impact events. On average, a company traded on a public US exchange (to be subject to the US securities laws, a company does not need to be domiciled in the United States, it just needs to have securities traded on a US stock exchange) faces a roughly 4% chance of incurring securities litigation, and the median settlement cost is about $8,750,000; factoring-in defense costs (given the nuanced and complex nature of SCA cases, even companies with sizable in-house legal staffs tend to use specialized outside law firms), estimated to aver-

---

7 According to a widely used industry benchmark, about 40% of initial SCA filings are dismissed during the initial discovery, though at least some of those initially dismissed cases are subsequently amended and re-filed.

age about 40% of settlement costs, the total median SCA cost is about $12,250,000. Those are just the economic costs – securities litigation also carries substantial though hard to quantify reputational costs, as being accused financial fraud often brings with it waves of adverse publicity.

In more tangible terms, according to the Securities Class Action Clearinghouse (2022), in the 25-year, post-PSLRA span from 1996 to 2021 there have been a total of 6,118 SCAs filed in federal courts; to-date (some of the more recent cases are still ongoing), 2,352 settlements arouse out of those lawsuits, adding up to a grand total of more than $127.5 billion. Those 25-year aggregates hide considerable cross-time and cross-industries variability, which is explored in more detail below, as a step toward uncovering potential future shareholder litigation trajectories.

Aggregate Frequency and Severity

The preceding overview suggests that the two core SCA tracking metrics are frequency, or 'how often,' and severity, or 'how much.' Starting with the former, Figure 9.2 shows the year-by-year (using the lawsuit filing date as the assignment basis) distribution of the 6,118 SCAs that have been recorded in the twenty-five-year span between 1996 and 2021; the dark-shaded bars highlighting years 1996, 2002, 2005, 2007, 2010, 2014, and 2017 relate the key post-PSLRA US legislative acts and the US Supreme Court rulings, summarized earlier in Figure 9.1, to the annual SCA counts, as a mean of visually exploring potential associations.

One of the most striking informational elements of the summary of annual SCA frequencies is the exceptionally high 2001 count (498 cases). Buoyed by a sudden influx of the so-called IPO laddering[8] cases which followed on the heels of bursting of the dot-com bubble of the early Internet era (between 1995 and 2000) characterized by excessive speculation of Internet-related companies, year 2001 set the all-time record for the number of securities fraud cases. Setting that single anomalous year aside, the second key takeaway is a distinct upward-sloping ebb and flow pattern, suggesting steady cross-time growth in average annual SCA frequency. However, there appears to be no visually obvious association between the incidence of securities fraud litigation and the distinct SCA-related legislative and legal developments (timing of which is highlighted by the dark-shaded bars in Figure 9.2). A potential alternative explanation of the gradual uptick in the annual incidence of shareholder litigation might be the gradual broadening of the scope of disclosure materiality. More specifically, traditionally rooted almost exclusively in financial performance measures, the definition of what consti-

---

8 Initial Public Offering, opening shares of a private corporation to the public in a new stock issuance. 'Laddering' is an illegal practice of offering a below-market price to investors prior to the IPO if those same investors agree to buy shares at a higher price after the IPO is completed.

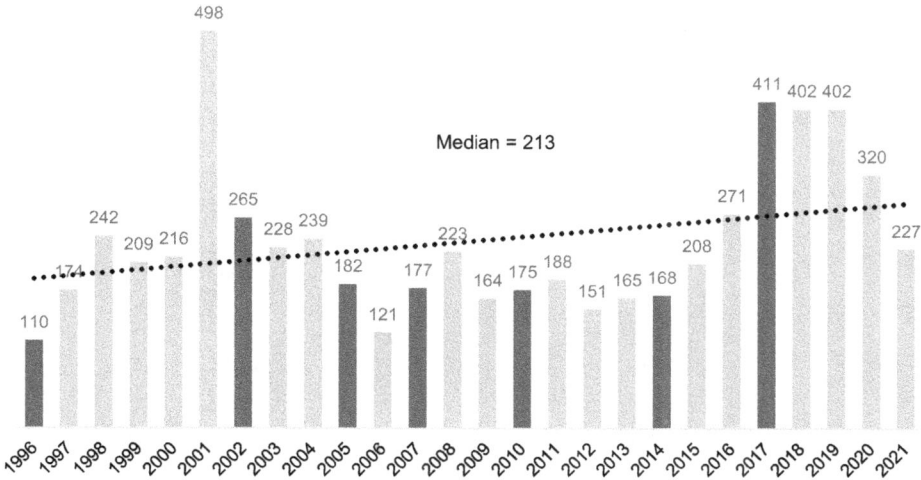

Figure 9.2: Annual SCA frequency: 1996–2021.

tutes 'material disclosure' is now beginning to encompass nonfinancial environmental, social justice, and governance, jointly known as ESG, considerations, resulting in public companies having to content with a broader array of potential securities litigation triggers, ultimately manifesting itself in higher average frequency of SCA litigation.

A similar, ebb and flow upward trending pattern characterizes the second key facet of shareholder litigation – severity, graphically summarized in Figure 9.3.[9] There are two key takeaways here: First, there again appears to be no obvious impact of the individual legal developments summarized in Figure 9.1 on the median settlement value. Second, there is a pronounced upward drift in annual median settlement amounts; however, that conclusion warrants closer examination in view of the potentially moderating impact of company size, which is rooted in the positive correlation between the magnitude of SCA settlements and the size of settling companies, as measured by market capitalization. More specifically, for all 1996–2021 SCA settlements ($n = 2,352$) for which market capitalization value was available around the time of settlement announcement ($n = 1,373$), the value of the Pearson correlation between Settlement Amount and Market Capitalization was .21 ($p < 0.01$). This empirically validated but also intuitively obvious association (i.e., larger company means potentially larger aggregate shareholder loss) suggests that the year-by-year variability in size-based mix of companies may have a material impact on average annual settlement values. Figure 9.4 offers a graphical assessment of that assertion.

---

9 The settlement part of the analysis encompasses reaches back to 1998, not 1996, because that was the first year for which analytically meaningful number of settlements for post-PSLRA shareholder class actions was available.

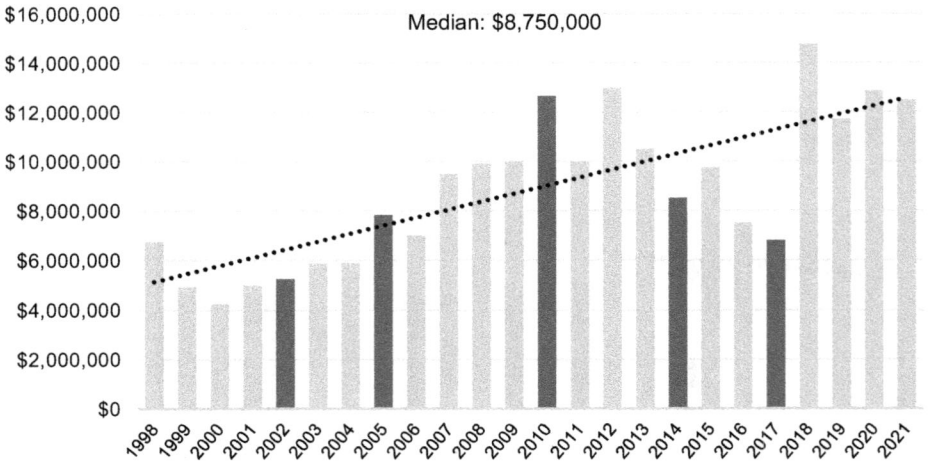

Figure 9.3: Annual median SCA settlements.

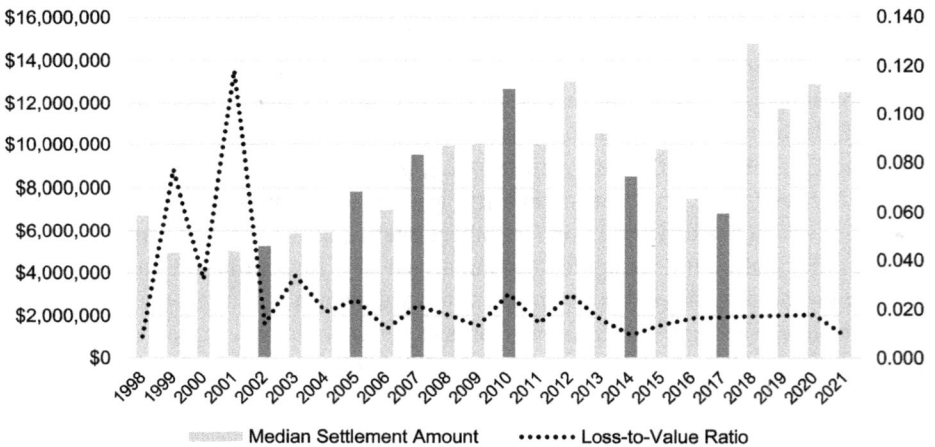

Figure 9.4: Median SCA settlement amount vs. loss-to-value ratio.

The trendline in Figure 9.4 depicts the relationship between loss-to-value ratio, which captures the relationship between the magnitude of SCA restatements and the magnitude of the corresponding market capitalization values, and the annual median SCA settlement values. The early, i.e., 1998 through about 2003, volatility can be largely attributed to a cluster of some of the most egregious, in terms of the underlying offenses as well as the resultant SCA settlements, examples of securities fraud: Enron, WorldCom, and Tyco International, all three of which came to light in 2001 and 2002 and resulted in the three largest-ever SCA settlements.[10] That early volatility aside, the overall conclusion that emerges from the long-term trend, and particular the most recent several years, is that there is a surprisingly stable relationship between the size of SCA settlements and the magnitude of the corresponding market capitalization, suggesting that the upward median settlement value trend in Figure 9.3 is really a manifestation of steadily increasing median market capitalizations.

Digging Deeper

Examination of aggregate frequency and severity, 25-year-long trends can be a source of informative topline insights, but may also obscure more nuanced effects, such as cross-industry differences. Moreover, conclusions drawn from long-term trends also implicitly discount the importance of recency, or the closeness of past outcomes, which can reduce the predictive power of those conclusions by blending the relatively recent patterns with comparatively older ones. Motivated by those considerations, the ensuing analyses aim to disaggregate the frequency and severity trends summarized in Figures 9.2–9.4 by delving into cross-industry differences in the context of a shorter timeframe.

Industry Definition and Data Recency

The notion of 'industry' is so widely used and familiar that most rarely stop to consider the basis for how industries are defined – those who look into that question invariably encounter an unexpected level of ambiguity. The reason for that is that there are numerous industry classification standards that have been developed over the past several decades by entities that span national governments, transnational bodies, and private organizations. National government-drafted industry classification schemas include the Standard Industrial Classification (the oldest industry classification taxonomy and the source of the ubiquitous SIC codes) created by the US government, the North American Industry Classification System developed by the US, Canadian and Mexican governments (intended to replace the SIC system of codes), the United Kingdom Standard Industrial Classification of Economic Activities drafted by the United Kingdom government, the Swedish Standard Industrial Classification developed by the government of Sweden, Australian and New Zealand Standard Industrial Classification created by governments of Australia and New Zealand, and the Euro-

---

10 The $7.2 billion Enron Corp. settlement is the largest-ever SCA loss; the WorldCom Inc. ($6.12 billion) and Tyco International ($3.2 billion) settlements are the second and third costliest; both Enron and WorldCom collapsed under the weight of their accounting scandals.

pean Union-developed Statistical Classification of Economic Activities in the European community. Transnational bodies-conceived taxonomies include International Standard Industrial Classification of All Economic Activities, and United Nations Standard Products and Services Code, both created by the United Nations. And lastly, there are numerous private interest-developed taxonomies, a group which is perhaps best exemplified by Standard & Poor's and MSCI co-developed Global Industry Classification Standard, and FTSE-developed Industry Classification Benchmark. Table 9.1 offers a summary of the ten best-known industry classification taxonomies, as seen from the perspective of applied, US-based users.

The competing taxonomies summarized in Table 9.1 differ, most notably, in terms of their orientation, which tends to be either production- (process similarities) or market- (demand characteristics) centric, geographic scope (national vs. global), classification units (companies, establishments, business lines, securities), and the number of hierarchy levels. As suggested by the substantial cross-taxonomy differences summarized in Table 9.1, the choice of industry classification schema can lead to conflicting descriptions of product market competition and firm characteristics across product market competition levels. In fact, different classification systems are seldom consistent for a given firm – for instance, a study by Krishnan & Press[11] found that mapping four-digit SIC codes to five- or six-digit NAICS (which was introduced in 1997 expressly to replace the SIC structure dating back to the 1930s) produced only 41.9% agreement; in a similar study, Bhojraj and colleagues[12] found only 56% agreement between GICS and SIC classifications. The absence of singular, universal framing of 'industry' is troubling, particularly considering the potential for substantive differences in the common practice of industry benchmarking. In fact, a recent study concluded that using different industry classification schema can produce material differences in benchmarking conclusions.

In view of the difficulty of choosing among so many comparably taxonomically robust schemas producing materially different industry groupings, the approach taken in this research is to instead follow the approach used by the US Securities and Exchange Commission (SEC), the key US securities laws enforcement agency. The SEC requires all registrants to identify a single primary SIC code, following which it divides all public filings, and thus the entities submitting those filings, into seven distinct segments: energy and transportation, financial services, life sciences, manufacturing, real estate and construction, technology, and trade and services. The resultant SIC-based groupings are analogous to *sectors*, which are the most aggregate company clusters (each encompasses multiple industries) used by NAICS, GICS and other taxonomies; the use of sec-

---

11 Krishnan, J., & Press, E. (2003). 'The North American industry classification system and its implications for accounting research,' *Contemporary Accounting Research*, 20(4), 685–717.
12 Bhojraj, S., Lee, C.M, & Oler, D.K. (2003). 'What's my line? A comparison of industry classification schemes for capital market research,' *Journal of Accounting Research*, 41, 745–773.

Table 9.1: Best-Known Industry Classification Taxonomies.

Industry Classification Scheme	Year Introduced	Orientation	Geographic Scope	Classification Units	Hierarchy Levels	Update
Standard Industrial Classification (SIC)	1938–1940	Production and Market	United States	Establishments	4	Last updated* in 1987
International Standard Industrial Classification (ISIC)	1948	Production	Global	Establishments	4	Last updated in 2006
North American Industry Classification System (NAICS)	1997	Production	North America	Establishments	5	Every 5 years
Global Industry Classification Standard (GICS)	1999	Market	Global (120 countries)	Companies; Securities	4	Annual reviews
Morningstar Category Global Equity Classification Structure	2000	Market	Global	Companies; Securities	4	Ad hoc
Industry Classification Benchmark (ICB)	2001	Market	Global (75 countries)	Companies; Securities	4	Biannual reviews
FactSet Revere Business and Industry Classification System (RBICS)	2002	Market	Global (78 countries)	Companies; Securities; Business lines	6	Annual reviews
Thomson Reuters Business Classification (TRBC)	2004	Market	Global (130 countries)	Companies; Securities	5	Ad hoc
Bloomberg Industry Classification System (BICS)	2011	Market	Global	Companies; Securities; Business lines	7	Annual reviews
Sustainable Industry Classification System (SICS)	2012	Sustainability	United States	Companies	2	Ad hoc

*By the US Department of Labor, which maintained the official SIC Code system comprised of 1,514 codes (across the 2, 3, and 4-digit levels); the more granular (6,7, and 8-digit) Extended SIC Codes have since been developed by private companies – those are updated on continuous basis.

tors is also analytically appropriate in view of the relatively small average annual SCA filing counts (median = 213), and even smaller settlement counts.

The second key trend disaggregation consideration is *recency* of data, or the closeness of SCA filings and settlements. The broad 25-year perspective captured in Figures 9.2–9.4 confounds numerous legal developments (summarized in Figure 9.1) with broad economic events, such as the 2007–2008 global financial crisis, and more general societal trends, such as the relatively recent intensification of interest in the impact of ESG considerations. Moreover, it also dilutes micro trend changes – for instance, while it is well-established that median based estimates are unaffected by outliers, it might be less obvious that data time horizon choices can also have a pronounced impact on statistical estimates. For example, the median number of SCA filings for the full 1996–2021 25-year period is 213 (see Figure 9.2), whereas the median number of SCAs for just the most recent 10 years (2012 through 2021) is 249. In short, given that recent outcomes are generally more indicative of the future, the data recency question needs to be carefully considered. But what, exactly, should be the line of demarcation between data that are recent and those that are not? While it is not always easy to arrive at a truly objective answer to that important question, analyses of legal trends are commonly tied to statutes of limitations of applicable laws, which offers a convenient basis for objectively delimiting between 'recent' and 'old' data. For securities laws, the statute of limitations applicable to civil monetary penalties (manifesting themselves in the form of the earlier discussed SCA settlements) was set by the US Supreme Court in its 2013 ruling[13] to be 5 years from the date of the underlying violation. Using that as the basis for data recency, the ensuing analysis will focus on 2017–2021 SCA filings and settlement trends.

Recent Cross-Industry SCA Trends

Zeroing-in on the most recent 5 years of SCA filings and settlements (each selected separately, i.e., all SCA 2017–2021 filings and, separately, all SCA 2017–2021 settlements), in conjunction with also breaking down the all-companies aggregate trend into seven SEC-defined industry sectors paints a picture of considerable cross-segment variability, as graphically summarized in Figure 9.5.

Erudite Analytics,' a consultancy, proprietary database of 8,965 public (i.e., traded on US stock exchanges) companies, each labeled with self-designated primary SIC code, coupled with SEC-reported total annual SEC Form 10-k filings, were utilized to develop the base annual company counts, onto which the Securities Class Action Clearinghouse-sourced listing of securities fraud litigation filings was overlaid, ultimately giving rise to SCA incidence rates summarized in Figure 9.5.

---

13 *Gabelli v. Securities and Exchange Commission.*

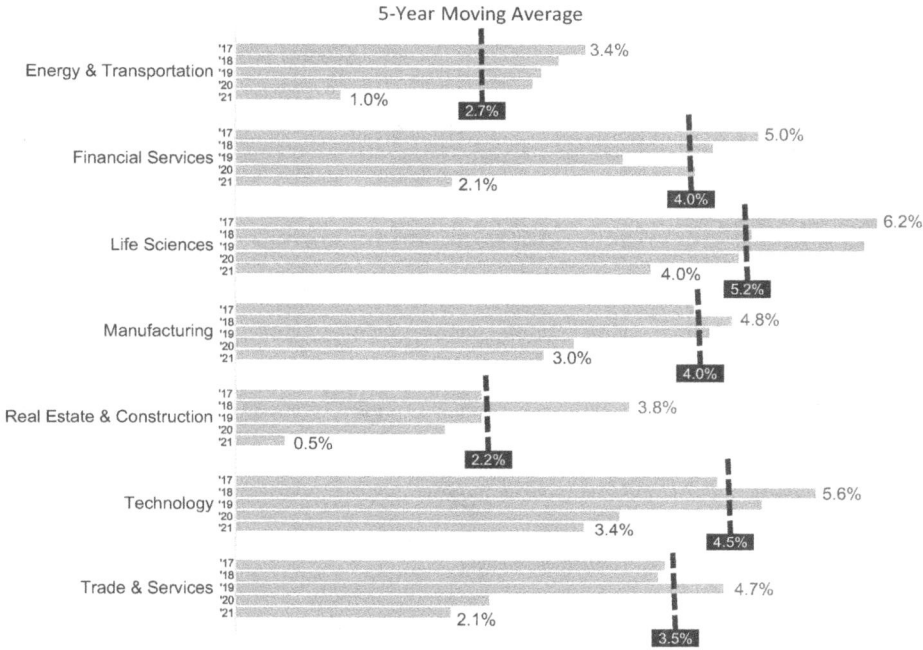

Figure 9.5: Sector-specific 2017–2021 SCA filing frequency.

As shown by the 5-year moving average along with the low and high 5-year frequency values, the incidence of securities fraud litigation varies considerably across the seven industry sectors, with life sciences exhibiting the highest overall incidence rate, and real estate and construction the lowest. It is also worth noting that the within-segment annual incidence rates fluctuate noticeably, which underscores the importance of framing the reported 5-year moving average as an approximation rather than an exact value. Still, the empirical evidence presented in Figure 9.5 suggests that based on the most recent trends, as a group, life sciences firms face the greatest probability of incurring shareholder litigation.

Given that approximately 40% of securities fraud cases are dismissed during the initial discovery (resulting in no settlement) and the remaining cases may take up to several years to be settled, annual settlement counts are considerably lower, rendering parallel to Figure 9.5 settlement analysis statistically unsound (i.e., cross-time and cross-sector breakdowns would result in prohibitively small sample sizes). More specifically, at a sector level, the average annual number of settlements ranges from only about 4 for real estate and construction (it is by far the smallest, number of companies-wise, of all seven SEC groupings) to a high of 32 for life sciences. With that in mind, Figure 9.6 offers a comparison of 2017–2021 median settlement values for all sectors combined.

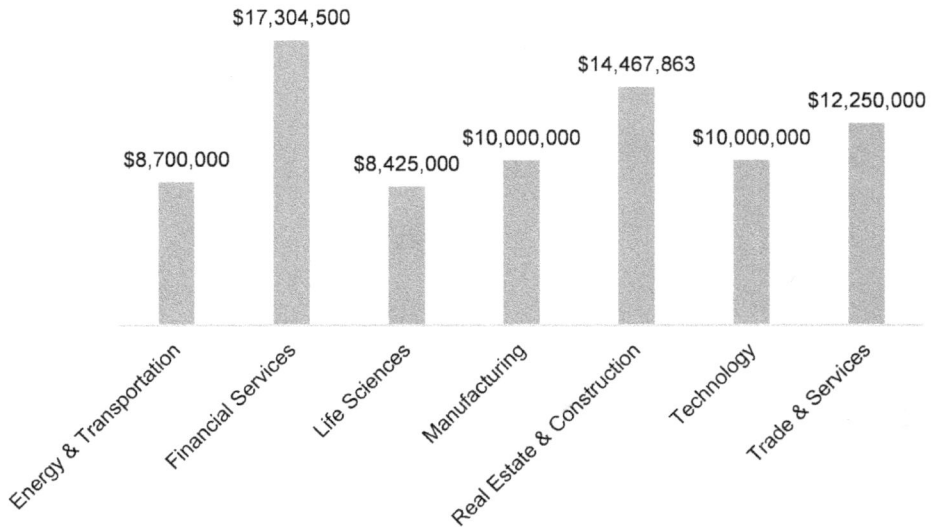

Figure 9.6: 2017–2021 median SCA settlement values.

Once again, considerable cross-sector variability is evident, with median settlement values ranging from a low of $8.425 million for life sciences companies to a high of $17.305 million for financial services firms. However, as noted earlier, the magnitude of SCA settlements is positively correlated with market capitalization, thus at least some of the variability depicted in Figure 9.6 could be due to cross-sector company size differentials. Examining company-specific market capitalization values recorded about the time individual settlements were announced yields supporting evidence: financial services firms boasted by far the largest median market capitalization of $3.241 billion, while life sciences companies recorded the lowest median market capitalization value of $446 million. Figure 9.7 offers an overall SCA settlement vs. corresponding market capitalization value comparison.

While clearly evident, the settlement amount-market capitalization association appears to be strong for financial services and life sciences organizations, which fall on the high and the low end, respectively, of the settlement amount-market capitalization spectrum – that association, however, is less clear for the remaining five sectors. For instance, Manufacturing companies boast the second highest market capitalization ($1.872 billion), but their median settlement value of $10 million is noticeably lower than real estate and construction ($14.468 million) and trade and services ($12.25), both of which exhibit significantly lower market capitalization values ($1.182 billion and $923.6 million, respectively), which suggest the need for more in-depth analysis. Consider Table 9.2.

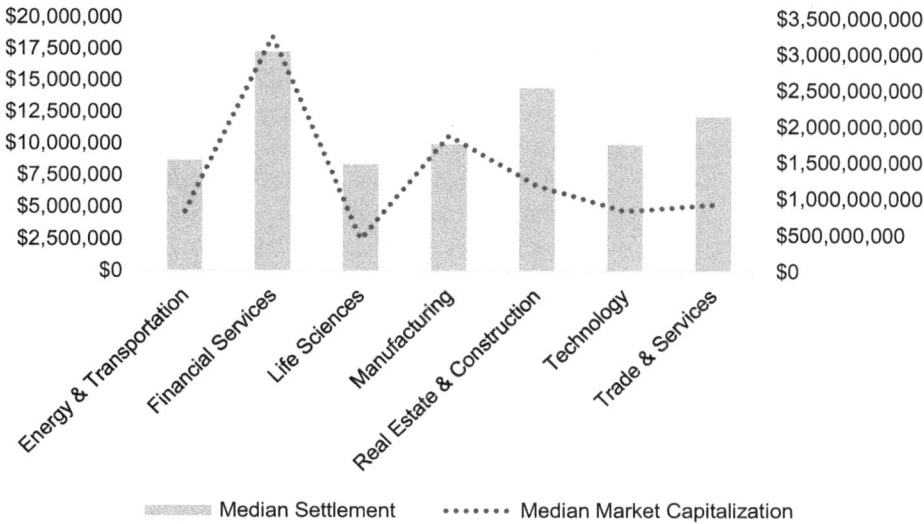

Figure 9.7: SCA settlement vs. market capitalization.

Table 9.2: Fair Share Index.

Sector	Share of:			Fair Share Index	
	Companies	**Filings (#)**	**Settlements ($)**	**Frequency**	**Severity**
Energy & Transportation	13%	9%	18%	0.69	1.80
Financial Services	13%	14%	24%	1.07	0.57
Life Sciences	18%	25%	23%	**1.35**	**2.70**
Manufacturing	15%	16%	9%	1.04	0.29
Real Estate & Construction	9%	5%	6%	0.58	0.52
Technology	13%	15%	10%	1.13	0.88
Trade & Services	18%	16%	11%	0.91	0.65

The goal of the Fair Share Index (FSI) summarized in Table 9.2 is to amalgamate and systematize the frequency and severity cross-sector comparisons discussed earlier, while also factoring-in important mediating considerations, such as the impact of company size on the size of settlements. FSI is rooted in the idea that, everything else being equal, a large group of similar companies, as exemplified by industry sectors, that accounts for a certain proportion of all companies, can be expected to also account for a proportional share of all SCA lawsuits (frequency) and a proportional share of total market capitalization-weighted SCA settlements (severity). For instance, given that the life sciences sector represents approximately 18% of companies in Erudite Analytics' SCA Tracker database (which encompasses primarily companies traded on NYSE and NASDAQ, but also a sizable cross section of OTC traded firms), that sector can then be expected to account for about 18% of SCA filings, and also about 18% slice of the aggregate, size-weighted SCA settlement amount. If that was the case, the life sciences sector would be deemed to exhibit average exposure to the threat of shareholder litigation (in the context of either or both SCA dimensions). If, on the other hand, life sciences accounted for larger than expected share of filings or settlements, it would then be deemed to have heightened SCA incidence or severity exposure; conversely, if it accounted for a smaller than expected share of filings or settlements, it would be deemed to exhibit subaverage SCA exposure (numerically, the FSI is centered on 1.0, thus values greater than 1.0 indicate heightened and values smaller than 1.0 indicated subaverage SCA exposure). Also, given that due to random fluctuations alone the chances of any sector's frequency or severity FSI equaling exactly 1.0 are low, the FSI estimation logic should be framed as deviation-adjusted range, computed here using the established concept of average absolute deviation, as follows:

$$\text{AAD} = \frac{1}{n}\sum_{i=1}^{n}|x_i - m(X)|$$

where $m(X)$ is the average frequency or severity FSI value, n is the frequency or severity record count, and x_i is the individual frequency or severity FSI values.

Using the above AAD calculation and the 'Share of' values shown in Table 9.2, the average frequency deviation was estimated to be 0.21, and the average severity deviation was estimated to be 0.68. With those estimates as additional inputs, sector-specific 'Fair Share Index: Frequency' values smaller than 0.79 or greater than 1.21 point toward subaverage or heightened, respectively, SCA frequency exposure, and 'Fair Share Index: Severity' values smaller than 0.32 or greater than 1.68 point toward subaverage and heightened, respectively, SCA severity exposure. The examination of sector values in Table 9.2 points to the life sciences sector as the one that exhibits clearly heightened SCA incidence and severity exposure, suggesting that, overall, life sciences firms are more likely than others to be sued by their shareholders, and those suits are also likely to lead to disproportionately large (vis-à-vis the company size) settlements. Also worth noting is the heightened energy and transportation sector's value of the Severity FSI; when interpreted jointly with the sector's lower than expected Frequency FSI value, the evidence in Table 9.2 suggests that energy and transportation firms are comparatively less likely to be sued by their shareholders, but when sued, those firms face considerably higher than suggested by their size settlement costs.

Key Takeaways

The domain of executive risk is not well understood outside the relatively small universe of corporate directors and officers and those involved in providing (insurance professionals) and procuring (corporate risk managers) executive risk related insurance coverage, commonly referred to as 'directors' and officers' (or simply D&O) coverage.' It is that relative anonymity of that critical facet of organizational functioning that makes executive risk a good case study of the importance of understanding the broader context as the basis of informationally sound interpretation of data patterns of interest. With that in mind, the primarily baselining-focused research summarized here had two core objectives: Firstly, to offer a conclusive summary of the key securities fraud litigation trends that emerged since the passage of the seminal norm-setting legislative act known as Private Securities Litigation Reform Act (PSLRA), which reframed the core aspects of how allegations of misconduct levied against corporate directors and officers are prosecuted. Secondly, to offer a more forward-looking and more granular examination of more recent trends, with an eye toward highlighting differences among distinct industry sectors.

Examination of the ebbs and flows of the aggregate, 25-year post-PSLRA trend of securities fraud litigation filings did not reveal clear association between the number of SCA filings and key post-PSLRA legislative and judicial enactments, suggesting that, overall, the incidence of securities litigation is driven largely by market forces and events, such as the 2007–2008 global financial crisis or the stock option backdating scandal (which reached its high point between 2005 and 2007). Severity-wise, the aggregate trend analysis revealed a surprisingly stable – particularly over the most recent several years – relationship between the magnitude of SCA settlements and the associated market capitalizations, suggesting that the observed cross-time variability in the median settlement amount is driven largely by fluctuations in median company size. In other words, after adjusting for annual differences in market capitalization-expressed company size, the median SCA settlement amount was remarkably flat over the past several years.

The 'deeper dive' part of the analysis focused on the most recent five years, and a more granular examination of sector-level SCA frequency and severity trends, revealing several interesting findings. First, there are persistent and considerable differences in SCA incidence across industry sectors, even after within-sector, cross-time variability is taken into account. Second, the association between SCA settlement amount and market capitalization that emerged in the earlier, aggregate analysis is even more pronounced when compared across industry segments, with very large cross-sector settlement magnitude differences closely paralleling differences in market capitalization. Third, after correcting for the confounding effects of sector size (i.e., the number of companies) and company size (i.e., median market capitalization), a single sector, life sciences, emerged as clearly exhibiting abnormally high exposure to the threat of shareholder securities litigation.

Chapter 10
Benchmarking Case Study – Micro Standards

The macro case study summarized in the preceding chapter offered an illustration of how systematic baselining can be used to develop a better understanding of patterns hidden in time series data; the goal of this chapter is to illustrate how benchmarking can be used to assess more micro-level phenomena, here in the form of company-specific exposure to the threat of shareholder litigation. Moreover, given the importance of rooting data analyses – not just those related to comparative assessment, but in general – in sound understanding of the broader background, this case also begins with foundational overview of the key concepts and ideas related to the topic at hand.

The case study outlined here is built around what is perhaps the most seen application of benchmarking, which is to contextualize magnitudes of outcomes of interest. In a broader sense, that intuitively obvious sensemaking activity comprises a core part of an emerging management philosophy commonly referred to as management by the numbers. An application of the general principals of evidence-based decision-making, management by the numbers is tantamount to using objective, typically data analysis derived insights, as the basis of making a wide array of managerial decisions; it is typically contrasted with intuitive decision-making, which emphasizes subjective beliefs and experience. Interestingly, while the idea of managing *by* the number seems intuitively obvious, its application is often confused with what could be characterized as managing *to* the numbers; not surprisingly, the understanding of that not always clear but critical distinction is an important part of understanding of the broader benchmarking context.

The Broad Context: The Art and Science of Managing

The practice of management, defined as a general process of controlling things or people, is inherent to organized living and thus can be considered to be as old as human civilization. The very functioning of early civilizations, the emergence of cities and states, and the building of the great monuments of human communities in the form of pyramids, temples, churches, and palaces required controlled, organized efforts. Not surprisingly, the earliest evidence of somewhat formalized management practices dates back more than six millennia, to around 4500 BCE, and the organized record keeping developed by early Sumerians; however, it was a Babylonian king, Hammurabi, who oversaw the development of more systemic and formally codified control practices some 2,500 years later. Still, it was the work of a Greek philosopher Xenophon (a student of Socrates), household management, that is commonly credited with giving rise to management as a separate domain of study and practice.

https://doi.org/10.1515/9783111001296-010

While those early contributions framed the practice of management in terms of general processes and oversight related considerations, the process orientation of modern management practice is generally attributed to the far more recent work of Frederick W. Taylor, an American mechanical engineer. Taylor is widely recognized to be the first to approach managing of work through systematic observation and study;[1] in his seminal work published in 1911 and titled *The Principles of Scientific Management*, he summarized his theory of effective job and incentive compensation design as a mean of achieving higher productivity. His ideas were widely adopted and, together with other contributions, most notably those by Frank and Lillian Gilbreth, gave rise to what it now known as *scientific management*. It is worth noting that though groundbreaking, scientific management is inescapably grounded in the Industrial Era's conception of work and management of work, much of which was built around application of direct human effort to manufacturing processes; still, its numbers orientation is just as applicable to other management contexts, as evidenced by the well-known expression: 'In God we trust, all others bring data.'[2]

Scientific Management in the Age of Data

One of the greatest minds of antiquity, Plato, argued in his seminal work *The Republic* that kings should become philosophers or that philosophers should become kings.[3] The roots of Plato's reasoning are not merely that philosophers – or nowadays, highly educated individuals – are better equipped to make informed choices, but also because, according to him, highly knowledgeable individuals are more inclined to make just choices. His reasoning was rooted in the idea that if those who value knowledge above other pursuits were to take on the task of governing by becoming kings, it would be more out of desire to seek the attainment of larger goals than just for the sheer desire to rule. But if, as Plato reasoned, philosophers could not become rulers,

---

1 Taylor's primary focus was *time*, thus his studies came to be known as 'time studies'; his contemporaries, Frank and Lillian Gilbreth, who were industrial engineers, were focused on identifying the most efficient *ways* of accomplishing tasks, thus their research came to be known as 'motion studies.' What is today known as 'time-and-motion' studies, and sometimes erroneously entirely attributed to Taylor, represents a subsequent merging (by others) of the two distinct areas of research.
2 The expression is popularly attributed to W. E. Deming, an American business theorist, economist, and industrial engineer, but there is no written evidence to substantiate that claim (it didn't come out of any of his writings).
3 The exact quote, translated into English reads: 'Unless, said I, either philosophers become kings in our states or those whom we now call our kings and rulers take to the pursuit of philosophy seriously and adequately, and there is a conjunction of these two things, political power and philosophic intelligence, while the motley horde of the natures who at present pursue either apart from the other are compulsory excluded, there can be no cessation of troubles, dear Glaucon, for our states, nor, I fancy, for the human race either.'

then rulers should try to become more philosopher-like, meaning more knowledge-able, to become more just as rulers. Applying those lofty ideals to the comparatively humble context of organizational management suggests that those in the decision-making roles should seek knowledge in the form of objective evidence.

The emphasis here is on equating knowledge with objective evidence,[4] which then brings into scope familiarity with basic data analytic concepts, believed to be necessary to correctly interpret the often statistically nuanced meaning of bench-marking. At issue here is the often-confused distinction between managing *to* the numbers and managing *by* the numbers. The notion of 'numbers' takes on a very dif-ferent meaning in those two contexts, as does the idea of managing. In the case of the former it entails setting of explicit numeric targets to be reached by whatever means are deemed (generally subjectively) most appropriate, whereas in the case of the lat-ter it entails using objective (and often numerically expressed) evidence to make the most appropriate – in view of objective evidence – decisions. It follows that while managing 'to the numbers' requires little-to-no statistical fluency, being able to man-age 'by the numbers' calls for an appreciable degree of statistical prowess, or in Pla-to's words, for kings to become philosophers.

The timeless wisdom of the great thinker's advice manifests itself here in two key benefits: Firstly, greater understanding of the core concepts used in extracting mean-ing out of raw data can be expected to translate into heightened propensity to use data analytic outcomes, which means more robust and systematic learning from ob-jective evidence, which in turn can be expected to diminish the impact of cognitive bias that accompanies (everyone's) subjective beliefs. That, in turn, can bring to light previously unnoticed opportunities, and it can also be the guiding light in situations where choices are shrouded in ambiguity. Secondly, basic statistical proficiency can also allow users of objective evidence to be more skeptical of inferences drawn from data, and even be able to identify situations in which available data are of limited informational value. As discussed in the earlier chapters, by and large data are incom-plete and messy, and the informational value of data can vary considerably across decision contexts. Moreover, even overtly robust data can be thought of as being com-prised of informative 'signal' and noninformative 'noise,' which means that data de-rived insights are approximately, not absolutely correct – appreciating that difference is an essential part of sound utilization of data analytic insights, and it is rooted in basic statistical literacy.

---

4 The general idea of knowledge can be seen as stemming from two distinct sources: explicit, or fac-tual and objective (e.g., what one learns in school), and tacit, which is interpretive and subjective (e.g., what one learns through experience); content-wise, it is comprised of three distinct dimensions: se-mantic (ideas, facts, concepts), procedural (behaviors, habits, skills), and episodic (events, experiences, emotions). For a more in-depth overview, see Banasiewicz, A. (2019). *Evidence-Based Decision-Making: How to Leverage Available Data and Avoid Cognitive Biases*, Routledge: New York.

Interestingly, while the general distinction between the ideas of managing 'to' vs. 'by' the numbers might be intuitively obvious, in practice that distinction can be easily blurred. With that in mind, a more in-depth exploration of conceptual and practical differences between those two different managerial mindsets seems warranted.

The Idea and Practice of Managing by the Numbers

As evidenced by the brief historical recounting of origins of modern management practice, while the idea of managing by the numbers may seem new it is not – in fact, the mindset of using objective evidence as the basis for making decisions predates not just the modern informational infrastructure, but even the scientific precursors of that infrastructure.[5] Long before the Internet and electronic data, business organizations began to publish their financials in the form of balance sheet, income statement, and cash flow statements as a way of attracting investors, who used those documents as proof of companies' profit-making abilities. The same organizations also invested considerable time and effort into streamlining workflows as a way of increasing efficiency; in a sense, long before the advent of robotic process automation, commercial enterprises saw their workers as not much more than biological robots . . . Looking past the numerous and well-known social implications of that mindset, which are acknowledged here but examination of which falls outside of the scope of this analysis, time-and-motion studies of scientific management, together with initially voluntary[6] publishing of financial statements effectively transformed the management of, at least public, companies into de facto management by the numbers.

But what, exactly, are 'the' numbers? The most visible manifestation of the idea of 'managing by the numbers' is the use of financial statements, which in the context of the general management setting sketched out in Figure 6.1 comprise the outcomes of organizational management processes. While there are numerous types of financial statements, the 'big three' are: (1) balance sheet, which is a summary of the organization's assets, liabilities, and capital, at a point in time, (2) income statement, which captures revenues and expenses during a period of time, and (3) statement of cash flows, which summarizes all cash inflows and cash outflows during a period of time. In that context, 'the' numbers are the bottom lines of balance sheet, income statement,

---

5 While in the sense of philosophy the origins of modern scientific thinking can be traced back to Aristotle, the third of the famous trio of ancient Greek philosophers (Socrates, his student Plato, and then Aristotle, who was Plato's student), the rise of modern science as a larger societal movement is commonly traced back to the Age of Enlightenment (also known as the Age of Reason), which dominated the world of ideas in Europe during the seventeenth and eighteenth centuries.

6 In the United States, starting in early 1930s, following the passage of the Securities Act of 1933, which governs issuance of new securities, most notably stocks, to the investing public, and the Securities Exchange Act of 1934, which governs trading of securities in secondary markets (such as the New York Stock Exchange of NASDAQ), all public companies, which are those with securities trading on public exchanges, are required to publish their financial statements each year.

and the statement of cash flows, thus managing by the numbers is tantamount to managing organizations with an eye toward financial statements-captured outcomes.

It is considerably less obvious what managing by the numbers entails within the confines of the process dimension of commercial activities. The earlier discussed scientific management ideas are well-suited to repetitive, assembly line-like work geared toward tangible industrial output, but quite a bit less so to other work contexts; in a more general sense, those principles are meaningful primarily to manufacturing organizations, which, as of 2019, accounted for a little more than 11% of the total US economic output, and employed about 8.5% of the total workforce. In other words, scientific management-rooted conception of managing commercial work-related inputs, throughputs, and outputs 'by the numbers' is not directly applicable to managing more than 90% of organizational workforce.

An even more fundamental trouble with that Industrial Era-rooted conception of management by the numbers is evident in epistemic and ontological foundations[7] of those ideas, which can be summarized here by simply asking if that overt characterization is in alignment with the implied meaning. In other words, is managing organizations by setting explicit performance targets tantamount to truly managing 'by' the numbers, whether those numbers represent production efficiency or aggregate financial results?

In principle, managing 'by' the numbers could be expected to notionally parallel piloting a plane in a mode known as 'fly-by-wire,' which replaces conventional manual flight controls of an aircraft with an electronic interface. In that mode, automated flight control systems use computers to process flight control inputs and send corresponding electrical signals to the flight control surface actuators that control the key functions such as speed, direction, and altitude. Similarly, an organization managed by the numbers could be expected to tie many of its decisions to objective numeric evidence, thus effectively removing the 'human factor' from many organizational decisions. In an abstract sense, organizational management could, under those circumstances, be reduced to a simple stimulus-response model,[8] but is that even feasible, and if so, would it be desirable?

In a very general sense, organizational management entails numerous strategic and tactical alternatives; dealing with the resultant uncertainty is the essence of decision-making. Using the fly-by-wire analogy, the rational, in the stimulus-response sense, decision model would entail objectively estimating the relative advantage of each of the available decision alternatives ('inputs' in Figure 6.1), and then choosing the one with the highest estimated value. Such a mechanically rational approach

---

7 Both of distinct branches of philosophy; ontology is concerned with how concepts are grouped into more general categories and which concepts exist on the most fundamental level, whereas epistemology is focused on differences between justified beliefs and subjective opinions.
8 Expressed through a mathematical function that describes the relationship (f) between the stimulus (x) and the expected (E) outcome (Y), where $E(Y) = f(x)$.

would effectively do away with nonquantifiable considerations, and it would shield decision-making processes from the ubiquitous cognitive bias, and group-based evaluation-warping effects, such as groupthink. But, and that is a big 'but,' such a fly-by-wire algorithmic decision-making model is highly dependent on the availability, validity, reliability, and completeness of decision-driving data. While nowadays organizations tend to be awash in data, those data are generally messy and informationally incomplete, meaning are in need of substantial pre-use processing, and even more importantly, only contain a subset of factors that shape or outright determine observed outcomes. And though data preparation is ultimately a manageable problem, informational insufficiency may not be, as not everything that needs to be known (to auto-decide) is knowable – for instance, it is hard to imagine how the highly personal attitudinal determinants of brand choice could be systematically captured along with other, more visible (e.g., price, promotional incentives) choice influencing factors.

Appreciating the Difference: Managing to the Numbers
It is hard to escape the conclusion that while 'managing by the numbers' is a widely used label, it may be a misnomer or an aspirational goal, at best. Aircraft are routinely flown-by-wire because their onboard computer systems are able to capture the required data that are produced by a carefully designed array of sensors; the ensuring auto-processing of flight details produces electrical signals which in turn cause the flight control actuators to appropriately adjust the key operating elements, such as speed or direction of flight. All that is possible because (1) the required operational decision-making is narrowly defined (getting from point A to B, in generally straight line or via a set of straight lines), (2) the needed data are readily available, and (3) barring a rare malfunction, data are valid and reliable. While such perfect conditions may describe some specific organizational decision-making contexts, the vast majority of organizational choices need to be addressed under less perfect conditions, which renders implementing of managing by the numbers processes far more, even prohibitively difficult. In fact, what is often characterized as managing 'by' the numbers is really managing 'to' the numbers.

The ubiquitous financial statements, which offer a concise way of systematically capturing the key financial aspects of business entities, provide natural management targets; similarly, in educational setting, standardized test scores provide natural instructional targets. In both contexts, those are outcomes of organizational decisions, and decisions that directly impact or even shape those outcomes are commonly made with an eye toward maximizing those outcomes. Business organizations aim to maximize their value, while educational institutions typically aim to maximize test scores-implied quality of their education, now commonly codified in endless rankings. Those, and other, types of organizations do not manage 'by' the numbers, they manage 'to' the numbers because their respective numbers are merely performance goal posts, not fly-by-wire-like operational actuators.

Managing to specific revenue or profitability targets is quite common among for-profit business organizations because it offers unambiguous goals and incentives, but it is frequently accompanied by several negative side effects. Focusing on a specific target, such as the attainment of a specific level of profitability, tends to frame success in terms of only meeting that target, often called the 'threshold effect,' in addition to also diverting attention from other outcomes, such as revenue; even more incredibly, it can also give rise to what is known as the 'ratchet effect,' which manifests itself in unwillingness to reach the stated target in fear that doing so will lead to the target being raised in the future. Focusing on more relative-minded rankings tends to mitigate the threshold and ratchet effects, but can produce other adverse side effects, perhaps best exemplified by 'teaching to the test' by educational institutions that see that as a mean of achieving higher rankings (which are largely based on comparisons of measurable outcomes, such as average test scores).

The roots of the problem of confusing managing *to* the numbers with managing *by* the numbers run deep, as illustrated by the recent case of the Boeing Company, an aerospace focused manufacturer, and Pacific Gas & Electric, or PG&E, an electric utility company. In March 2019, Boeing 737 Max, a variant of the company's best-selling Boeing 737 aircraft (itself the best-selling plane in commercial aviation history) was grounded worldwide after 346 people died in two separate crashes. While the underlying fact pattern that led up to those tragedies and the subsequent grounding is complex, some of the more striking aspects of that case include evidence that the company historically renowned for its meticulous designs made seemingly basic software design mistakes that are now believed to have played the key role in those crashes. According to long-time Boeing engineers, what should have been a routine development project was complicated by the company's push to outsource that work to lower-paid contractors, some being paid as low as $9/h; moreover, the company's decision to sell as 'extra' premium options certain safety features, most notably those known as 'angle of attack indicators,' may have also played a role. Those Boeing decisions share one thing in common: they are both geared toward shoring up of company's profitability, a key manifestation of managing to the numbers.

A possibly even more egregious example of managing to the numbers gone awry is offered by PG&E choosing profits over safety. As reported by the *Wall Street Journal*,[9] the company knew for years that hundreds of miles of its electric power lines, some as old as a century, needed to be upgraded to reduce the chance of sparking a fire. Once again, the company's bottom line focus compelled it to not to invest in replacing unsafe transmission lines; the nightmare scenario came true in 2018 when a felled power line sparked what eventually became the deadliest wildfire in California's history, claiming 88 lives, causing more than $30 billion in potential legal claims, ultimately pushing

---

9 https://www.wsj.com/articles/pg-e-knew-for-years-its-lines-could-spark-wildfires-and-didnt-fix-them-11562768885

PG&E to file for bankruptcy protection. It is worth noting that while the 2018 wildfire is notable as being the largest, the company's power lines are believed to have caused more than 1,500 California wildfires in the span of just 6 years, and time and time again, the pursuit of profit trumped maintenance investments.

While the cases of Boeing and PG&G are just two, somewhat extreme examples of management to the numbers gone awry, they are nonetheless illustrative of potential dangers of that mindset. There is a fundamental difference between striving to reach predetermined performance outcomes and allowing objective evidence to permeate the full spectrum of organizational decision-making, which is the essence of the difference between managing *to* the numbers and managing *by* the numbers.

The Role of Assessment Standards

The idea of purposeful and systematic use of rich varieties of organizational data to manage by the numbers can be more formally characterized as *evidence-based management* practice, a still relatively novel but increasingly more popular management philosophy.[10] Central to that decision-making approach is the notion of evidence, framed here as facts supporting or justifying beliefs or inferences, where facts can represent scientific truths, as exemplified by the π (pi) ratio or the speed of light, or methodologically sound data analytic outcomes, as exemplified by assessment standards in the form benchmarks or baselines. Simply put, the development of sound state or outcome assessment capabilities is one of the core prerequisites to implementing systematic evidence-based management practices.

The role played by benchmarking and baselining differs based on the type of decision. Coarsely categorized, decisions can be grouped into two broad categories of routine and nonroutine; the former tend to be recurring and formulaic, while the latter as irregular and nonstandard. Also implied in that distinction is the availability of relevant data: Recurring decision-making typically involves solving the same or very similar problems over and over again, a process that often manifests itself in outcome data that could be used to construct explicit benchmarking and baselining mechanisms; in general, that is not so for nonroutine decisions. Given those general characterizations, it follows that routine decisions lend themselves to decision automation, at the core of which are algorithmic resolution mechanisms which not only are a natural fit for data derived assessment standards, but in fact, are dependent on availability of those standard. Moreover, even looking past decision automation, routine decision-making in general can benefit greatly from data derived assessment stand-

---

10 For a more in-depth overview, see Banasiewicz, A. (2019). *Evidence-Based Decision-Making: How to Leverage Available Data and Avoid Cognitive Biases*, Routledge: New York.

ards, the availability of which has been shown to greatly reduce the impact of cognitive bias and other undesirable influencers.

While nonroutine decision-making may not naturally lend itself to the direct use of objective assessment standards, it can quite often benefit from indirect use of those decision-making aids. Nonroutine decisions tend to be focused on more complex problems, which in turn may encompass a wider range of direct and indirect factors; in that sense, dealing with nonroutine problems often entails addressing a mosaic of multiple, narrower in scope and interconnected considerations, some of which may lend themselves to objective assessment. In other words, the availability of data derived assessment standards may indirectly contribute to nonroutine decisions by enhancing the validity or the reliability of at least some of the parts of the larger problem at hand.

When considered from the perspective of decision-making inputs, the impact of objective assessment standards is perhaps most visible in the context of the distinction between 'data,' 'information,' and 'knowledge.' *Data* are simply facts, which when processed and refined by means of summarization or contextualization become *information*; the relevant and objective information that offers decision-guiding insights becomes *knowledge* when it exhibits higher decision-making value. The progressively greater utility associated with the data → information → knowledge progression suggests that transforming often readily available data into unambiguous insights in the form of benchmarks and baselines has the potential to thoughtfully use available data as means of developing factually sound and deep understanding of phenomena under consideration, and by doing so to contribute toward efficient and effective completion of tasks.

Building on the general ideas outlined above, the next section offers a continuation of the shareholder litigation case study, first outlined in the previous chapter. Here, the threat of shareholder litigation is looked at from the perspective of a singular company, where the goal is to assess the absolute – i.e., company-specific – as well as the relative – i.e., company vs. peers – exposure to that risk.

Benchmarking Exposure to Shareholder Litigation

The two fundamental questions that encapsulate exposure to risk of shareholder litigation as well as other potential threats are: How likely is it to happen, and if it did, what would be the expected impact? Or stated more succinctly, what is the likelihood and the expected impact or severity? Also important in many applied settings, such as assessment of executive risk, is the idea of relative exposure – how does our risk exposure compare to that of our peers? And given that often the company-specific exposure might be higher or lower than that of its peers, softly implied in the relative exposure assessment is the question of 'why' – why is our exposure higher or lower than our peers'? Figure 10.1 shows an example of summary report that encapsulates answers to those questions.

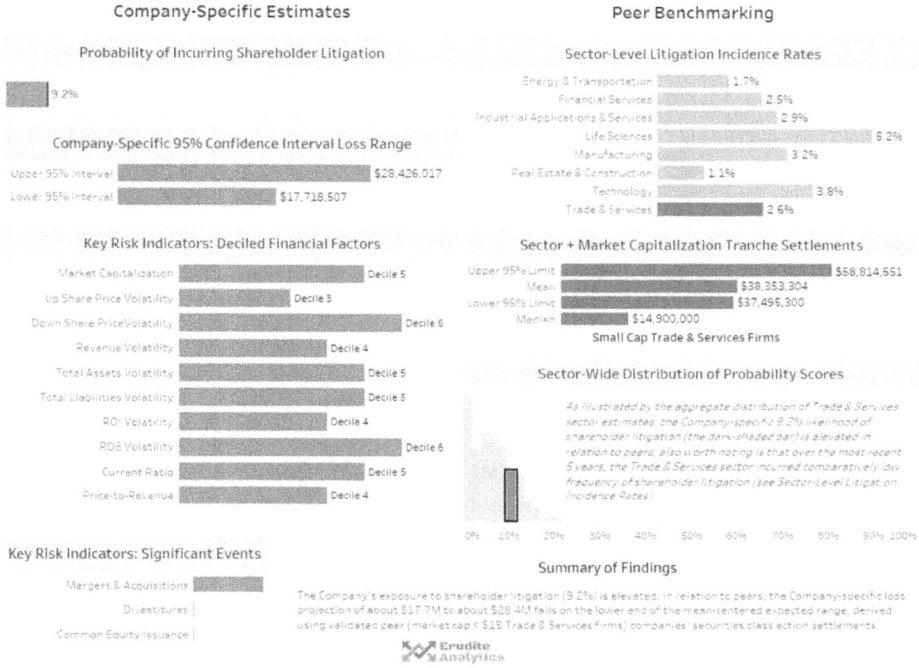

Figure 10.1: Sample benchmarking scorecard.

Aiming to succinctly summarize multiple and diverse sources and types of insights focused on assessing and contextualizing a sample company's exposure to securities litigation, the scorecard depicted in Figure 10.1 combines the results of company-specific predictive modeling, and industry-wide descriptive benchmarking. Content-wise, the former, grouped under the company-specific estimates heading, are topline summaries of complex, multivariate statistical models' forecasts, whereas the latter, grouped under the sector-level benchmarks heading, capture comparatively (in the methodological sense) simple, peer-based averages and confidence interval-based ranges. The intended purpose of the scorecard is to offer an easy to grasp, highly con-clusive summary of the most pertinent aspects of SampleCo's exposure to the threat posed by securities litigation; lastly, the target audience of the scorecard is the organi-zational executive management and its board of directors.

Breaking down the content of the shareholder litigation exposure summarizing scorecard shown in Figure 10.1, the company-specific estimates section captures the key highlights that succinctly communicate the two key dimensions of risk exposure: Likelihood, framed here as the probability of incurring a shareholder lawsuit in the upcoming 12 months (8.3% for SampleCo in Figure 10.1), and severity, or the expected cost, framed here in terms of monetary settlement amounts,[11] expressed as a 95% confidence interval range in Figure 10.1 ($23,066,260–$36,688,750). Also shown are two blocks of key risk indicators: deciled financial factors, which list financial metrics, and significant event, which identify specific point-in-time organizational actions, that together emerged (based on comprehensive analyses, most notably the multivariate predictive models mentioned earlier) as the strongest predictors of securities litigation.

Complementing the company-specific assessment is the comparative benchmarking shown under the heading of peer benchmarking in Figure 10.1, the goal of which is to offer an evaluative frame of reference for the two key risk dimensions of likelihood and severity. The core value of benchmarking, in this situation, is to provide an interpretive context for the company-specific estimates outlined above. Even though SampleCo's 8.3% likelihood of incurring shareholder litigation is obviously a lot closer to 0% than it is to 100%, the 8.3% value is nonetheless informationally somewhat unclear because most users tend to evaluate such estimates not in the context of the underlying absolute range (i.e., 0–100%), but rather in the context of what they deem to be the 'typical' exposure, which in the context of risk assessment often takes the form of a peer group average. That idea, framed as *assessment paradox* in Chapter 1, is rooted in the observation that some magnitudinally precise value can be informationally unclear, if those magnitudes are not intrinsically informative. To that end, without an evaluative frame of reference, in the form of an appropriate benchmark, the 8.3% probability of incurring shareholder litigation is not immediately seen as high or low, but once put in the context of the appropriate benchmark (the average shareholder litigation incidence of 2.9% for industrial applications and services firms highlighted in Figure 10.1), the company-specific estimate lends itself to far easier interpretation.

A very similar logic applies to the second dimension of risk exposure – the potential magnitude of loss (i.e., severity). Admittedly, the range of potential settlement related costs is more self-explanatory than the likelihood estimate, but here as well peer benchmarking can further enhance the informational value of that dimension of exposure assessment. However, interpretation of severity related benchmarking information is somewhat more nuanced, as it requires more abstract statistical thinking. The Sector + Market Capitalization Tranche Settlements shows several distinct values which can be grouped into two common expressions of the general idea of 'average,' as in typical, values: the mean and the median. The 'standard' statistical advice is to use the median when data are non-normally distributed because the median is unaffected by outliers; given the aggregate distribution of shareholder litigation settlements exhibit

---

11 In the realm of shareholder litigation, virtually all lawsuits that survive the initial discovery phase (i.e., are not dismissed on factual or procedural grounds) are settled out of court; out of the over 6,500 shareholder lawsuits that have been filed in the post-PSLRA era, only 10 went to jury trial (with roughly half won by defendants).

very strong positive skew,[12] that recommendation seems quite appropriate in this context. However, just focusing on the median can lead to systematic undervaluation of the potential risk exposure because, intuitively, a median value of let's say, $10 million implies a range of approximately $20 million, unless other information is presented to warrant a different conclusion – that is exactly the reason for also including (in the Sector + Market Capitalization Tranche Settlements section) the mean value, but in the somewhat nonstandard context of separately estimated upside and downside confidence intervals. The difference between the downward (i.e., the lower 95% confidence interval) and the upward (i.e., the upper 95% confidence interval) is quite significant: $19,941,351 to $18,802,188 (mean and lower 95% confidence interval, respectively) vs. $19,941,351 to $38,336,543 (mean and upper 95% confidence interval, respectively), which underscores the very high potential upward volatility in shareholder settlement amounts. In short, the goal of that part of benchmarking is to underscore that although the typical, i.e., median, settlement amount is moderate, the potential for the upward escalation of that cost is considerable.

The company-specific and benchmarking information summarized in Figure 10.1 are used as a part of publicly traded companies' risk management efforts.[13] In a very general sense, those efforts are focused on two distinct risk management undertakings: risk mitigation and risk transfer. A high-level overview of the nature of each of those two related, but distinct, activities is offered next, as it is necessary to appreciating how more in-depth benchmarking efforts are used to further the general goal of reducing companies' exposure to the threat of shareholder litigation.

Risk Mitigation and Risk Transfer

Management of risk is a multistep process that typically begins with risk identification, followed by risk assessment, and risk response, which can take the form of one of four possible actions: acceptance, avoidance, mitigation, or transfer. Identifiable but uncontrollable (from the standpoint of a business or other organization) threats, as exemplified by changing social sentiments or various political risks, are typically accepted, in view of implausibility of other response options, whereas threats that are identifiable and controllable, such as applicable (to a particular organization) regula-

---

12 Using all available post-PSLRA settlements (over 2,900 in total), the overall mean of about $52.3M is several times larger than the median of $8.75M – the very sizable mean vs. median difference is one of the most visible manifestations of the positive skew of shareholder settlement data (also worth noting that selecting a smaller subset of peer companies can be expected to yield similar results); for the more technically inclined, the associated coefficient of skewness is 17.48.

13 It is worth noting that while shareholder litigation is primarily of concern to companies traded on public US stock exchanges, a number of private (i.e., not publicly traded) companies are also focused on that risk, though considerations driving their interest fall outside the scope of this analysis.

tory risks, are usually targeted for avoidance activities, often taking the form of specific organizational policies and enforcement mechanisms.[14] Many other identifiable threats – including the risk of shareholder litigation – confronting organizations are managed with the help of various risk mitigation and/or risk transfer mechanisms – it is those risk exposures that are particularly in need of robust choice-informing inputs.

The depth and complexity of organizational risk management efforts are not always fully appreciated. The threat of shareholder litigation that is the focus of this case study (as well as the baselining analysis highlighted in Chapter 9), is itself a subset of a broader domain known as *executive risk*, which encompasses numerous other – i.e., legally and analytically distinct from securities laws violations focused shareholder litigation – risks associated with the discharge of executive organizational duties, including employment practices, fiduciary duties, or product liability. To paint a clearer picture, Figure 10.2 shows a conceptual summary of the totality of threats that jointly comprise executive risk.

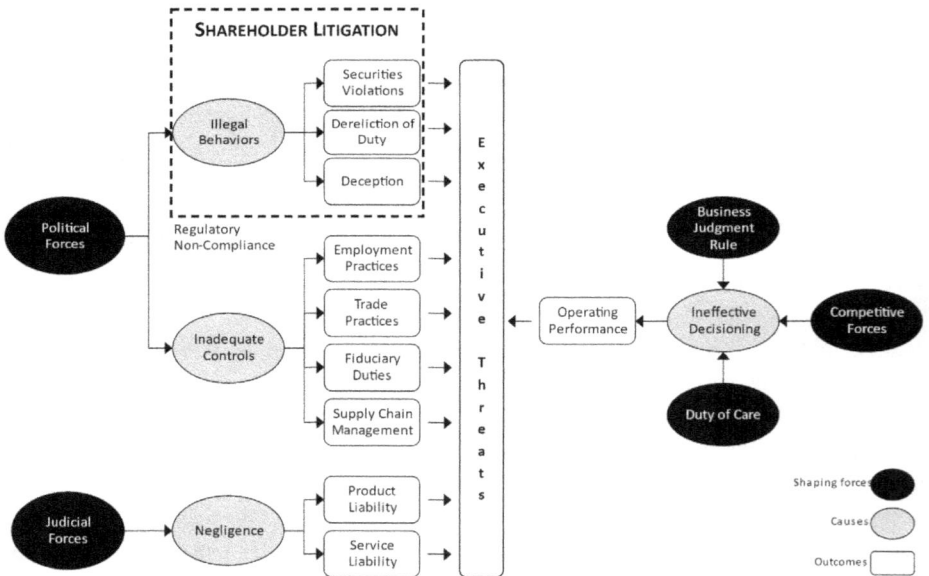

Figure 10.2: The scope of executive threats.

---

14 For a more in-depth overview of organizational risk management see Banasiewicz, A. (2016). *Threat Exposure Management: Risk, Resilience, Change*, Lightning Source: La Vergne, TN.

It is instructive to note that each of the 'outcomes' identified in Figure 10.2 and falling outside of the highlighted domain of shareholder litigation – employment practices, trade practices, fiduciary duties, etc. – comprises its own risk management and informational focus, inclusive of domain specific exposure estimation and benchmarking. And though largely corollary to shareholder litigation assessment informing benchmarking, it paints a picture of the scope of informational needs that are at the core of applied risk management efforts.

Turning back to risk response, the remaining two alternatives – risk mitigation and risk transfer – are the heart and soul of applied risk management efforts, because they entail making speculative choices based on limited and imperfect information. Recalling the two key dimensions of risk exposure – likelihood and severity – risk mitigation is primarily geared toward reducing the likelihood of an undesirable event of interest materializing, whereas risk transfer is geared primarily toward reducing the severity, or the cost dimension (which is why risk transfer is also at times referred to as risk financing). Both response options implicitly recognize that some threats, as exemplified by the risk of shareholder litigation, cannot be fully eliminated because, in the case of shareholder litigation, they emanate from choices made by independent other parties' (i.e., shareholders) interpretation of organizational outcomes (typically, financial results) and surrounding circumstances (most notably, organizational disclosures, or lack thereof, associated with financial results of interest). With that in mind, risk mitigation calls for insights into factors that heighten the chances of litigation, while risk transfer calls for insights that inform procurement of insurance coverage.

Before delving into specifics of risk mitigation- and risk transfer-aiding benchmarking, a quick note regarding the term 'risk transfer' might be in order. To start, the term itself is a bit of a misnomer – as it is intuitively obvious, the chances of an undesirable event impacting a particular organization, or any other entity, cannot be shifted onto any other entity. So, it is not the possibility of, in this case, a shareholder lawsuit being filed against a particular company that is being transferred, but rather the financial responsibility for any potential damages, typically in the form of legal defense expenses and potential monetary settlements. In view of that, risk transfer discussed here can be more accurately characterized as post-event compensatory arrangement, given that it entails the transfer of financial responsibility connected to covered (by the insurance contract) loss causing, adverse events.

Deeper Dive Benchmarking

The summary scorecard shown in Figure 10.1 is just that – a summary of multiple facets of SampleCo's exposure to the threat of shareholder litigation, as seen from the perspective of the two key dimensions of likelihood and severity. In some situations, most notably when the goal is to merely refresh prior assessment efforts, such summative assessment might be sufficient; other contexts, however, might call for more granular analyses, offering more granular assessment of likelihood and severity of shareholder litigation.

Risk Mitigation: Reducing Likelihood

Singling out of factors that lead to shareholder litigation calls for basic grounding in legal rights and obligations of directors and officers of public companies, and while there are numerous considerations that come into focus here, of most fundamental rights of directors and officers are embodied in the legal concept of business judgment rule, while their core obligations are encapsulated in the (also legal) notion of duty of care. The *business judgment rule* states that directors and officers of a corporation are clothed with the presumption of being motivated in their conduct by a bona fide regard for the interests of the corporation whose affairs they direct and manage. The origin of that legal doctrine can be traced back to a 1945 shareholder action in which the company's shareholders alleged that corporate directors failed to obtain the best price available in the sale of securities by dealing with only one investment house. The court, however, reasoned that errors in the exercise of honest business judgment should not subject decision-makers to liability for negligence in the discharge of their appointed duties, an opinion which gave rise to business judgment rule as used today.

Keeping in mind the interplay between corporate managers' rights and obligations, while the business judgment doctrine effectively extends a certain degree of immunity to corporate decision-makers, it nonetheless requires managers to act in good faith and in the best interest of the company, a requirement which forms the basis for another key legal principle known as the *duty of care.* That doctrine effectively limits the immunity offered by the business judgment rule by requiring organizational managers to adhere to a standard of reasonable care while performing any acts that could foreseeably harm others. When considered jointly, the business judgment rule and the duty of care form the base standard of directors' and officers' liability by stipulating that organizational decision makers they have the freedom to act, so long as they act in good faith and in the best interest of the company, as determined by in a manner in which a reasonably prudent person in a like position and in similar circumstance would act. How does that translate into the threat of shareholder litigation?

In the most direct sense, it can be used as a lens through which management actions, most notably statements regarding current financial situation and future prospects are evaluated – where all financial disclosures time, complete, and accurate? Again, management assumptions, strategies, and ultimately actions may – in retrospect – turn out to be ineffective, even disastrous, but so long as management acted in good faith and fully, completely, and timely disclosed all pertinent information, they cannot be held liable for business outcomes of their choices. In other words, the broadly framed liability trigger in shareholder litigation is completeness, timeliness, and accuracy of management disclosures, not the efficacy of their decisions. It is important to note, however, that under the US securities laws, corporate managers can be held liable for any materially false filings of public disclosures, even in the absence of any discernible intent to deceive.[15] However, in order for disclosure errors to trigger shareholder litigation there has to be a corresponding and attributable precipitous drop in the stock price; in other words, there has to be clear evidence of economic harm to shareholders.[16]

Also pertinent to assessing the likelihood dimension of the risk of shareholder litigation is the presence of any material events. In the context of shareholder litigation, material events are developments that can be expected to have significant impact on companies' share price, most notably initial public offerings (a private company selling its shares to the public), issuance of new shares, and mergers and acquisitions; in general, those events significantly heighten disclosure requirements and scrutiny, which ultimately increases the chances of incomplete or inaccurate disclosures.

And lastly, allegations of violations of securities laws are subject to statutes of limitations, though the exact timeframe is a bit complicated: Securities claims need to be filed no later than 2 years from the time plaintiffs become aware of potential violations or 5 years (10 for the SEC) from defendants last culpable act; in practice, 95%+ of all claims are filed within 3 years following last culpable act, thus risk of litigation predicting models tend to use the most recent 3 years of data. Figure 10.3 offers a summary of the preceding considerations, put in the context of benchmarked stock price trend.

What likelihood of incurring shareholder litigation information is communicated by the chart shown in Figure 10.3? Firstly, the chart shows a clear divergence of stock price trends of SampleCo and the peer group average, which underscores that the downward slide in SampleCo's stock price was not driven by larger market forces, which is an important consideration that factors into the legal notion of *loss causation* (which requires that the defendant's, in this case corporate directors and officers as a group, misrepresentations proximately caused the plaintiff's, here shareholders as a group, economic loss). And secondly, it also shows the presence of two material events in the form of mergers and acquisitions (M&A) during the timeframe of interest. Taken together, the reference information contained in Figure 10.3 suggests that Sam-

---

15 More specifically, US securities laws make no distinction between cases where management has committed deliberate fraud (i.e., took affirmative steps to hide the truth) and cases where reported information merely contain misstatements that could have been discovered in the course of due diligence.
16 While the broader discussion of this topic falls outside the scope of this book, it is also worth noting that the US Securities and Exchange Commission can levy fines, which can be substantial, on offending organization even if disclosure errors are not accompanied by precipitous stock price declines.

SAMPLECO SHARE PRICE VS. PEER AVERAGE
Most Recent 3 Years

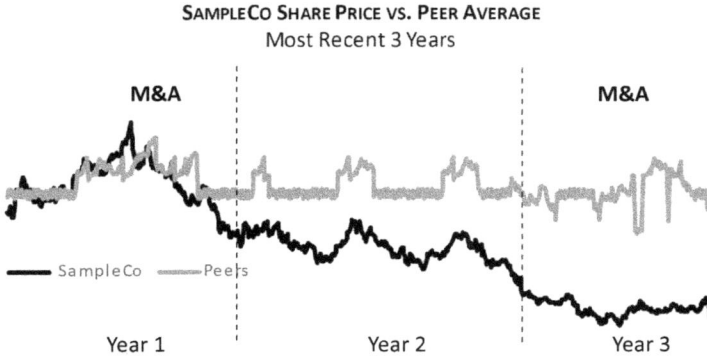

Figure 10.3: Drivers of likelihood: share price volatility and material events.

pleCo's exposure to shareholder litigation is greater than the average exposure of the company's peer group.

The initial conclusion suggested by Figure 10.3 is, however, quite nonspecific in terms of numerically expressed probability as it does not offer operationally clear assessment of the average exposure of like-companies to shareholder litigation. Rectifying that shortcoming, additional risk exposure benchmarking details are shown in Figure 10.4.

The left-hand-side bar graph shows average frequency is shareholder litigation computed for each of the eight SEC classification-defined industry sectors (as discussed in Chapter 9); the highlighted sector – industrial applications and services – is the SampleCo's broadly defined peer group, which exhibits comparatively moderate 2.9% average probability of incurring shareholder litigation. A more tailored likelihood benchmark is offered by the right-hand-side graph, which breaks down the overall 2.9% estimate into market capitalization size-based tranches[17] – here, SampleCo falls into the highlighted small market capitalization based tranche which exhibits a higher litigation frequency of 4.5%. Hence the initial general conclusion derived from the graph in Figure 10.3 can be further refined by stating that based on the combination of its share price behavior and the presence of two distinct material events, SampleCo's likelihood of incurring shareholder litigation is greater than 4.5% (to arrive at a more numerically explicit estimate requires the use of company-specific predicting modeling, which falls outside the scope of this overview).

---

17 Tranches are based on the standard, FINRA (Financial Industry Regulatory Authority) definitions which are: under $50M in market capitalization – Nano tranche, $50M–$250M – Micro, $250M–$2B – Small, $2B–$10B – Mid, and $10B + – Large (FINRA also uses Mega tranche for over $200B companies, but that group is too small for the purposes of shareholder litigation tracking).

SECTOR-LEVEL SECURITIES LITIGATION FREQUENCY
(MOST RECENT 5 YEARS)

Energy & Transportation — 1.7%
Financial Services — 2.6%
Industrial Applications & Services — 2.9%
Life Sciences — 5.2%
Manufacturing — 3.2%
Real Estate & Construction — 1.1%
Technology — 3.8%
Trade & Services — 2.6%

INDUSTRIAL APPLICATIONS & SERVICES DRILL-DOWN

Large — 12.3%
Mid — 7.9%
Small — 4.5%
Micro — 1.7%
Nano — 1.2%

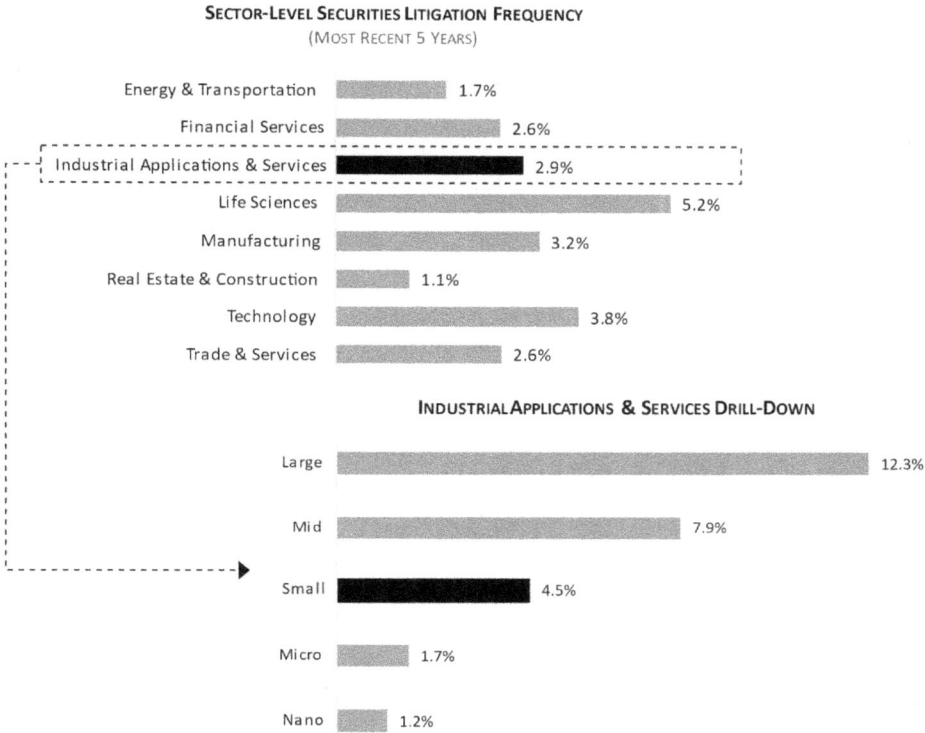

Figure 10.4: Likelihood benchmarks.

Risk Transfer: Managing Potential Costs

As noted earlier, the idea of risk transfer is tantamount to procuring insurance coverage (known as directors' and officers', or D&O, liability insurance). One of the key challenges here stems from what can be characterized as the intangibility of the threat of shareholder litigation. In contrast to insurance procurement decisions that are driven by replacement costs, as exemplified by home insurance (which is driven by the cost of the structure since land cannot destroyed), potential shareholder litigation related liability does not have clearly defined economic loss basis. The company-specific market capitalization offers a very broad indication since larger value companies tend to incur larger settlements (due to proportionately larger shareholder losses), but analyses of historical settlement trends clearly indicate that shareholder litigation related settlements reported by similarly sized and otherwise (e.g., industry classification) similar companies can vary by several orders of magnitude. That variability manifested itself earlier in the summary scorecard shown in Figure 10.1; consequently, benchmarking of risk transfer-informing potential settlement cost needs to be framed in the context of estimation ranges that can capture the underlying variability of historical outcomes.

Although the likelihood and severity dimensions of risk are independent from the standpoint of estimation, they nonetheless have a common informational foundation in the form of historical shareholder litigation filings and dispositions (specifically, settlements) data. With that in mind, the SampleCo vs. peers share price behavior comparison discussed in the context of likelihood benchmarking also offers a point of departure in severity benchmarking. Consider Figure 10.5.

SAMPLECO SHARE PRICE VS. PEER AVERAGE
Most Recent 3 Years

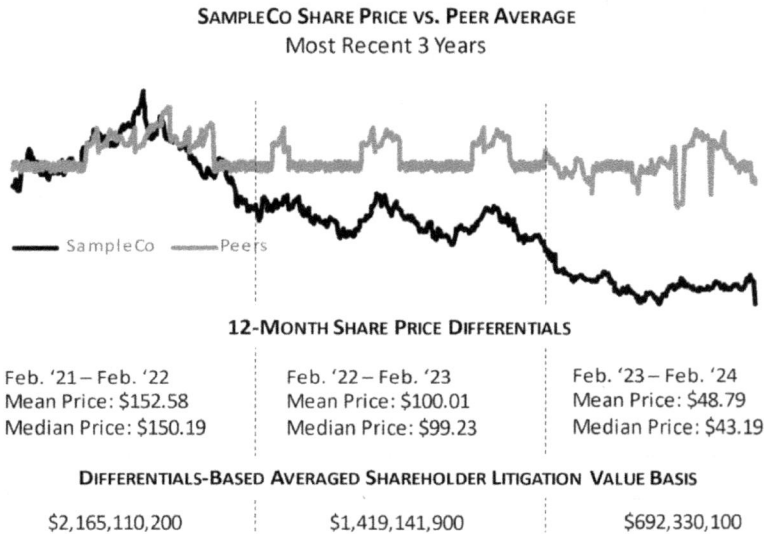

— SampleCo ——Peers

12-MONTH SHARE PRICE DIFFERENTIALS

Feb. '21 – Feb. '22	Feb. '22 – Feb. '23	Feb. '23 – Feb. '24
Mean Price: $152.58	Mean Price: $100.01	Mean Price: $48.79
Median Price: $150.19	Median Price: $99.23	Median Price: $43.19

DIFFERENTIALS-BASED AVERAGED SHAREHOLDER LITIGATION VALUE BASIS

$2,165,110,200	$1,419,141,900	$692,330,100

Figure 10.5: From share price volatility to value basis.

There is a lot of detail in the above chart, but it all can be condensed to a small handful of severity assessment-informing takeaways: First, as noted earlier, SampleCo's downward share price slide appears to be driven by company-specific rather than market-wide factors. Second, when interpreted in the context of *loss causation* (once again, understanding of the broader data context cannot be overemphasized!), the declining company value translates into more-or-less proportionately decreasing severity. And third, implied in Figure 10.5 is lower, in terms of the amount of coverage, than peer companies' insurance coverage needs; more on that later.

The next piece of the risk transfer-informing severity assessment puzzle is offered by the summary of peer group specific shareholder settlements. Here, there are multiple points of comparison, starting with the high-level sector-level contrast shown in Figure 10.6.

Information contained in Figure 10.6 offers a broader context for the industry sector level (industrial applications and services) benchmarks included in the summary

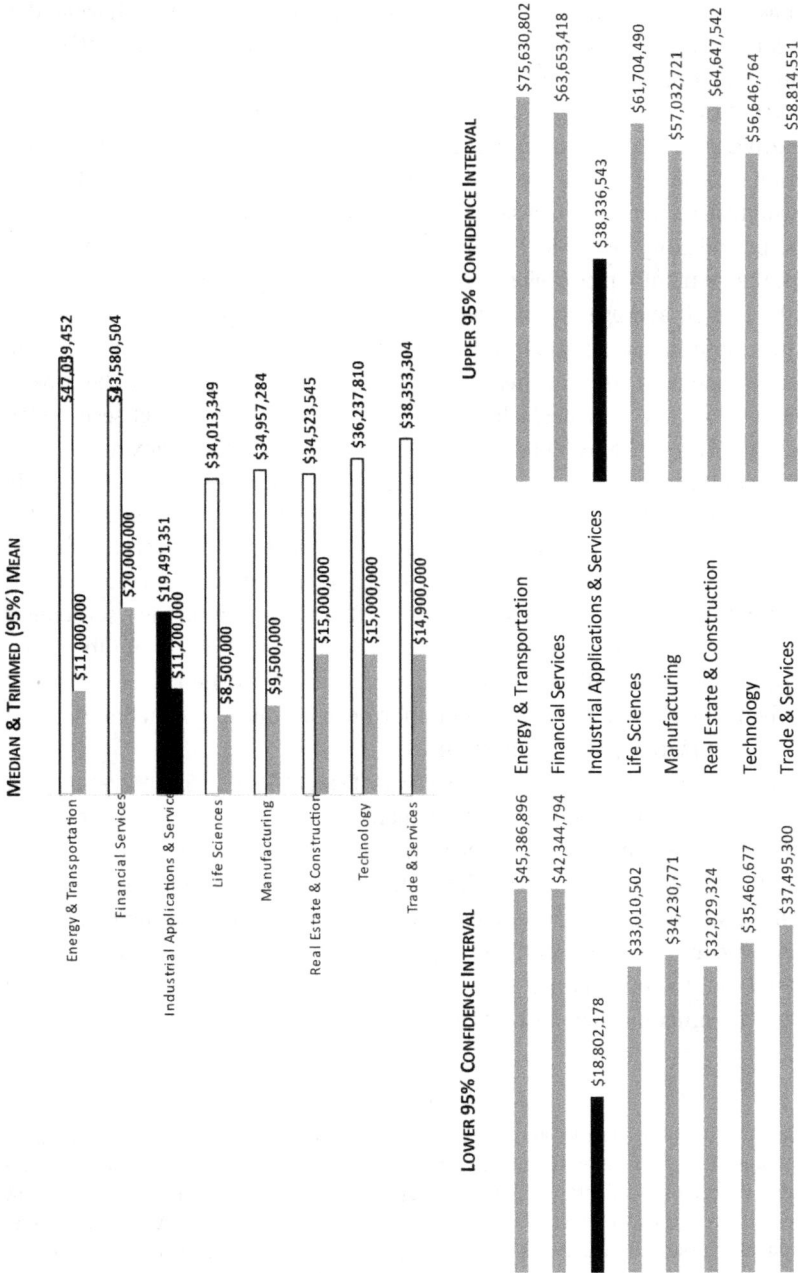

Figure 10.6: Sector-level contrasts.

scorecard shown in Figure 10.1. More specifically, it frames the median shareholder litigation settlement value as well as the trimmed mean-centered average settlement range[18] in the context of the same estimates computed for other sectors, with the goal of contextualizing the values of the sector of interest. That context clearly indicates that, in a relative sense, industrial applications and services firms' average shareholder litigation settlement values are noticeably lower than those of other sectors.

The cross-industry sector average settlement amount differences can be made even more explicit by indexing sector-level expected (as in average) settlement amounts across sectors, the result of which yields average percentage-expressed sector-level deviations from the overall average. Furthermore, to narrow the scope of comparative assessment to just those industrial applications and services firms that fall into the same market capitalization-based size tranche, the aggregate sector assessment can be broken down into five distinct size tranches, which are also indexed to the overall sector-wide average. Figure 10.7 shows the resultant cross-sector and within-sector indexing.

The additional informational granularity offered by Figure 10.7 reveals that while at the aggregate level, the average industrial applications and services sector firms' shareholder litigation settlement value is about 15% lower than the overall – i.e., all sectors combined – average, within the industrial applications and services sector, small market capitalization (i.e., those in the $250M–$2B range) companies' settlement value trended about 13% higher than what could be expected by the size of those companies. The somewhat contradictory conclusions suggested by the cross-sector and within-sector benchmarking underscore the importance of tailoring benchmarking to the specifics of organizations being benchmarked.

Adding further clarity to the contrasts offered by Figures 10.6–10.8 captures the key highlights of the distributional summary of settlement values for SampleCo's peer group, which is small market capitalization industrial applications and services company.

Mirroring the mean vs. the median all-companies difference, the distribution of settlement values suggests a relatively modest typical (i.e., median) settlement value, while also underscoring a comparatively high settlement cost escalation potential. Keeping in mind that the information shown in Figure 10.8 describes SampleCo's peer group, it offers the much-needed reference background for evaluation of SampleCo-

---

18 A brief explanation might be warranted here: As a nonparametric estimate that imposes no distributional assumptions, the point estimate-expressed median can be used with non-normally distributed data (because the median estimate is not distorted by outlying values); the same, however, is not true for the mean, the estimate of which is directly impacted by outlying values. At the same time, when data are positively skewed, as is the case with shareholder litigation settlements, and the outlying values do not lend themselves to trimming or outright elimination (because they represent legitimate values boosted by seriousness and veracity of underlying allegations), the median understates the true magnitude of the expected average settlement value; *the nonsymmetric confidence interval*-expressed mean estimate is used here to recast the expected average settlement as a range of possible values that take into account the underlying distributional skewness.

CROSS-SECTOR DIFFERENCES
(0% = Average)

Energy & Transportation   -17%

Financial Services   51%

Industrial Applications & Services   -15%

Life Sciences   -36%

Manufacturing   -28%

Real Estate & Construction   13%

Technology   13%

Trade & Services   12%

INDUSTRIAL APPLICATIONS & SERVICES DRILL-DOWN
(0% = AVERAGE)

Large   -21%

Mid   -24%

Small   13%

Micro   2%

Nano   0%

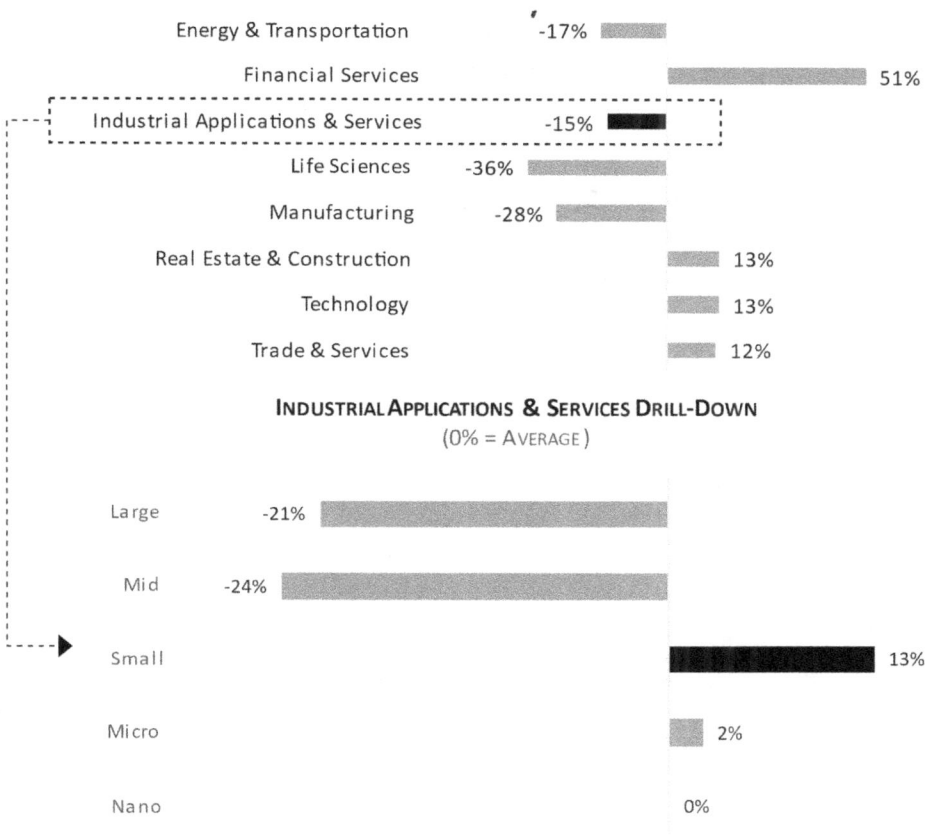

Figure 10.7: Cross-sector and within-sector indexing.

Metric		Settlement Amount
	Mean	$11,346,525
	Median	$3,875,000
Quartiles	25	$1,912,500
	50	$3,875,000
	75	$13,375,000
	Maximum	$74,000,000

Figure 10.8: Distributional summary of peer companies' settlements.

specific projections, yielded by company-specific predictive estimation processes, discussion of which falls outside of the scope of this book.

Relating information contained in Figure 10.8 to share price differentials-based averaged litigation value basis captured in Figure 10.5 can yield a yet another interesting benchmarking perspective, in the form of shareholder litigation value basis-implied expected settlement ranges. That somewhat confusing sounding idea is in fact simple: The persistent SampleCo's downward share price slide captured in Figure 10.5 implies gradually decreasing valuation basis for potential shareholder litigation settlement – in other words, everything else being the same, progressively smaller market capitalization suggests a corresponding decrease in expected settlement values. Figure 10.9 captures the resultant extension of the logic first shown in Figure 10.5.

SAMPLECO SHARE PRICE VS. PEER AVERAGE
Most Recent 3 Years

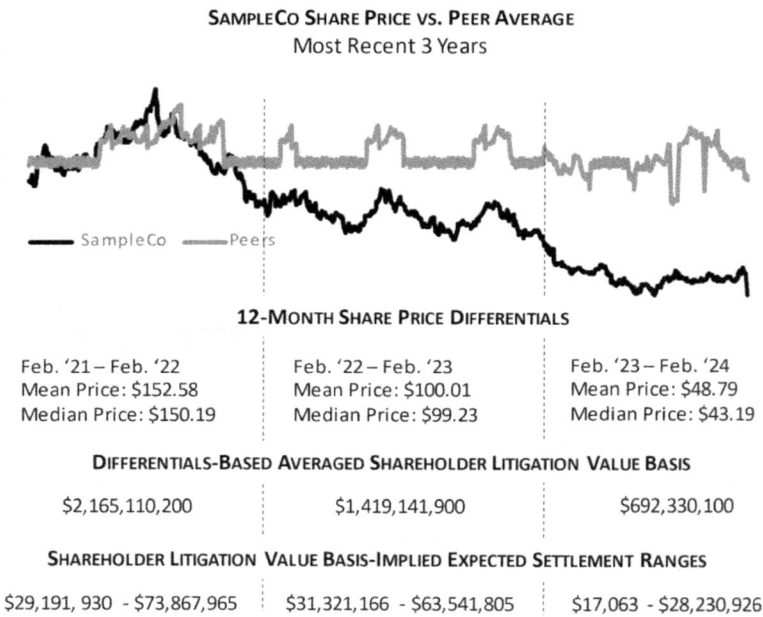

—— SampleCo —— Peers

12-MONTH SHARE PRICE DIFFERENTIALS

Feb. '21 – Feb. '22	Feb. '22 – Feb. '23	Feb. '23 – Feb. '24
Mean Price: $152.58	Mean Price: $100.01	Mean Price: $48.79
Median Price: $150.19	Median Price: $99.23	Median Price: $43.19

DIFFERENTIALS-BASED AVERAGED SHAREHOLDER LITIGATION VALUE BASIS

$2,165,110,200	$1,419,141,900	$692,330,100

SHAREHOLDER LITIGATION VALUE BASIS-IMPLIED EXPECTED SETTLEMENT RANGES

$29,191,930 - $73,867,965	$31,321,166 - $63,541,805	$17,063 - $28,230,926

Figure 10.9: Share price volatility-implied shareholder settlement ranges.

It should be noted that the differences shown by the three expected settlement ranges shown above represent not only decreasing market capitalization basis, but also differences in share price volatility contained in each of the three distinct 12-month periods. Together with other points of reference, the information captured in Figure 10.9 offers a robust context for contextualizing company-specific (not shown here) exposure estimates.

Implicit in the overview of benchmarking and baselining laid out in this book is the idea that data used to produce the various assessment standards are not only accessible, but that accessing and using those data will not violate any applicable laws or regulations, nor will it create any ethically questionable situations. Those important but not always well understood considerations are addressed next.

The Tug of War: Informational Needs vs. Rights of Others

Consider the question of who owns and who has the right to use data generated by wearable technologies, such as the ubiquitous fitness trackers and smart watches. The popularity of those technologies continues to grow as the now established categories of smart watches are joined by new embodiments of the wearable technology concept, including smart glasses, smart jewelry, and even smart clothing. The incredibly detailed and accurate data captured by those devices could inform an ever wider set of organizational decisions – for instance, health insurance companies could offer more lifestyle-tailored pricing, effectively rewarding healthy and punishing (in terms of premium pricing) unhealthy ones; at the same time, it is hard to not see that as invasion of individuals' basic right to privacy. At issue here are two broad considerations: legality and ethics, which can be seen as external (laws) and internal (ethics) systems of controls, or what is permitted by applicable legal statutes, and what is permitted by one's internal moral compass.

In the United States, laws governing data rights and responsibilities are enacted at the federal (US Congress) and state (individual state legislatures) levels; in general, federal statutes regulate the collection, storage and use of sensitive nonpublic personal information, while states tend to legislate disclosure requirements after a security breach of nonpublic personal information occurs. In short, the US data protection is a patchwork of individual federal and state laws that cover different aspects of data privacy, like health data, financial information or data collected from children; it is worth noting that other jurisdictions favor more comprehensive approaches, perhaps best exemplified by the European Union's General Data Protection Regulation. One of the more notable shortcomings of the ad hoc US approach to data protection is that data collected by many companies is unregulated in most states, which effectively allows business companies to use, sell or share your data without any notification.

The recent explosion of interest in generative artificial intelligence (AI) and other AI technologies brought into the spotlight numerous ethical considerations regarding potentially biased data used in training of the machine learning algorithms that are at the core of those systems. Of course, unlike written laws which are meant to convey uniformly interpreted meaning, ethical standards, which reflect human sense of rights and wrongs, are inescapably individualized, so much so that what might be seen as biased or unethical by one individual may be seen as fair and reasonable by another. Moreover, whereas applicable laws are binding and can be enforced, ethical beliefs are neither binding nor enforceable, meaning that one person's interpretation of right or wrong cannot be imposed on another person.

The combination of written and generally unambiguous data protection laws and unwritten and highly interpretive ethical standards is at the heart of how individual business and nonbusiness organizations approach accessing and utilizing data that are available to them. Keeping in mind that some data related practices might be legal but at the same time might be deemed, at least by some, unethical, organizational data access and use policies might differ across otherwise similar organizations. The reason for that is that those policies generally combine legal and ethical considerations, and the former tend to reflect the key aspects of organizational culture, which in turn is shaped or at least strongly influenced by ethical standards by organizational founders or key managers. Recognizing that it is difficult to offer a succinct summary of the highly nuanced and interpretation prone ethical data privacy mindsets, the ensuing section takes a closer look at the more easily discernable key legal considerations.

Responsible Data Capture and Usage

The ever-expanding digitization of personal and commercial interactions translates into ubiquitous data capture, but the relentless recording of interactions and events is not always evident. As noted earlier, when looked at from the perspective of data privacy, the United States is a complex patchwork of sector-, jurisdiction-, and medium-specific laws and regulations. Filling the void created by the US Congress' slow progress in that regard, individual states, territories, and even localities have been enacting their own laws, resulting in hundreds of data privacy and data security laws aimed at regulating collection, storage, safeguarding, disposal, and use of personal data collected from their residents. Needless to say, staying abreast of those laws and complying with their various provisions can be a challenge, especially for organizations that operate in multiple jurisdictions. Still, forward-thinking commercial and noncommercial organizations aim to go beyond black letter laws by actively considering ethical data capture and usage implications, with the goal of going beyond avoidance of noncompliance precipitated punishment by voluntarily instituting positive data privacy practices built around notions of integrity and transparency.

Broadly considered, responsible data capture, stewardship, and usage can be considered in three somewhat distinct prevention contexts: (1) unauthorized data access, commonly referred to as data breach, (2) improper data access, and (3) publication of de-anonymizable data. Unauthorized data access typically, though not always, entails malicious outsiders aiming to steal or damage information, while improper data access entails authorized data users using data in unethical or even illegal manner; publication of identity-discoverable data is comparatively more obtuse a threat as it is a manifestation of publishing – internally or externally – data that were overtly anonymized but that nonetheless contain details that make de-anonymization possible.

Unauthorized Data Access

Confidentiality is a key consideration in implied or explicit consent granted by those whose information is contained in data captured by commercial, nonprofit, and governmental entities. Perhaps the most obvious violation of the promise of confidentiality is unauthorized data access, commonly known as *data breach*. Some basic data breach statistics illustrate the extent and root causes of that growing problem: In 2019 more than 2,100 individual data breach events have been reported, and that number more than doubled in 2020 and continued to increase in years after; surprisingly, in roughly 50% of individual data breach cases the exact number of compromised records could not be determined. Cause-wise, trends reported over the past several years suggest that about 62% of breaches can be attributed to malicious outsiders, about 22% to unintended accidental lapses caused to organizational insiders and about 12% to malicious insiders, and about 2% apiece to hacktivists and state sponsored actors. The bottom line is that as more and more of commercial and private life is going online, so is crime, and according to experts in the field of data security, when considered from the perspective of individual organizations, some form of organizational data breach is essentially unavoidable. As commercial and noncommercial organizations continue to amass more and more data and as those holdings become more distributed throughout their organizational ecosystems, organizational exposure to malicious or unintended data breaches will continue to grow.

Securing organizational data is, in principle, an undertaking comprised of two parts. The first part entails access control in the form of authorization and authentication, while the second part takes the form of obscuring data, which can be achieved via a variety of means, such as data masking, where letters and numbers are replaced with proxy characters, encryption, which uses algorithms (called cipher) to scramble data, or tokenization, where sensitive data are replaced with random, not algorithmically reversible characters. In that sense, access control can be thought of as the first line of defense in efforts to protect data against unauthorized access, and the multifaceted undertaking of making data unreadable to intruders by means of *data obscuring* can be considered the second line of defense in that fight.

An important consideration in data security is *access mining*, which entails the collection and selling (illegally, typically on the dark web[19]) of access descriptors. Gaining unauthorized access to data is a problem that is so pervasive that there are numerous established (illegal, of course) marketplaces for selling and buying illegally obtained access credentials. For example, one such marketplace, Ultimate Anonymity Services, offers some 35,000 credentials with an average price of $6.75 per credential.

---

19 The dark web is the World Wide Web content that is not visible to search engines, and requires specific software, configurations, or authorization to access.

Improper Data Access

In many regards, making sure that those with legitimate data access rights do not abuse those rights might be the most undefined challenge of responsible data ownership. The reason for that is that illegitimate data access encompasses an impossibly broad array of behaviors ranging from malicious, as in the case of a disgruntled employee's intentional theft, to just plainly stupid, as in the case of a bank employee looking up friends' account balances. Putting in place explicit data usage policies is usually the first, obvious step that an organization can take to diminish that threat. A more formalized approach is to institute explicit access control protocols, which can be vertical, horizontal or context defined. Vertical access control assigns different access rights to different users, while horizontal access control grants limited access, meaning that specific user profiles are granted access only to specific subsets of data. In a more operational sense, vertical and horizontal protocols can manifest themselves in discretionary access control, where access rights are determined on case-by-case basis, mandatory access control, which groups potential users into explicit categories with differentially defined access rights, or role-based access control, in which functional responsibilities are used as basis for assigning specific data access rights. Altogether different, context-dependent access controls tie access rights to a specific data usage purpose or application, allowing differential access based on the underlying informational purpose.

Still, there are no panacea-like access control choices as each of the above outlined alternatives is based on assumptions that might be sound most of the time, but not all the time. At issue here is an inherent tradeoff between data security and data usability, where strengthening of one comes at the expense of the other. By and large, outside of mandatory record keeping situations, data is a utilitarian asset that should be used to justify the expense of ownership (hardware, software, personnel, etc.), but making data usable, in the sense of access, inescapably heightens the chances of improper data access. Given that, it is difficult to draw a conclusion other than some type of unauthorized or improper data access is another of a growing number of risks that cannot be completely eliminated, but which can be mitigated with multipronged risk reduction and risk transfer (i.e., purchase of protective insurance coverage) strategies tailored to uniqueness of individual organizations' datascapes.

Publication of De-anonymizable Data

While keeping data secure is generally technologically the most challenging aspect of responsible data capture and usage practices, internal and external sharing of data or data-derived information is likely the most procedurally vexing. Definition-wise, once data leave a secure environment they can be considered to have been 'published,' in a sense of having been made available for wider consumption, even if it is just limited to specific organizational stakeholders. Moreover, within the confines of data privacy related considerations, the definition of *publishing* is relatively broad as it encompasses not just raw data but also data-derived information in the form of summaries and other data analytic outcomes. The key threat associated with publishing of data or information where personally identification and other confidential details have been masked or outright deleted is that what might overtly appear to be anonymous, may in fact contain traces of confidential details.

Looking beyond masking of overtly individually identifiable data details, a common step toward further reducing the risk of inadvertent publication of confidential information is to normalize data, which entails reorganizing of individual data elements in a way that reduces redundancies, creates logical dependencies, and groups all related data. Among the core informational benefits of *data normalization* is reduced variability which gives rise to tighter distributions thus making individual values seem less unique, or less identifiable. However, data normalization does not eliminate the possibility of there being combinations of additions and subtractions, through a general process of database querying, of individual data records that might cause de facto revealing of private information.

A considerably higher privacy assurance is offered by what is today considered the state-of-the-art approach, known as *differential privacy*. Broadly characterized, it is an approach for publishing information about a dataset by describing the patterns of groups within the dataset while withholding information about individuals in the dataset. The core appeal of the differential privacy approach is that it offers strong privacy guarantees that are rooted in the fact that it is a semantic privacy notion, meaning it is built around data processing algorithms rather than specific datasets. The basic idea here is that the effect of making a single substitution in the database is small enough to assure privacy in the sense that review of published information is unlikely to reveal if a particular individual's information was included.

Since first being introduced in the early 2000s,[20] differential privacy algorithms gained widespread usage not only with traditional numeric and text data, but also with newer types, including social networking and facial recognition. Social networking platform operators use a two-step anonymization process: first, computing (using differential privacy methods) parameters of a generative model that accurately captures the original network properties, which is then followed by creating samples of synthetic graphs. A somewhat similar approach is used by providers of facial recognition technologies, which process biometric information using third-party servers. Biometric information delivered to an outside third-party can be considered a significant privacy threat as biometrics can be correlated with sensitive data such as healthcare or financial records, but the use of an appropriate variant of semantic differential privacy algorithms can offer strong assurance of privacy protection.

---

20 Dwork, C., Kenthapadi, K., McSherry, F., Mironov, I., & Naor, M. (2006). 'Our data, ourselves: Privacy via distributed noise generation,' in *Advances in Cryptology-EUROCRYPT*, pp. 486–503, Berlin: Springer.

List of Figures

https://doi.org/10.1515/9783111001296-011

List of Tables

https://doi.org/10.1515/9783111001296-012

Index

www.ingramcontent.com/pod-product-compliance
Lightning Source LLC
Chambersburg PA
CBHW081059220326
41598CB00038B/7156